sewing with nancy's
Favorite Hints

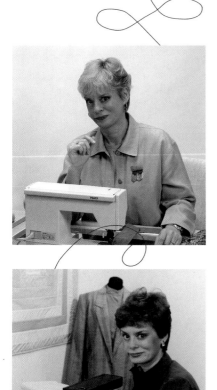

sewing with nancy®
20th anniversary

Twenty years of great ideas
from America's most popular
television sewing series.

Published by

Krause Publications
700 E. State St.
Iola, WI 54990-0001
Telephone 715-445-2214
www.krause.com

Please call or write for our free catalog of publications. Our toll-free number to place an order or obtain a free catalog is 800-258-0929 or please use our regular business telephone, 715-445-2214.

Editorial: Amy Stalp and Pat Hahn of Nancy's Notions
Illustrator and designer: Laure Noe
Photographer: Dale Hall

Library of Congress Catalog Number: 2002105105

ISBN: 0-87349-447-4

Printed in the United States of America

Dedicated to...

Gail Brown, Mary Mulari, and Natalie Sewell, three colleagues and true friends who have made great contributions to Sewing With Nancy. *Best of all, they have been anchors in my life.*

Nancy

Introduction

When I taped my first *Sewing With Nancy* program, I secretly thought, "I'm not cut out to do this!" The first anniversary of the show was a milestone, so were the 5th, 10th, and 15th years.

Now that we're celebrating our 20th anniversary, I reflect on my TV show and realize, as I've known all along, that the TV studio is my classroom and the main objective is to "share the love of sewing."

This book is an extension of *Sewing With Nancy*. You'll read in print many of the same elements that you see on air. In the following pages you'll find:

"Nancy's Favorite Techniques" – At the end of each chapter you'll find timesaving techniques for projects that relate to the topic of the preceding pages. Much like my TV show, these techniques are streamlined for ease of sewing.

"Hundreds of Hints" – Each week on PBS, I pass along hints from viewers. This is where I get to learn from you! The hints are organized by topic.

"Guest Spots" – Occasionally I invite special teachers to be part of the program. You'll read comments from several of my guests or read their favorite tip.

"Why I Sew With Nancy" – Several months ago we asked our viewers why they tune into the show. In this column, you'll see that the reasons are as varied as the viewers.

"Behind the Scenes" – I show you what goes on during the taping and pre-taping. It's rather like sitting at the teacher's desk!

I hope that you enjoy this book as it celebrates the joy of sewing. Thank you for being part of *Sewing With Nancy* for the past 20 plus years!

Nancy Zieman

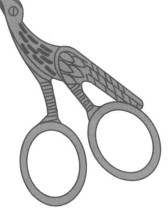

Table of Contents

CHAPTER ONE

Cure for the • cluttered *sewing room*

I have a dream – a dream where everyone has a sewing room with ample closet and shelving space, all the latest equipment, notions right at their fingertips, and all the time in the world to practice their craft.

Unfortunately for many of us, this is only a dream. Space in our homes or apartments is limited, and we just never have enough time to organize everything we have. In this chapter, you will find oodles of ideas from people just like you who found simple solutions to the problem of having small or unorganized sewing spaces.

Armed with these ideas, you can tackle the clutter in your sewing room and emerge victorious and ready to create!

So Much Fabric, So Little Space

If your fabric stash has taken over your sewing room, your house, or your life, the following hints will help you take control of your life and organize your stash once and for all.

Take a walk on the organized side

I have found a way to store the leftover fabric from my various sewing projects so I can find it easily when I need it. I stacked two quilted vinyl shoe storage chests in my sewing room. They have clear vinyl zippered windows so I can see at a glance the color of fabric I am looking for. With 24 cubbyholes of paperboard dividers in each, there is plenty of room to group like colors next to each other. Now I can throw away all the boxes that used to hold my scraps.

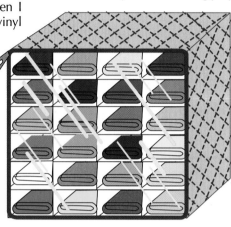

Evelyn Dostal,
David City, Nebraska

It's like having a fabric store at home!

When I find a fabric print that I just can't live without, I usually purchase three to four yards of it. Because I won't be using it for a while and don't want a lot of semi-permanent wrinkles in the fabric, I ask the clerk at the fabric store for an empty cardboard bolt. At home, I wrap my fabric around the bolt and place it on a shelf. It doesn't take up much room and I am always able to see exactly what fabric I have in my stash.

Pamela Johnson,
Conifer, Colorado

Towel racks to the rescue

The fabric hanging on a rack against the wall on the set of *Sewing With Nancy* was my inspiration for hanging fabric in my own home. I purchased an over-the-door towel rack and use it to hang fabric for the project I'm working on or fabric for a future project.

Audrey Myers,
Union City, Pennsylvania

Quilt strips "hung out" to dry

I can't always finish my quilt projects as soon as I would like to, so I purchased a wooden clothes drying rack and hang my quilt strips on the rungs. This keeps everything together and also keeps the fabric from becoming wrinkled or lost in the shuffle. The clothes rack is inexpensive and takes up very little space. I also use the rack to hang other sewing projects if I can't finish them right away.

Theresa Szynskie,
Papillion, Nebraska

Guest Spot

Mary Mulari, prolific author and designer, has been the most frequent guest on Sewing With Nancy! *Series topics such as "Adventure in Appliqué," "More Sweatshirts With Style," and most recently, "Made for Travel," feature Mary's creative touches. Here's what Mary had to share about taping the show.*

"If my face and name are familiar to sewing enthusiasts, it's because of my guest appearances on *Sewing With Nancy*. It has been a pleasure and honor to work with Nancy and share my projects on 23 television shows.

"I enjoy helping Nancy plan the shows when I'm the guest, sewing the step-by-step portions of the projects, working on the taping details at Nancy's office in Beaver Dam, and then traveling to Madison to the TV studio early in the morning. Vicki, the Make-up Wizard, is always cheerfully waiting there to do our make-up and I count on her to help me select my jewelry for each show we tape.

"When I present seminars, the loyal viewers of *Sewing With Nancy* often say, 'You have a better sense of humor in person than on TV.' My response to that is, 'Would you like it better if Nancy and I told jokes to each other while you're waiting to get the latest sewing information?' (But sometimes when we do a live stage presentation together, we do get to tell jokes and be funny!)

"And, by the way, I look younger in person too!"

Mary Mulari

A closet full of fabric

I hang my fabric stash on padded hangers to avoid fold lines, cover the fabric with muslin to keep it clean and dust-free, and hang it in a closet. I also put a swatch of the fabric on the outside of the muslin cover so that I know what is there. I have found this keeps the fabric in my thought process. (However, it does not keep me from buying more fabric!)

Susan Cosby, Chicago, Illinois

When I purchase a new fabric, I serge both cut raw edges, wash and iron the fabric, and put it on a hanger with two other pieces of fabric from the same color family. I then hang it with all of my other fabrics, according to color. This keeps the fabrics together and ready to use.

Trish Hamm, Madison, Wisconsin

File this one under "Fabric"

I fold and hang fabrics over hanging file dividers purchased at an office supply store and put them into a large legal size metal filing cabinet. When I open the drawers, it's easy to see fabrics at a glance and I can remove one piece without digging through and disturbing a stack of fabric. As I fold the fabric, I also measure it, write the yardage on a piece of paper, and pin it to the fabric.

Mary Long, Bella Vista, Arizona

Organizing fabric doesn't have to be a three-ring circus

I love fabric. Whenever I go to a fabric store, I usually purchase at least a quarter yard. As a result, I have quite a stash, so I catalog what I have available.

- Glue a swatch of each fabric to an 8½" x 11" sheet of paper.
- Write down the measurement and whether or not the fabric has been washed.
- Arrange the sheets by color, insert them into plastic page protectors, and add them to a three-ring binder.
- When a particular fabric is gone, just mark "gone" under the swatch, or delete the page from the binder. You can always add more sheets to this "book" of fabric.

Pat Ganascioli, Burdett, New York

It's in the cards

I insert 8½" x 11" clear business card holder sheets, purchased at the local office supply store, into a 2" loose-leaf notebook. Using my business card as a guide, I cut swatches of the fabrics in my fabric collection and insert them into the pockets. Each sheet holds 20 fabrics (10 on the front and another 10 on the back). I sort my fabrics by color value and I carry this notebook with me whenever I go to the fabric store. It guides me in purchasing new selections and helps me use up what I already have.

Darlene Griffin, Draper, Utah

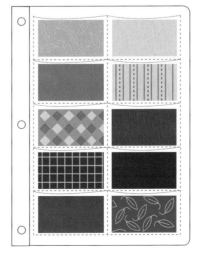

Behind the Scenes

Take 1

I love to teach – *Sewing With Nancy* is my classroom!

Twenty years ago when I first stood in front of a TV camera, I gave new meaning to the word nervous! Once I started imagining that I was teaching to a room filled with people, the TV studio became a comfortable classroom.

From the beginning we've offered 26 new shows every year – most are organized into three-part series. We gather new ideas and notions, keep a running file on topics, and develop scripts and samples when we feel we have a great series. Some series take months to organize; others take weeks – just like your sewing projects at home.

Since I've most likely been in your family room or living room – vicariously through TV – I'd like to show you my TV classroom in this "Behind the Scenes" column. You'll see snapshots of the various phases of TV production and I'll give you a brief commentary of the production steps. You may also learn some Sewing With Nancy trivia! I hope you'll enjoy the tour.

why i sew with nancy

Nancy is the Julia Child of sewing.

Vivian Spinelli, Tracy, California

I sew with Nancy because:
- *She is such a pleasant and friendly woman. I almost feel like she is actually in my home giving me a free sewing lesson.*
- *She sews beautifully and knows how to teach her techniques. I can count on one hand how many times, in all the years I have watched her, I wanted her to clarify something further.*
- *She shares viewers' hints, so it is clear she does not consider herself the only one who knows it all, but she is a friend.*
- *Her subject matter is diverse and interesting. Even if she is teaching something that may not be my first choice of sewing activities, I find I can use her techniques on other projects.*
- *She has always moved with me. I left the Navy in 1993 and no matter where I was stationed (always in the U.S.), Nancy was there to greet and teach me.*

Debby Tinker, Springfield, Virginia

Nancy makes me feel like I can do anything. She allows me to believe that she is "one of us," not above us. She empowers me!

Patty Bragg, Benton, Arkansas

As a true professional, Nancy makes things look easy. But, she remembers to tell me that I must practice! I thank her for her kindness, her enthusiasm, and her smile.

Toni R. Duesing, Marietta, Georgia

Picture this

Something that has helped me for several years is an inexpensive purse-size photo album that I bring shopping. In it I have index cards on which I've glued swatches of fabric from my various sewing projects. I have separate cards for each family member, and I divide them (or use more than one card) into sections for pants/shorts, blouses, etc. I also have a couple of cards (along with paint chips) for the things I've made for our home. Each of the cards goes into one of the album sleeves. Having this album in my purse makes it easy to check whether or not some fabric or accessory that I'm looking at will blend with what I already have.

Pauline Houck,
Maplewood, Minnesota

Like all of us, I have lots of fabric just waiting to be sewn into something beautiful. Unfortunately, I have trouble remembering what I have! I purchased a photo album with pockets for 3½" x 5" photos. I created a form on my computer with spaces for width, total yards, fabric content, name, date purchased, where purchased, price per yard, total price, as well as a space for a swatch of the fabric. I organize the cards by type of fabric (wool, linen, knit, etc).

Width: _____ Total yards: _____
Width: _____ Total yards: _____
Fabric content: _____
Name: _____
Date purchased: _____
Where purchased: _____
Price/yd. _____ Total price: _____

Whenever I purchase fabric, I fill out and file the form in the photo album. It took me some time to get started. I had to fill out a form (to the best of my memory) for my whole stash. But now, whenever an idea comes to mind, I can quickly go through my file to see what fabric I have that's appropriate.

Claire Spinelli, Morganville, New Jersey

Fabric footnotes

Recently I have been making appliqué designs on sweatshirts. Most of the patterns require a very small amount of fabric, so I have many remnants. When I go to the fabric store to purchase patterns and fabrics, I cannot always remember what fabric colors/patterns I already have. To eliminate purchasing the same or very similar fabric:
- Tape small strips of each fabric on a 3" x 5" index card.
- Write how much of each fabric you have under each swatch.
- Take the cards along when planning to purchase another pattern or more fabric.
- Keep all fabrics of the same color family together on one or more cards.
- To add fabrics, simply tape another piece on the appropriate card.
- When all of a fabric has been used up, just remove the fabric strip.

Shirts/blouses (Amy)

Note from Nancy

Over the past 20 plus years of collecting sewing and quilting hints, this suggestion (or ones very similar) has been submitted well over a hundred times. Since it would be fruitless to list everyone who has submitted this idea, I give you my collective "thank you!"

P.S. Selfishly, I wish someone could organize my stash of fabrics with this system.

Frazzle-free prewashing

I have just started quilting and I am a big time fabricoholic. Every time I buy new cotton or cotton blend fabric for quilting, I wash it as soon as I have a machine load. I cut the corners at a diagonal; this keeps the fabric from fraying when it's being washed and is much easier to handle when I start to cut it. It works every time!

Alta Sumerlin, Redmond, Oregon

I've used many methods to prevent the edges of fabric from raveling when I prewash it. I've been doing a lot of piecework lately and had to wash 10 to 12 quarter yard cuts. I didn't want to pink, zigzag, or serge the fabrics because it was too time consuming. So I put all those pieces into a large pillowcase-size mesh laundry bag before I washed them. The fabrics didn't ravel much, and they didn't come out twisted and knotted together as they did when I didn't use a bag. The entire bag can be thrown into a dryer, too.

Joan Rader, St. Petersburg, Florida

That's what friends are for!

When my husband unexpectedly received a job offer 1,200 miles from our home, I wondered how I could justify taking the several boxes of fabric I had accumulated. Some of my pieces had practically become old friends! I decided to use the fabric as packing material for china, crystal, pottery, and bric-a-brac. Our things were moved not-so-gently across the country and put into storage for nine months before being moved again to our current home. I am happy to report that none of the pieces protected by the fabric were broken, although we had some breakage of items wrapped in paper and plastic. Now, if I ever find the time, I'll use my fabric, but it is comforting to have these old friends with me.

Tonette Skube, Bardstown, Kentucky

Color me clean

Since I don't always use a fabric right after I purchase it, I had a hard time remembering care instructions for all of the fabrics. To solve this dilemma, I made labels on my computer to remind me of how to care for each fabric.

- Use one color paper for the machine-wash labels and another color for the dry-clean-only labels to make the difference more obvious. I can fit eight or more labels on one sheet of paper.
- When you begin a project and cut the fabric, remove the label and attach it to a swatch of the same fabric.
- Tack the swatch up on a bulletin board. If the fabric must be dry cleaned, you can make a permanent label for the garment.

Tiffany L. Harrison, Baltimore, Maryland

Tag your fabric

In the past when I got an urge to sew I wasted a lot of time going through my stash, remeasuring everything because I could never remember how much was in each piece. So I made some tags from old index cards, punched a hole in each of them, and used a large safety pin to attach a tag to the fabric. Now, all I have to do is look at the tag to find out the width and yardage. I make sure that when the tag goes on, the fabric has been preshrunk and measured and is ready for my new creation!

Myrna O'Brien, De Land, Florida

That's a "wrap"

- Prewash washable fabrics. Press the fabric if necessary.
- Fold the fabric lengthwise, meeting selvages. Then fold it again, meeting selvages to the fold. (For long pieces of fabric, this is easier to do on the floor.)
- Wrap the folded fabric around a 10" x 20" piece of mat board. **(Note:** *It is easier to slide the fabric off the mat board if the fabric is wrapped near one end of the board rather than at the center.)*
- Slide the fabric off the board and store it in a drawer or on a shelf.

Rosalyn Bullock, Jamestown, Ohio

All Your Quilting Supplies in a Row

You've heard of *10•20•30 Minutes to Quilt*? With these organizing hints,
you can always have your supplies ready to go when the creative urge strikes.

Quilt blocks on the go!

I like to keep all of the quilt blocks for one quilt neatly together and ready to quickly pack up to take to class. To make a quick Quilt Block Carrier:

- Cut a 23" square of flannel. Serge or clean finish the edges.
- Wrap one end of the flannel around a cardboard gift-wrap tube, just far enough to cover the tube. Topstitch close to the tube.
- Stuff the tube with fiberfill to create a pincushion.
- Cut two round pieces of fabric slightly larger than the diameter of the cardboard tube opening. Glue the round fabric pieces in place to cover the ends of the cardboard tube.
- Cut two 36" pieces of ribbon for ties and fold the ties in half.
- Position the ties on the wrong side of the carrier.
- Measure and mark 6" from each corner on the end opposite the cardboard tube.
- Place the folds of the ribbons at the marked positions, meeting the fold to the fabric edge.
- Tack the ribbons in place.
- Place quilt block pieces on the flannel, then cover with another piece of fabric. Stack additional quilt blocks on top, separating each layer with a piece of fabric.
- No more lost pieces. The carrier is ready to roll up and put in my quilting tote.

Hattie Vickerman, Romulus, Michigan

Note from Nancy

Hattie's Quilt Block Carrier could be made a variety of sizes to fit your quilting needs. To make a larger carrier, securely tape two cardboard tubes together or shorten the tubes by cutting them with a serrated knife.

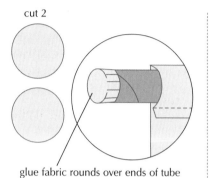

cut 2

glue fabric rounds over ends of tube

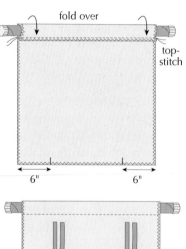

fold over

top-stitch

6"   6"

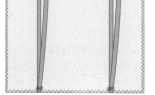

tack ribbons in place

fabric to separate layers

Get a grip!

I've seen several ways of holding and storing a rotary cutting mat, but the best I have found is a pants hanger. It has plastic grippers that hold the mat securely.

Mildred Hudson, Springtown, Texas

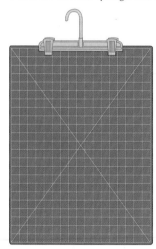

When I purchased the second largest rotary cutting mat, I read that the mat should be stored flat and out of the sun. That's all well and good, but where do I have room for that?

As a solution, I use a wooden pants hanger and close it around my mat. If the mat slips out of the hanger grips, fold a piece of scrap fabric over the mat area that will be clipped. (The hanger works better if the mat is centered.)

I hang the mat inside the bedroom closet door or on an over-the-door clothes bar. It's out of the way, yet easy to use.

Krysta Sutterfield, Worthington, Ohio

I use large binder clips found in office supply stores (often used to hold thick stacks of paper together) to hang my rotary cutting mats and some of my rulers. I can now hang up some of the items that previously cluttered my sewing area.

Cheryl Birchard, Independence, Iowa

Resourceful Ribbon Storage

Hang in there, as *Sewing With Nancy* viewers share ways to satisfy your sweet tooth and organize your ribbon collection.

No-frills ribbon and trim dispensers

Small zip-closure plastic bags are an easy way to store silk ribbons.

- Insert the ribbon in the bag, leaving one end of the closure open and extending the end of the ribbon through that opening.
- Pull the end and remove as much of the ribbon as you want.
- I also use these bags for storing laces. By standing the bags up in a shoebox, I can easily see the ends so I can select the color or size I need.

Audrey Boonstra, Ada, Michigan

While working with yards and yards of trims, I devised an easy way to keep trims organized. I used a large (gallon size) clear zip-closure plastic bag.

- Place trims in the lower half of the bag. Stitch, forming a pocket around each trim.
- Insert trims in the upper half of the bag. Stitch pockets around the trims, using the same method.
- After stitching, snip off the lower corners of the bag to create an opening for the trim to feed through. The trims in the upper half of the bag feed through the zip-closure top.

Ann Ward, Holbrook, Arizona

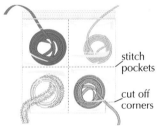

stitch pockets

cut off corners

Keep your ribbon hanging around!

I have around 50 spools of fabric ribbons that I use for sewing and craft projects. The spools took up a large amount of space in my storage tubs. Each time I needed a specific color, I had to sort through all of the spools. As a solution, I untwisted the top of a wire hanger and threaded the spools onto the hanger, organized by color. I then twisted the top of the hanger closed. Now the spools of ribbon hang in my craft closet. The hanger works like a dispenser, I can easily choose the color I need, and the spools take up less space.

Penny Wadham, Grand Prairie, Texas

Refreshing ribbon storage

I do a lot of sewing and crafts using ribbons, and those ribbons were always a mess! I took a two-liter soda bottle and used a sharp knife to cut off the top about 3" from the opening. Most fabric stores will save the empty cardboard spools from ribbons for you. I wound my ribbon onto those spools, placed the ribbon spools in the cut-off bottle, and now I can easily see the colors and how much I have of each ribbon. To prevent dust and dirt from accumulating on the ribbons, I cut the bottom from another bottle at the groove mark, and use that section as a cover.

Gladys Haberer, Rathdrum, Idaho

Ship-Shape Sewing Machines

A needle here, a pair of scissors there… Use the following hints to get everything in order around your sewing machine, so when you sit down to sew, it's smooth sailing.

"Clearly" the best organizers

I put the sewing feet and special accessories for my sewing machine and serger in clear zip-closure plastic bags according to their use (decorative, hemming, etc.).

I insert an index card with all the pertinent information regarding each foot in that bag, coordinating the colors of the cards with the colors of the tabs in the instruction book that came with the machine, or just keep the same "sewing work" feet together.

Information on the card includes:
• Name of foot.
• Description of use.
• Page number where instructions for use of foot are found.

I even list the accessories that come with the machine and note that they are in the accessory box and list all the information that pertains to them. With this method, all I have to do is take a little bag out of a drawer. All the information and feet I could use for a particular function are in one place.

Joan Meuller, Sterling Heights, Michigan

Next, a trio of ideas for tracking needles

I often have several projects going at once. To keep track of my needles I cut a fabric swatch from each project. When I change needles, I poke the needle I removed through the fabric swatch and store it. When the needle is in the machine I keep its fabric swatch under the pressure foot. Whenever I sit down to sew I know which needle is in the machine by looking at the fabric swatch. This system really helps me keep track of needles in and out of my machine without having to guess what size they are, or whether they're for wovens or knits.

Amy Reges, Burdett, New York

To identify machine needles, I use little stickers, the kind you might use as price tags for a garage sale. When I change needles in my sewing machine and serger I write the size or the name of the needle on the sticker (i.e. size 80 or quilting), and stick this on my machine. Then, when I leave a project that I might not be able to come back to for a few days, I'll know what needle I have in the machine when I sew again. I also find that the stickers don't leave any sticky film after I take them off.

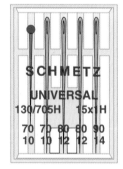

Marilyn Kenzik, Elyria, Ohio

When inserting a needle in my machine, I always place a pin with a colored head into the needle's slot in the needle package. This shows me exactly what size needle I have in the machine and where to put it when I change needles.

Sigrid A. Klein, Willow, Alaska

Basket of gadgets times three

I don't have a lot of cupboard or drawer space, so I use a plastic patio cutlery carrier about 5½" x 5" x 6" to store my seam ripper, rotary cutters, small and large rulers, marking pencils, chalk, paper scissors, and other small gadgets. Everything is together on the sewing machine table while I sew, and the carrier fits easily into the corner of a cupboard when I'm not using it.

Donalda Lockhart, Brockville, Ontario, Canada

My good old standby hint is simple, but I like to keep as organized as I can. I always keep a small wicker basket with a handle near my sewing machine to hold odds and ends as I am sewing (bobbins, threads, cleaning tools, etc.). That way the clutter is in one place instead of being strewn all over the room. When my clean-up time comes, everything is right there ready to be put away.

Lorelei Winkelman, Great Falls, Montana

Since I'm a collector of gadgets and like to keep them handy, I use a plastic- or rubber-coated wire silverware basket to the right of my machine for cutting tools and gadgets. It keeps them corralled and handy.

Mary Timme, Aurora, Colorado

Keep your scissors in "suspense"

I attached a clear plastic suction cup hook to the right side of my sewing machine. I hang my small trimming or embroidery scissors there so I always know where they are.

Susy Hanson, Statesboro, Georgia

No more walking on pins and needles

To dispose of my bent and broken needles and pins, I use an empty spice container with a shaker top. Needles and pins easily slip through the holes. Then you can screw the cap back on and dispose of them without fear of them hurting someone when the trash is emptied.

Cathy Francis, Norborne, Missouri

To dispose of needles and pins, I use a 35-mm film container with a hole punched in the lid. When it is full, I cover the hole with a piece of tape and toss it in the trash. This is very safe, especially for people with small children or pets.

Sue Murray, Woodridge, Illinois

Sticky notions

Using sticky back Velcro®, I put a piece of the loop side on the top of my sewing machine. Then I put a piece of the hook side on my seam ripper, pin cushion, Little Wooden Iron, or any other notion that I will be needing for a particular project. The notions stick to my machine; they are right at hand, don't fall on the floor, and don't get lost in my project.

Janet Fedor, Marion, Indiana

Needles no longer a nuisance

In the past, I had machine and hand needles stored in several places, and I was never exactly sure what I had or where to find a particular one when I needed it. To get organized:

- Purchase a three-hole binder from an office supply store, and insert plastic pages with pockets designed to hold baseball cards.
- Cut felt pieces (2¼" x 3") to fit in each plastic pocket, and insert hand needles into the felt or staple a needle package insert to the felt rectangle.
- To store machine needles, keep the needles in the packages. Insert the package and a piece of felt into a pocket.
- Add a label to each pocket, identifying size and type of needle, so the needle can be returned to the same pocket each time.
- Store the folder in your sewing area, where it is immediately available when you need it. (As a handy reference I slipped a needle/thread chart in the folder's pocket.)

When I'm organized I have more time for sewing!

Jan Dobbie, Portage, Michigan

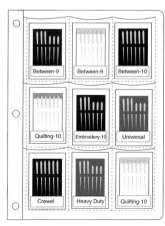

No-Nonsense Storage for Notions & Sewing Supplies

Pins, buttons, feet, snaps… the list goes on and on.
With these storage hints from viewers, you'll be "hooked" for life.

Hold everything!

Having frequently-used sewing notions close at hand is a real time-saver. Here's how I made an organizer for my notions:

- Cut a rectangle of quilted fabric large enough to hold your notions. (You may want to position your notions on a flat surface to determine the best size.) Finish the outer edges of the fabric by zigzagging or serging.
- Cut strips of clear vinyl the same width as the quilted fabric, but of assorted heights. These will be the pockets on the organizer.
- Encase the top of each pocket with wide bias tape. Zigzag the tape in place.
- Place the vinyl strips on top of the quilted fabric and zigzag stitch around the outer edges of the quilted fabric to secure the pockets.
- Stitch vertical pockets to hold the various accessories such as scissors, books, rulers, thread, etc.
- Attach four loops across the top and insert a large dowel through the loops.
- Add a strong cord at both ends of the dowel.
- Hang the organizer in your sewing area and you'll never have to search for your notions when you need them.

Optional: Add decorative accents such as silk roses and/or ribbon.

Bev Forde, Spanaway, Washington

bias tape

vinyl

stitch pockets to quilted fabric

"Eye spy" my notions

I use a hard-sided eyeglass case to hold my pins, thimble, sewing needles, scissors, seam presser, seam ripper, etc. I can take my quilt and my eyeglass case and go into another room all set to quilt. This is also helpful if I'm attending a class or traveling. I have everything in my compact, portable eyeglass case, ready to go.

Dorothy Kelly,
New Port Richey, Florida

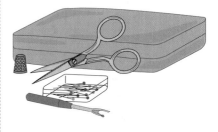

Zip up your projects

I use a metal shower ring and zip-closure plastic bags to keep my sewing projects organized. I usually have several projects started at one time and this makes it easy to find the one I need. (This is also a good method for storing sewing notions.)

- Punch a hole in the top of the plastic bags. (Any size bag works, and several fit on one shower ring.)
- Put the ring on a hanger in a closet or on the wall.

Sidney Morris, Benton, Arkansas

Goodbye strained carrots, hello buttons!

To store small items like buttons, snaps, and hook and eyes, I use empty baby food jars and label each jar with the item's name on the outside. I use three different sizes of jars and store them in stacking baskets that are also labeled with a tag on the outside.

JoAn Freemyer, Fairfax, Missouri

Hold everything – deluxe version!

This notions holder features a clear vinyl cover to keep my notions dust-free when not in use. Customize it to fit your sewing and quilting supplies.

Supplies needed:

- 1¾ yd. fabric, 60" wide
- Batting, 24" x 30"
- Clear vinyl, 24½" x 31"
- 50" piping, ⅛" wide
  (or purchased piping)

Making the holder:

- Cut two 24" x 30" fabric pieces. Sandwich the batting between them and machine quilt the layers together.
- Cut two 3" x 24" fabric pockets. Cut two 2½" x 24" strips to bind the pockets.
- Bind one 24" edge of each pocket. Turn the other 24" edge under ¼".
- Position the pockets on the holder. Stitch the lower edge of each in place.
- Cut the piping in half and place one section about 3" above each pocket. Straight stitch the ends in place.
- Straight stitch to divide both the pockets and the piping into sections.
- Cut two ties, each 2" x 12". Fold them in half with right sides together, meeting the 12" edges. Stitch a ¼" seam along the lengthwise edge. Turn the ties right side out and press.
- Fold the ties in half to mark the centers. Position the center on top of the holder approximately 6" from each side. Stitch the ties in place.
- Place vinyl over the holder and ties and stitch the vinyl to the top of the holder.
- Add hanging loops across the top of the holder.
- Bind the outer edges with remaining fabric using your favorite technique.

When the holder is not being used, the vinyl serves as a dust cover. To use the holder, roll up the vinyl and secure it with the ties so the vinyl is out of the way.

Maxine Walker, Knoxville, Tennessee

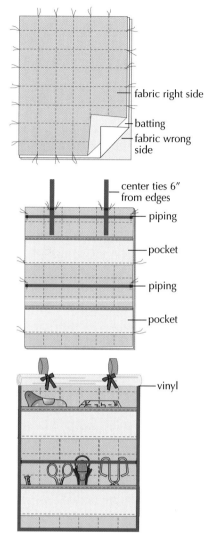

fabric right side

batting

fabric wrong side

center ties 6" from edges

piping

pocket

piping

pocket

vinyl

Note from Nancy

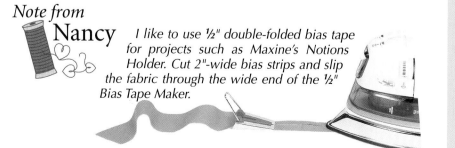

I like to use ½" double-folded bias tape for projects such as Maxine's Notions Holder. Cut 2"-wide bias strips and slip the fabric through the wide end of the ½" Bias Tape Maker.

Behind the Scenes

Take 3

Which came *first*, the TV show or the catalog?

You may wonder, as many people have asked me, "Which came first?" It's not "the chicken or the egg" answer, rather a simple one . . . the catalog.

I founded Nancy's Notions in 1979 in Virginia, Minnesota. My husband was transferred to Virginia, a town 60 miles north of Duluth, from Chicago. With his career move, I decided to start my own seminar and mail order business, Nancy's Notions.

Nancy's Notions was born on my kitchen table and my office/warehouse was housed in the second bedroom of our apartment. Seminars were the best way for me to acquire names and encourage orders.

After two years, I quickly realized that business travel was not the life for me. When I was asked to tape a pilot for cable TV in 1981, I thought it was worth the gamble, especially since it gave an option to encourage viewers to send for a free "catalog," initially a single-page flyer pictured below. Like my first TV show, my first catalogs were primitive at best!

It's in the bag!

Here is my way of keeping my thread clean and off the floor.

Use scraps of fabric to make a double thickness that measures about 7" x 54". (The length varies depending on the amount of hanging space you have.)

- Fold the top down and stitch to make a casing for a dowel.
- Use zip-closure plastic bags that have blue and yellow stripes at the top. (These bags are the only ones with a longer lip on the backside of the bag.)
- Measure 4" from the bottom of the fabric and position the bag, placing the yellow stripes next to the fabric.
- Zigzag across the two thin yellow stripes at the top of the bag, being careful not to catch the blue stripe.
- Attach additional bags, allowing 1½" between the bags.
- Insert a dowel rod in the casing, hang up the organizer, and fill the bags with thread.

Mary Rambo,
Wenatchee, Washington

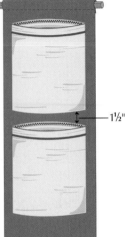

zigzag across yellow stripes

4"

1½"

I can see right through you

My bins of decorative threads were difficult to organize. Since I like my threads to be accessible and organized by color, size, and type, I've developed this inexpensive method of storage.

- Cut a 16" x 56" strip of clear vinyl and 1 yd. of ribbon.
- Fold up one long side of the vinyl 6".

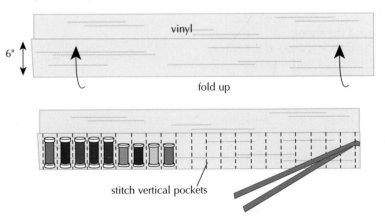

vinyl

6"

fold up

stitch vertical pockets

- Stitch vertical divisions through the two layers to fit your thread spools.
- Fold the ribbon in half and tack it to one end of the vinyl.
- Insert your threads; fold the flap down over the threads. Roll up the organizer, and secure with the ribbon tie.

Lynn Ortega, Seattle, Washington

Tidy Up Your Threads

Does organizing your thread have you
tangled up in knots? It doesn't have to with these timeless tips.

"Glamorous" sewing kits

Instead of discarding make-up cases, I recycle them into traveler's sewing kits.

- Cut one piece of grosgrain ribbon the width of one side of the opened case, and a second piece 4" longer.
- Stitch the two pieces of ribbon together, forming a T. Stitch each end and the center of the crossbar section of the T to one half of the opened case.
- Baste a variety of buttons in basic colors to the crossbar of the T, and slide a small pair of scissors behind the ribbon. Add pins and sewing needles to the tail of the T. Insert notions into the pockets.

Patricia Kirby, Bridgewater, New Jersey

All the colors of the rainbow

My sewing area is not very large, so I don't have room for thread racks. I do a lot of machine embroidery and have many spools of thread. I devised a system for storing threads, using a #10 cardboard envelope box (the 500 count size):

- Cover the outside of the box with fabric to coordinate with your sewing area.
- Use mat board to make two trays to go inside the box.
- Store up to 150 spools of thread neatly on the two trays and bottom row of the box.
- When sewing, take the two trays out and lay them on the table, exposing the bottom row.
- When done sewing, put the trays back inside and put the lid on.

This keeps my sewing area very neat and clean.

Carole Wardeh, Newark, Delaware

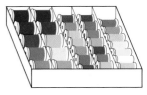

To keep my spools of thread organized, available, and portable, I use a blouse-sized gift box. I cut strips of cardboard from cereal boxes the height of the box to separate the rows of thread by size and color. They are always in order and accessible. I can put the cover on and easily take them from one place to another and it costs nothing to make.

Betty DeWitt, Elmhurst, Illinois

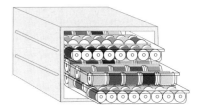

To store my thread spools so they are visible, free from dust, and easily accessible, I use a 9" x 15½" x 12½" three-drawer plastic container. To separate the rows of thread, I cut 1½" strips of balsa wood. I arrange the thread by color so it is easy to see my inventory.

Kathy Van Susteren, Milwaukee, Wisconsin

Thread under wraps!

Here's a tip to keep spools of threads from unraveling during storage.

- Cut a strip of lightweight vinyl the width of the thread spool and 1" longer than the distance around the spool.
- Wrap the vinyl around the spool. The overlapped section will adhere to the vinyl underneath and hold the thread in place.

Nina and Helen Fricks, Fort Smith, Arkansas

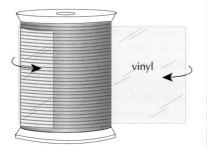

vinyl

Bobbins on the rocks!

I use a plastic ice cube tray in my sewing machine drawer to hold my many bobbins.

Euna Staniforth, Madison, Wisconsin

Take your thread rack to the next level

I place a drinking straw over the spool pins on my thread rack to increase its capacity. The straw can be cut down to hold two or three spools of thread or left as is to hold up to four or five spools.

Vicki Heckman, College Park, Maryland

Cut to the Chase

A cluttered sewing room seems "point"-less.
Cut through the red tape of scissors storage with these tips from our sharp viewers!

Garage sale finds to help get organized

Keeping my scissors safe, yet handy in my sewing room, is a priority. I found a small pipe rack at a garage sale. It has six holes, three on each side. The base has six indentations for the bowl of each pipe to rest in. Pipe racks can also be found in thrift shops and flea markets.

In the three back recesses I glued graduated sizes of felt, starting with the smallest piece, and built it up until it fit the edges of the recess. This provides padding for the points of my longest scissors. I keep my small scissors in the three front holes.

Dorothy L. Green,
Hartford City, Indiana
Pat Lindahn, Los Altos, California

I have several different scissors and small, thin sewing devices. At a second hand store, I purchased an upright oak knife stand traditionally used in kitchens to store knives. My husband drilled in the middle of some of the knife slots, allowing my scissors to slip neatly into the stand. The drilled hole accommodates the screws on the scissors. Now my collection of scissors and thin tools is located next to my sewing machine, readily available when I need them.

Vickie Popplewell, Butler, Missouri

Get to the point

Having a sharp scissors, especially at the point, is important when I sew. To keep each pair of my scissors super-sharp, I slip a small piece of vinyl tubing – found at any hardware store – over the tips. The tubing keeps the tips safe and sharp while they're in the drawer or in my bag on the road to my next quilting class.

Jeanne Halapoff, Kennewick, Washington

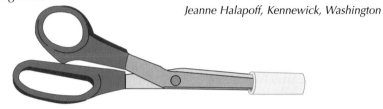

I use a cork to protect the ends of my scissors. It also protects my hands when I reach into my sewing kit while traveling.

Myra Nammack, Whittier, California

"A place for everything, and everything in its place"

I keep all my scissors in a dresser drawer lined with a sponge so they are always in the same location in the drawer. Here are the simple instructions:
• Cut a sponge sheet to fit the drawer, then outline each scissors with a pen.
• Partially cut out the scissors image with a razor blade or craft knife.
• Do not cut all the way through, so the scissors can sit in the cutout without shifting.
There's an added bonus – I can immediately see which scissors are missing.

Rosie Gastelum, Rancho Cordova, California

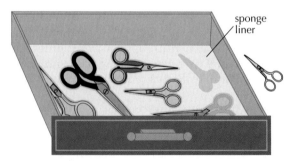

sponge liner

You've got the world on a string!

I string all of my scissors on ribbons at least 36" long, using a different color for each type. When I sew, I hang my thread-cutting scissors around my neck. I never have to search for them!

Sally Siegner,
Grand Bend, Ontario, Canada

The eyes have it

When I got new glasses, I saved my old eyeglass case and used it to store my rotary cutter. The case keeps my cutter safe and is an attractive addition to my quilting equipment.

Ida J. Wacker, Leavenworth, Kansas

Diary from a Sewing Room

From making memories to building a wardrobe,
put pen to paper and let these inspiring hints be your guide.

Making memories last

Keeping a sewing journal reminds me of all the items I have made over the years as well as who they have gone to. I write down any interesting things that happen while sewing the item or something about the event or the person I'm sewing for. This journal makes for interesting reading. I also include pictures.

Evelyn Romzek, Ubly, Michigan

I use a notebook as a sewing journal, taking time to list what the item is, the fabrics I used, sources, costs, pattern information, and project time span. I also list problems, successes, etc. I include photos when I can.

Susie Johnson, Morris, Illinois

I appliqué sweatshirts for 11 grandchildren, two daughters, and three daughters-in-law. I take pictures of all the sweatshirts I make and keep them in a special book with the name of the person and the year the garment was made.

Marlene Fast, Hastings, Nebraska

Note from Nancy

Lisa Boye sent me the hint many years ago to keep track of finished projects by pinning a swatch of fabric and noting details on a calendar. I've used Lisa's idea for years, since it's quick and easy. This hint was previously published, yet I wanted to thank Lisa again.

Mary, Mary, quite contrary, how does your wardrobe grow?

When assembling a new wardrobe, first make a basic suit or an outfit to build on, and keep a swatch of the fabric on a small card or notebook in your purse. Note what you made with the fabric on the card, such as a lined jacket, straight skirt, or slacks.

When shopping for fabric or ready-made clothes, use the card to check colors and designs. Each time you make a new item, put a swatch of fabric and the details on another card. Fasten the cards together on a ring or put them in a coupon organizer. If you make two complete suits in two different (but hopefully compatible) colors and styles, put one main color at the beginning and the other at the end. When you buy a new item, put it between the main suits, grouped according to color.

As your wardrobe grows, just fan out the cards to see where you might need a new basic item or where you can add something to perk up what you already have.

MaryAnne Cook, St. Louis, Missouri

Guest Spot

Nancy Cornwell, author of numerous fleece books and fleece fabric designer, joined me for a three-part series on "More Polarfleece® Adventures." During that series, we temporarily changed the name of the show to Sewing With the Nancys!

Nancy Cornwell

"As a sewer, when I watch *Sewing With Nancy*, I never give any thought to the mechanics of how the show is actually produced. I simply enjoy watching the programs and soaking up all the practical ideas and hints Nancy shares every week. Then I was a guest on the show – what an eye-opener as to what really goes on behind the camera!

"I smile when I think of the 'More Polarfleece Adventures' series we taped on a typical hot and humid Midwest summer day. There we stood, Nancy and Nancy, layered in fleece, wilting under hot glaring stage lights while the rest of the world was sunbathing and swimming. (I quickly learned that air conditioning fans don't run during the taping sessions because of the noise factor.) To say we were toasty and warm would be the epitome of understatement.

"To add spice and challenge, we had to compete with an energetic road crew jackhammering the streets throughout the entire taping session! Their sense of timing was exquisite. They were quiet while we rehearsed and immediately geared up the minute we started taping! It became a cat-and mouse game. (But, we won! The shows turned out great.)"

why i sew with nancy

I watch Sewing With Nancy *because Nancy looks at the camera, so it feels like she is speaking to the viewer personally. Nancy is a gifted teacher.*

Patricia B. Bonser, Springfield, Virginia

Nancy emphasizes one of the great benefits of sewing – individuality! She routinely reminds us that "you are the designer" and "the option is yours." What a refreshing approach in this world of instructors who admonish us that their way is the only correct way, and if we want to do it "right," we better follow their rules!

Valentina Goodman, Murray, Kentucky

Sewing With Nancy *gives me fresh, creative ideas and practical sewing suggestions, and it motivates me to work on my sewing projects that all too often must be put on the back burner.*

It is satisfying to know that there are others with the same interest, when it seems that there are few sewers left.

Myrtle Gibson, Safford, Arizona

Your methods are easy, practical, and professional. I use them when I teach sewing classes. Sewing should be FUN! That doesn't mean slipshod, but it shouldn't be tedious, either.

You are like a good and giving neighbor who I am pleased to have as a visitor every week via satellite.

Audrey Bergen, Hoquiam, Washington

Sewing With Nancy *is the first sewing show I ever saw and it really inspired me to learn to sew. Nancy has a lovely manner about her and makes sewing look simple and enjoyable. Watching her, I feel like I can sew anything.*

Maria Fortunato, Rahway, New Jersey

Patterns, Patterns, Everywhere

Do you need to organize your pattern collection but hate paperwork? Get the job done in a jiffy with help from these *Sewing With Nancy* viewers, who wrote the book on pattern storage.

The choice is clear

As my collection of patterns grows, carrying a variety of them with me to the fabric store becomes more and more difficult. Flipping through five or six patterns at a time and trying to focus on the correct sizing for yardage and notions can be very confusing.

To solve this problem, I make a copy of the pattern envelope and write on the back the fabric and notions for each view in my size only. I then laminate the copy so it doesn't get dog-eared.

The result is easy to carry, convenient to flip through, and less confusing when it comes to sizes. The laminated copies look and stay neat forever.

Vicki Mallonee, Portland, Oregon

Templates and books make a great team!

I love to quilt, but hate losing templates. Here is my system for organizing and storing quilting templates.
• Stitch or serge around a zip-closure plastic bag so it's slightly smaller than the size of a quilting pattern book.
• Tape the bag inside the book cover.
• Store the traced templates for patterns inside the bag.

A stick-on label tells me which templates are stored in the bag.

Kathy Ainger, Harvard, Illinois

Whenever I make quilting templates from a quilt book, I usually store them within the book pages. Naturally they tend to fall out and get lost. To prevent that:
• Cut the top off of a greeting card-sized envelope (preferably square rather than oblong), new or used.
• Tape the envelope sides to the stiff back cover of the book (towards the bottom), and insert the templates.

The envelope stores templates neatly. I also store small pieces of fabric used in the quilt, as well as a 3" x 5" card of its history.

Fran Johnstonbaugh, Oklahoma City, Oklahoma

Between the pages

Instead of trying to refold patterns to fit in the original envelope, I use top-loading vinyl page protectors and fold my patterns to fit, placing the picture of the pattern in front. I store the pages in a three-ring binder. It's a handy personalized pattern book!

Carol Boone, Freeport, Illinois

Ruler Rally

If your current method of ruler storage just doesn't measure up, consider the following hints the golden "rules" of organizing.

Pockets filled with rulers

Storing my large rulers and T-squares was a problem, so I made something to organize them.

- Use a length of heavy denim fabric approximately 10½" wide x 100" long.
- Fold the fabric in half lengthwise. The fold will be the bottom of the holder. Cut a 10½" x 50" rectangle of fusible interfacing; fuse the interfacing to the wrong side of the front.
- On the front, sew and cut open a series of buttonholes wide enough for each ruler. To position each buttonhole, start from the bottom and measure up 2" less than the length of the ruler.
- Fold the holder in half, wrong sides together. Stitch ⅝" seams along each open side.
- Use the largest buttonhole opening to turn the holder right side out.
- Add large eyelets across the top and use them to hang the holder on a wall.

Pamela Broesder,
Lexington, North Carolina

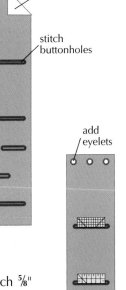

interfacing

wrong side

stitch buttonholes

add eyelets

Note from Nancy

Another option for hanging this ruler organizer is to hand stitch a quilt-type sleeve to the wrong side of the completed organizer.

- *Stitch a 6" strip, meeting right sides and long edges. Turn right side out.*
- *Hand stitch to the wrong side. Insert a dowel and hang!*

Ruler hang-ups

I use shower hooks to hold rulers and hang them on the rungs of a quilt rack. The rack is very portable and I can place it wherever I need it or store it in a closet. It takes up very little room and I can see at a glance everything I have and choose the ruler that works best for the project I'm working on.

Laureta Boyer, Port Richey, Florida

Sweet dreams are made of this

I have tried several ways of organizing my sewing and quilting rulers. I think I have found a way to keep them handy and organized in my small, crowded house.

For large rulers:

- Stitch slots to fit long rulers in a pillowcase.
- Add a bias tape hanger to the center, or to each corner for more stability.
- Store the organizer on a coat hanger and slip it in a garment bag.

For smaller rulers, use a heating pad cover. For triangles, circles, and my tailoring templates, I make cases appropriate for each.

- Attach the smaller ruler organizers to a multiple skirt hanger's clips.
- Write the ruler size with permanent pen at the top of each pocket so you know where to store it when not in use.

Louise Patterson,
Lake Charles, Louisiana

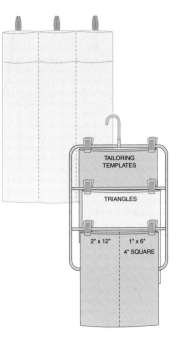

TAILORING TEMPLATES

TRIANGLES

2" x 12"   1" x 6"
4" SQUARE

Fully Furnished Sewing Room

What do PVC pipe pieces, shoeboxes, wood blocks, and dishwasher racks have in common? They will all help you arrange your sewing room for optimal storage space!

Table for one, please

I love to quilt but live in a small apartment. My cutting mat fits on my kitchen table or card table, but both tables are too low to use for any extended period of time.

To remedy this, I had four pieces of PVC pipe cut 30" long. I slip these over the legs of my card table. The top of the pipe fits right into the leg hinge, making the table 34" high – just the right height for me to use for cutting. When not in use, the folded card table and four pieces of pipe take up very little storage space.

Pat Kesler, Le Mars, Iowa

My husband slid pieces of PVC pipe over the legs of a heavy-duty folding table to raise it up about 6" or 7". This is my cutting table. I can also stack large plastic bins or plastic shelving units underneath.

Peggy Nelson, Janesville, Wisconsin

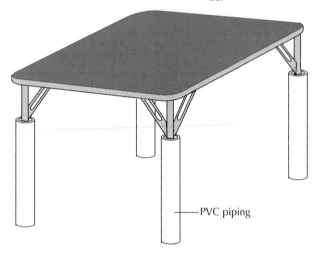

PVC piping

A chip off the old block

With the help of a friend I am now able to easily raise and lower tables I use for sewing and cutting out patterns. We glued four 1½" x 6¼" pieces of wood together and drilled 1" deep holes in the center of the top board to accommodate the legs of almost any table. Put the blocks of wood under each leg of a table to make it about waist high. I can lay out and cut out patterns without my back giving way. This is very handy; I can easily move these back-saving risers from one table to another.

Claire Collins, Rogers, Arkansas
Bonnie Kauffman, Keene, New Hampshire

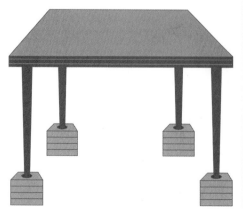

Take the next step

While reorganizing my small sewing room, I wanted a place to store my quilt and sewing magazines. While looking through some possibilities, I found a shoe organizer box. It worked perfectly! I arranged the magazines according to date with old issues on the bottom. It works nicely to have them in order and since the organizers stack well, I can store many magazines.

Elaine Feder, Green Lake, Wisconsin

No more dirty dishes!

We recently replaced our dishwasher. My husband hung the old racks and the silverware basket on my sewing room wall. What a great organizer this has been for tools, interfacing, notions, etc.!

Pat Druetzler, Indianapolis, Indiana
Ina Westbrook, Visalia, California

You're on a roll!

I use a three-drawer plastic cart with casters to organize my sewing items: one drawer for patterns, another for thread for the serger and sewing machine, and the third drawer for odds and ends such as zippers, scissors, fusible interfacing, etc. The great thing about it is that it can be moved into a closet for storage when not in use.

Mary Lou Ederer, Saginaw, Michigan

Hide and seek

My husband and I moved to a smaller home a couple of years ago and my sewing room is now much smaller. I realized that I must find more storage for my stash of fabrics, etc. After donating some to the Rescue Mission, I got the idea to put a plywood cover on a plastic container and cover it with fabric to match the sunroom decorations. Now it hides a big supply of sewing supplies and also serves as a table for a lamp. That allowed me to keep things that I would have had to give or throw away.

Elizabeth Lehman, Mt. Vernon, Illinois

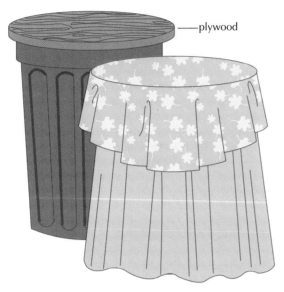
plywood

Empty nest sewing room

I never thought of having a sewing room until I started watching your show. After my children moved out, I converted one of their bedrooms into my sewing room. But my husband and I needed to have beds for visits from our children and their families and I wanted to be able to use every part of my room, so my husband designed and built a cutting table, which is actually stacked twin beds.

The mattresses are stored under the bottom bed. My husband gave a smooth finish to the top bed and painted it white so it could give me more light. Then he recessed a yardstick into it for me. The height is perfect, so I don't have to bend over and hurt my back.

Juavue Handy, Streamwood, Illinois

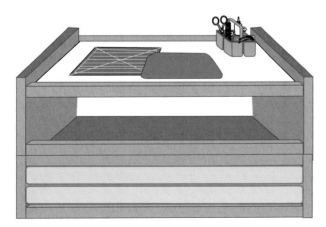

Take 4

Sewing With Nancy's first studio – my living room!

In 1981, I was asked to do a pilot for cable TV. Back then if you asked someone if they had cable TV, their common response was, "What's that?" In other words, the cable TV market was miniscule, allowing start-up, low-budget production companies to test uncharted waters.

The first Sewing With Nancy program was taped in my home; it was quite an experience! The ceilings in our living room were the standard eight feet in height, resulting in a "light burn" (much like a sunburn) due to the close proximity to the intense lighting. Of course, the light burn could have been a result of standing in front of the spotlights for over 13 hours . . . the time it took to tape the first show.

When I look back at that show today, I cringe at my delivery, presentation, and cadence – it's blackmail material! Thankfully, I'm the only person who knows where that tape is hiding!

Clever Organizers

Though it's hard to believe that there is life beyond sewing, these organizers will keep you moving through all walks of life.

Frequent flyer organizers

I developed a portable travel paper organizer for my daughter who was preparing to leave for a year of touring. She has traveled before and misplaced papers, causing some difficult situations. I used a scrap of reinforced vinyl, some clear vinyl scraps, and bias strips to make the case. Ultrasuede® could also be used. The case measures 9½" x 14", has a Velcro closing, and has room for her passport, visas, vaccination certificate, tickets, and an extra pocket for incidentals. The case folds flat, takes up little room, and hopefully will keep her papers safe.

Ruth Brockie,
Fort Frances, Ontario, Canada

Dough on the go!

I revised the basic ideas from your TV program on making a lingerie bag to make money organizers for my children. They were using envelopes to store their money, but the envelopes always fell apart since they often like to count the money!

Supplies needed:
• Six 7" x 12" fabric rectangles
• Six 7" zippers
• 32" length of grosgrain ribbon

Making the organizer:
• Make three zippered bags.
• Position zipper tapes along the 7" edges of one rectangle, right sides together. Stitch along the tapes.

- Meet a second fabric rectangle to the unstitched edges of the zipper tapes, right sides together. Stitch along the tapes.
- Open one zipper part way to provide an opening for turning the bag right side out.
- Meet the cut edges of the rectangles, right sides together, positioning the zipper teeth at the upper and lower edges. Stitch the side seams, catching the zipper tapes.
- Turn the bag right side out.
- Repeat, making two more bags.

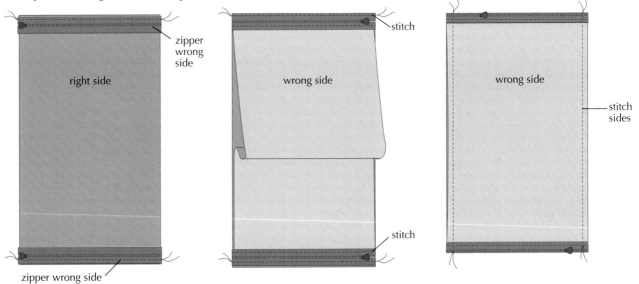

Assembling the organizer:

- Stack the three bags, positioning the second bag 1" down from the first, and the third bag 1" down from the second. Pin or clip the bags together.
- Center the ribbon lengthwise on the back of the bags.
- Stitch across all three bags 6" from the top of the third bag, forming six compartments.
- Fold the bags on the stitching line and tie with the ribbon.

My daughter and son put a slip of paper inside each bag to let them know what the money in each pocket is for – church, fun, savings, presents, clothes, and pet supplies.

Susan Kumba, Burlington, Wisconsin

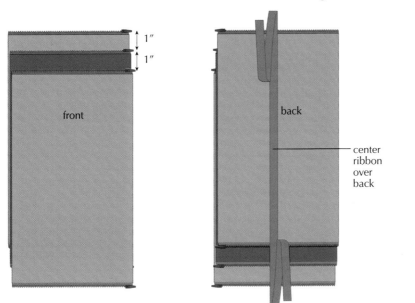

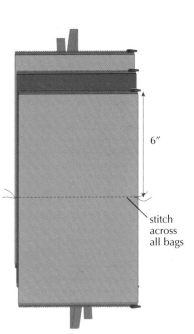

Organizing Ideas for a "Juggler"

In a simplistic form, there are two organizational types: the "juggler" – a multi-task person who has many projects going at once, and a "singular" – a diligent individual who starts a project and methodically finishes it prior to starting another project. A juggler can't be a singular, and vice versa.

Generally, the singular is more disciplined than the juggler; organizing isn't as difficult since there's only one project to keep on task. On the other hand, the juggler's projects can easily get out of control.

For many years, I tried to be a singular, saying to myself, "Just finish this project before starting another one." I'd find myself walking away from my sewing area, wishing to divert my mind to another project and ultimately taking longer to finish one project than if I had two going at the same time.

Box each project

When my sons were in kindergarten, each child had a plastic crate with his/her name on it to store mittens, scarves, and papers. Like the kindergarten classroom, my sewing area is filled with boxes or box-type holders: plastic boxes, shoe boxes, storage baskets, even tins.

After I've purchased the fabric for a project, I gather the pattern or book, the coordinating thread, interfacing (if applicable), zippers, etc., and store them in a box – a see-through plastic box is the organizer of choice! That box becomes a safe-haven for all the uncompleted components. When you have time to begin the project, all the "ingredients" are in one place.

This first step may seem obvious. Yet if you fall into the habit of stacking all the components on a tabletop or at the corner of a counter, you're much more likely to misplace the thread, or worse, lose a pattern piece. Besides, boxed projects can be easily and quickly stored away.

Don't hide your sewing machine in a closet

If you enjoy the art of sewing and quilting and strive to be organized, dedicate an area of your home to your hobby. Assign a corner of a bedroom, den, or basement as *your* space. An accessible sewing machine will allow you to enjoy the art of sewing and quilting at a moment's notice.

Hang up your patterns

If you enjoy apparel sewing, consider hanging up your favorite patterns in lieu of folding the pieces and placing them in the envelope. I keep my favorite skirt and top patterns ready to sew, hanging in my closet!

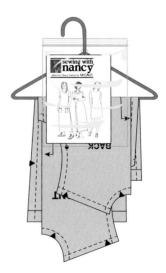

Drape pressed pattern pieces over a hanger, pinning the smaller pieces to the larger ones. Place the pattern envelope in a plastic bag, hole-punched at the top; hang the plastic bag over the hanger.

When you're finished with the pattern, hang it back in the closet.

Two for the time of one

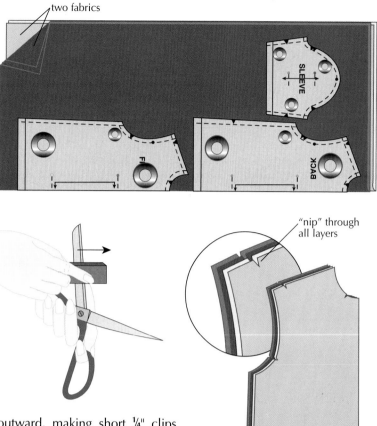

two fabrics

SLEEVE

BACK

"nip" through all layers

Often when sewing a simple t-top, I'll make two tops at the same time. This technique would also be great when making home décor accessories or outfits for kids.

- Cut out two projects at the same time. Choose fabrics that are the same width. Stack and pin the layers together along the folded and selvage edges before laying out the pattern.
- Since it's difficult to pin through the layers of two folded fabrics, only use a few pins to hold the pattern to the fabrics at each grain line end. Anchor the remaining pattern edges to the fabrics with pattern weights.
- Use 8" dressmaker shears for cutting the multiple layers. If your shears need sharpening, use a sharpening stone to ensure clean-cut edges. Work along the beveled surface of the knife edge blade, sliding the stone upward, working from the tip of the blade to the shank. After honing, wipe the blade clean.
- Nip notches instead of cutting them outward, making short ¼" clips through all the cut layers. Use V-clips to indicate the center backs and fronts on the garment, collars, and facing.
- If possible, sew the two like projects in tandem, choosing a thread color that could blend with both fabrics. For example, use a light gray for the inner seams thread if sewing one light yellow and another medium blue top. When you add topstitched details, change to matching thread colors. **Note:** *Obviously, this technique would not work if sewing one white and one brown top.*

Quilting on the go

I'm smitten with landscape quilting. To pass the time while riding in the car, I cut shapes for a flower garden quilt. I keep a shoe box filled with wonderful floral fabrics and a scissors between the bench seats, and I place cut-out pieces in envelopes also stored in the shoe box. (The only downside is arriving at a destination with a lap filled with fabric lint.)

Roll-up your patchwork

When working on a patchwork project, I keep a large terry towel handy. To store the unfinished project, place the various blocks and/or strips on the towel, then roll. The patchwork pieces stay separated and intact. When I'm ready to continue the piecing project, I simply unroll the towel and find all the pieces just as I left them.

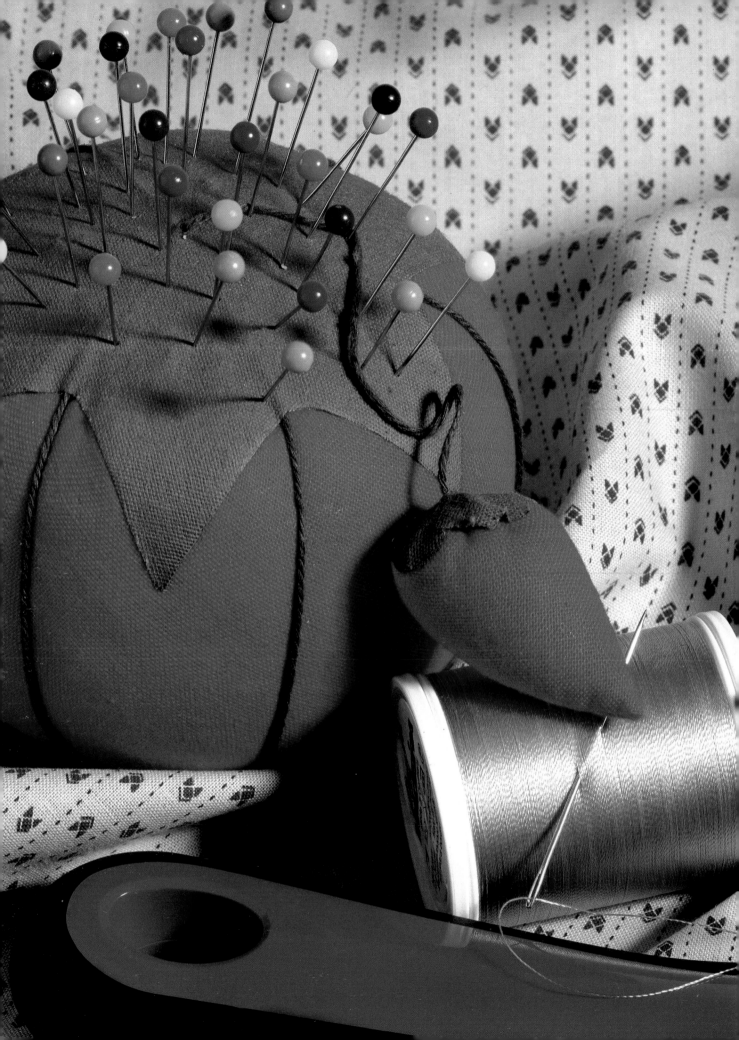

CHAPTER TWO

Nifty
notions
and groovy
gadgets

Seam gauges and rotary cutters and shears, oh my! Every sewer knows that a well-stocked sewing room is definitely something worth singing about.

Having the right tools for a project can make all the difference. Notions make sewing projects quicker and easier, and will help you achieve a polished look.

In this chapter, viewers of *Sewing With Nancy* share ways to use the old favorites, as well as some surprises that will have you singing a new notions tune.

Super Substitute Notions

When you have a job to do but don't have the right tool, these hints
will help you to think outside the sewing room to discover substitute notions
in the most unexpected places.

Weighing the options

When cutting out a pattern, I like to use weights instead of pins but to have the number of weights I want is a costly venture.

As an economical solution, I buy various widths (from 2" to 4") of metal washers at a farm equipment dealership to use as weights. They are perfect because they have a hole in the center that makes them easy to handle.

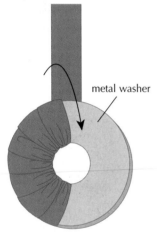

metal washer

- Cut 1" to 1½" strips of cotton knit fabric.
- Feed the strips through the hole and around the washer to cover it.
- Secure the end with a little hot glue.

A friend made me a weight holder with a 6" base and a piece of doweling set into the middle of the base. It holds the weights neatly and I can move it around easily.

Diane Gabruch, North Battleford, Saskatchewan, Canada

Old computer mouse pads make great pattern weights. They do not slip, are heavy enough to hold firmly, and can be cut into all sorts of shapes, allowing you to cut small pattern pieces easily without using pins.

Bernadette Traiger, Lawrence, Kansas

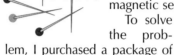

Kids' Hint

This seam guide has "sole"

When I was teaching my niece to sew, she had difficulty maintaining a uniform seam width. I have a magnetic seam guide, but it tends to migrate.

To solve the problem, I purchased a package of Dr. Scholl's Molefoam® padding that has adhesive on one side. I cut a narrow strip and attached it to the bed of my machine at the ⅝" mark. It is easily moveable, so I can reposition it depending on the size of the seam.

Carol M. French, Mexico, Missouri

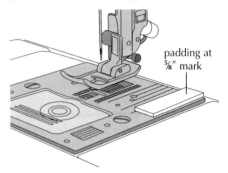

padding at ⅝" mark

Batten down the fabric!

I sew a lot with velvet, satin, faux fur, fleece, and other slinky fabrics, and tried many different tactics to keep the fabric from slipping. Double pinning helps stabilize the fabric, but takes too long. On an impulse, I reached in my basket of plastic clothespins and "pinched" the fabric together every 3" or so. The clothespins reach far enough into the fabric that I get the same result as with double pinning in about one-quarter the time.

Gail E. Steuart, Tucson, Arizona

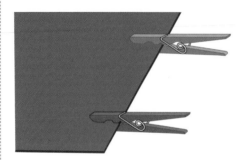

Hints from your hairdresser

It is often difficult to "pin" a pattern into Ultrasuede, and weights don't always hold a pattern down sufficiently. Instead of traditional pins, I buy professional hair styling tape from a beauty supply house, "pin" across the pattern edge at strategic points to hold the pattern down, and then cut at the cutting line. The tape leaves no marks on the Ultrasuede, and won't harm the pattern.

Sonya Breidbart, Scarsdale, New York

hair styling tape

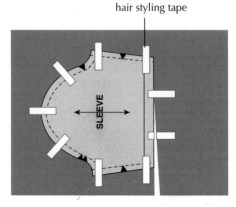

SLEEVE

Good for your smile and your serger!

Use a dental floss threader to thread the upper and lower looper of a serger.

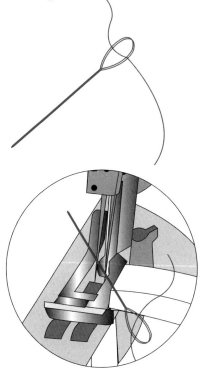

Note from Nancy

Since the introduction of sergers, this popular hint has been submitted countless times. I give my collective "thank you" to all who have sent me this valuable idea.

Spin cycle

Here's an easy way to turn straps or tubes right side out without using a conventional notion:
- Attach a safety pin to one end of a narrow ribbon approximately 2" longer than the tube.
- Pin the safety pin through one layer of the tube fabric.
- Tuck the ribbon inside the tube as you sew, being careful not to stitch into the ribbon.
- After sewing, just pull the ribbon and it will turn your tube right side out!

Connie Mashburn, Fort Wayne, Indiana

It's in the mail

Here's a good use for all of those self-sticking address labels I receive in the mail. I make circles with a paper punch and use the circles to mark dots, darts, shoulder seams, seam allowances, etc. when I cut out pattern pieces. The circles go on and come off easily without marking the fabric.

Dorathy J. Kimrey, Brooksville, Florida
Jane J. Davis, Charlottesville, Virginia

Reinventing the tracing wheel

My tracing wheel had picks that tore patterns. Since I often use patterns several times, I needed to use something else. I use a pizza cutter; it does not cut the paper, and it makes a bold and fine tracing line on the fabric.

Eva Krawchuk,
Winnipeg, Manitoba, Canada

Clean and "make-up!"

I keep a long-handled, fluffy make-up brush at my sewing machine. In the few seconds that I wait for a bobbin to fill, I can brush and clean all around the inside of the open bobbin case area. It's amazing, there's never any buildup of fuzz!

Adding one drop of oil and working it into the brush really helps to pick up lint and fuzzies around the bobbin and under the throat plate of my machine.

Dolores Ketelsen,
Albuquerque, New Mexico
Judy Snow, Lowell, Ohio

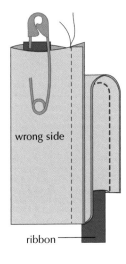

wrong side

ribbon

Behind the Scenes

Take 5

"R & D" at Sewing With Nancy

Most companies have "R & D" (Research and Development) departments. At Sewing With Nancy we have one too. Only for us, we commonly refer to this department as "The Sewing Room!"

Donna and Kate are the master seam-sters of this room, designing projects for TV, sewing the step-by-step samples, and testing and sewing projects for Nancy's Notions catalog. Some days you can literally see the steam coming out of the room.

In TV production, one of our challenges is determining the number of samples to create. We obviously have the finished project completed, but the big question is how many in-process steps to make to show you the process. On average, we have four process steps. After 20 years of programs, we have multiple cabinet files of current programming and boxes filled with older shows.

You may wonder why we keep the samples. If you ever call our customer service department and ask, "How did that zipper go into the jacket Nancy demonstrated on 'Sew 'n Go Separates'?" someone will go to the file, pull the sample, and give you the details over the phone.

"Wooden iron" alternative

Use a spring-loaded clothespin as a pressing aid.
- Remove the spring.
- Put the flat sides of the two pieces together.
- Tape, glue, or wrap the pieces together.

This can then be used as a "wooden iron." A single side of the clothespin could also be used in this manner but it is not as strong as the two pieces. It's a very inexpensive sewing tool.

Jackie McVay, Marysville, Washington

Note from Nancy

The "wooden iron" alternative and the Little Wooden Iron can be used to open seams or press seams to one side when quilting. Either notion is ideal for foundation piecing or "pressing" small seams.

Sharpen your ripping skills

While ripping out some quilting stitches, I realized my seam ripper was old and dull. I have used the knife sharpener that came with my cutlery set to sharpen my potato peeler for years. So, I used the knife sharpener on my seam ripper instead of buying a new one. It worked great!

Karen McDonald, Duluth, Minnesota

"Pitcher" perfect

In my sewing room, I have a "notion" that would normally be found elsewhere that is very useful to me. I use a gravy separator pitcher to fill up my iron. It has a narrow spout that feeds from the bottom of the pitcher. I don't have to tip the pitcher very much so I don't spill water all over my ironing board. This pitcher can be found wherever kitchen tools are sold.

Carol A. Brown, Batavia, Illinois

Raise the bar

While making a faux chenille vest, I found it quite time consuming to cut between the fabric layers, and the point of my scissors kept piercing through the bottom layer of fabric. To remedy this, I placed one of my Celtic Bias Bars™, 12" aluminum bars generally used to press narrow strips, in the channel where I needed to cut. The bar helped guide the scissors through the fabric and also prevented me from cutting the bottom layer of fabric.

Pam Overfield, Akron, New York

Note from Nancy

If you like making faux chenille, you'll be excited to know that there is a rotary cutter designed especially for chenille. This cutter combines a rotary cutter and guide in one tool! The cutter easily cuts through up to seven layers of fabric while the guide fits between the stitched channels and protects the bottom fabric layer.

Guest Spot

The elegantly English Angela Madden, author of eight books, has shared her techniques with American viewers on two Sewing With Nancy series – "Creative Celtic" and "Paradise Flowers." Not only did Angela find fame among U.S. sewers with those shows, she found a few nonsewing fans as well.

Angela Madden

"Around the time that 'Creative Celtic' was airing on PBS, my nonsewing United Kingdom neighbor was on holiday in the States. To pass time, she turned on the television in her hotel room.

"She was enjoying the variety of American shows and topics she found, when – to her amazement – she found me! The person she had always known as 'the lady from three doors away' was on a show called *Sewing With Nancy*.

"Upon returning to the U.K., my neighbor rushed round to see 'if I knew that I was on television in the States.' I could hear the excitement in her voice as she described to me what I had done and said on this U.S. television show. She talked very quickly, wanting to know every detail about what it was like to go on TV, and what it was like to be famous.

"Just like many neighborhoods in the U.K. and in the States, the news of my fame quickly spread. Needless to say, my standing in our neighborhood rocketed!"

Angela Madden

Fantastic Feet

Thought you knew everything that your machine presser feet were capable of? These hints will introduce you to some surprising new uses and leave you feeling footloose and fancy-free.

It "seams" so easy!

Using my bias binding foot to apply Seams Great® works beautifully. It is so much easier to fit the fabric edge into the fold of the Seams Great with the binding foot.

Yvonne Becker, Millford, Delaware

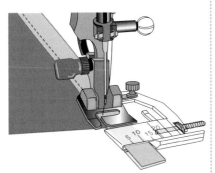

Note from Nancy

Seams Great is lightweight bias-cut, ⅝" wide tricot on a roll. It curls around the edge of the fabric and can be applied with a zigzag or straight stitch.

Tiptoe through the stitches

Previously, it always bothered me that I could not see the marks for the stopping and pivoting points when I stitched collars and lapels because the front of my presser foot covered the marks. I discovered that if I use an open toe embroidery foot, I could stitch more accurately in those areas.

Emma Sloan, Trussvile, Alabama

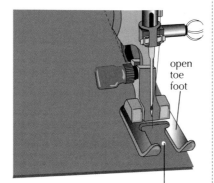

open toe foot

stopping point

Hole in one

Here is my solution to couching when you don't have a cording foot. I place plastic tape on top of my special-purpose or open toe presser foot. Puncture the tape at the center of the foot's needle opening, making the hole the width of the trim you are using. Insert the trim down through the hole, from top to bottom and from front to back. Then attach the presser foot. Adjust the stitch width so the stitches catch the fabric on both sides of the trim.

Caroline Thomas, Yorktown Heights, New York

"Zippy" stitching guide

I found that I could stitch perfect ¼" seams using my zipper foot as a guide. Place the edge of the foot against the edge of the fabric for uniform seams every time.

Emma Magielda, Amsterdam, New York

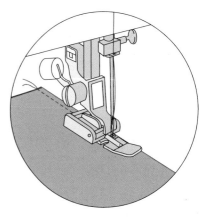

Note from Nancy

Not all zipper feet are exactly alike. Test stitch on a sample and measure from the stitching line to the cut edge to determine the seam width. If the measurement isn't exactly what you want, adjust the needle position if your machine has that feature. Then test again.

Between you and me

When sewing on vinyl, leather, or plastic, instead of purchasing a seldom-used Teflon™ foot, use tissue paper or wax paper between the plastic and the pressure foot. Everything will glide through the machine evenly and smoothly, and you can see through the paper to sew a straight line. When you are finished sewing, it is easy to tear the paper away, much like tear-away stabilizer.

Elaine Austin, Puyallup, Washington
Gayle Faraday, Pittston, Pennsylvania

On Pins & Needles

Sewing With Nancy viewers pin down problems like threading needles
without straining your eyes, keeping pins around when you need them, and more.

Pincushion "corsage"

It was frustrating when I couldn't find my pincushions. So I made one that always stays on my wrist.

- Cut two round pieces of fabric approximately 5" in diameter.
- Pin the circles right sides together. Stitch around the outer edge with a ¼" seam, leaving an opening for turning.
- Turn the cushion right side out, stuff it with fiberfill, and stitch the opening closed.
- Cut a length of ½" wide elastic the measurement of your wrist minus about ¾".
- Center the cushion over the elastic. Attach the elastic to the pincushion.

I have worn out two of these pincushions over the years, but I always have my pins handy.

Lyn Harris, Madrid, Iowa

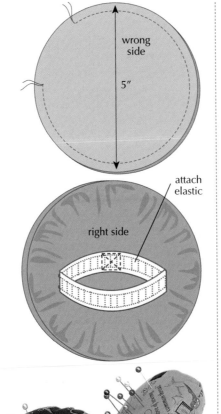

wrong side

5"

attach elastic

right side

Note from Nancy

To prevent sticking yourself with pins, add a plastic template to the underside of the pincushion, or use a child's plastic bracelet instead of elastic.

Staying in the loop

To prevent thread from slipping out of the eye of a needle for hand sewing:

- Double the thread and insert the thread loop through the eye of the needle.
- Bring the opposite end of the thread through the thread loop.
- Pull the thread through until the loop is tight against the eye of the needle. The needle will never come unthreaded!

Norma Beadel, Davenport, Iowa

The "eyes" have it!

When threading a needle, hold something white behind the eye to see the needle eye clearly. This works for both hand sewing and machine needles.

Darlene Minter, Snellville, Georgia

I am able to thread my machine needle much easier with a white background. Cut tiny ¼" x ½" pieces of white sticky back paper from videotape or computer labels, peel off the paper, and stick them to the shanks of all your presser feet.

white area

Nora Yeager, Bolivar, Pennsylvania

Threading a machine needle with monofilament thread is difficult for me, even when I use a needle threader, because the thread is clear. To remedy this:

- Place an index card or small piece of cardboard next to the sewing machine.
- Place the thread on the card and rub a permanent marker over the end, covering about ¾" of the thread. The colored end makes the thread tip more visible and easier to insert through the needle.

Lavon Dorsey, Osage, Iowa

With "aging" eyes, I find that if I put a little Fray Check™ on the end of the thread, the thread becomes stiff after it dries and is easy to thread through the needle.

Shirley Hunziker, Altoona, Iowa

Instead of moistening the thread to insert it into the needle, try moistening the eye of the needle instead. It works every time.

Eileen LaMonte, New Port Richey, Florida

Get a leg up on lost needles

I often misplace my threaded needle when working on my projects. Here's the method that works for me, virtually eliminating my problem:
- Cut four 4" squares of high-loft fleece. (You could use wool, flannel, or anything soft.)
- Layer the squares. Stitch along the edges.
- Serge the edges to finish them.

When sewing, I simply pin this pad to the thigh area of my pants with two safety pins. I can safely place my needle and thread into this "pad," knowing that it is always in the same place when I need it. I am free to move around, and I don't have to search for that elusive needle and thread.

Gayle Page-Robak,
Selkirk, Manitoba, Canada

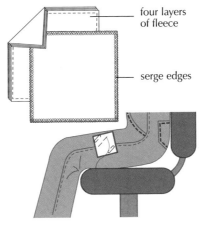

four layers of fleece

serge edges

Put your pins to the grindstone

To sharpen pins and needles, I make self-sharpening pincushions out of felt and stuff them with unsoaped steel wool pads purchased in the grocery store. I also make them for baby shower gifts and present them with diaper pins inserted. Disposable diapers have been known to tear or have the tabs come apart. That's the time to have an old-fashioned diaper pin handy. I've been making and giving both of these items for 35-plus years, and they are always well received.

Sandy Baney, Houston, Texas

A new spin on used needles

Here are a couple of uses for used sewing machine needles.
- Use them instead of tacks or push pins on a bulletin board.
- Use them to hang pictures on the wall. The needles leave only a very small hole in the plaster and are really very strong.

Vicki Heitman, Spokane, Washington

Finding your needle in a haystack

After completing a hand sewing session, leave a short piece of thread in the eye of the needle before putting it away. If the needle drops, it is much easier to spot the colored thread than it is to see just the needle alone.

Barbara Ellinger, West Jefferson, Ohio

"Berry" smooth sewing

To eliminate tiny unseen burrs and reduce the risk of a snagged seam when doing heirloom sewing:
- Unthread the needle after every few seams.
- Raise the presser foot to its highest position.
- Pass the needle through emery cloth, or the "strawberry" from a tomato pincushion.

Barbara Karon, Seminole, Florida

Magnetic personalities

One day while looking for something to hold my pins I looked at my refrigerator and saw magnets! I turned over an advertising magnet and put pins on it; my pins were no longer a problem. The magnet held the pins and did not get in the way because it is flat. Another good point: The magnet was free.

Kathie Martin, Allen Park, Michigan

While working on the car, my father and brother used a magnetic wand to lift out small metallic objects they dropped. After dropping pins on the floor and having to stop my sewing to retrieve them, I went to the automotive parts store and bought one of these magnetic wands. Now when I drop a pin, I reach for my wand, pick up the pin, and do not have to get up. There are several styles of wands; I found the telescoping one the most useful.

Claudette M. Arnold,
Richmond, Virginia

Needle ID in one "felt" swoop

After removing sewing machine or serger needles from the package, it is very difficult to tell whether they are for knits, denim, or regular cotton fabrics. Now I use a permanent felt-tip marker and stroke it across the needles in the package before removing one. Then I know at a glance what type it is.

Barbara Campbell,
Winnipeg, Manitoba, Canada

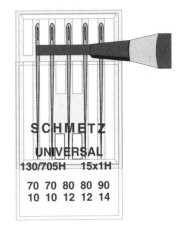

Tried & True Thread Tips

Thread: it runs through every sewing project, yet how can something so basic be so troublesome? The following hints will help you to ease your tangled mind and get your thread running smoothly.

Two's company, three's a crowd

Using a few pieces of children's Tinker Toys®, I made a great gadget for keeping decorative threads separated when using several at one time for embellishment with a multicord foot.

- Run a cord long enough to go around your neck through the center of two round wooden pieces. Knot the end.
- Attach a long dowel piece to one side of the round piece, thread your spools of thread, and attach the other end of the dowel to the other round piece.
- *Optional:* Stick smaller dowels into the round piece, perpendicular to the thread spool, to keep the thread spool away from your body.
- If you're using longer spools of thread, just add another round wooden piece and another dowel.

Kathy Yedinak, Ephrata, Washington

When working with two or more decorative threads at one time, it is very easy for the threads to become tangled. To keep the threads separated:

- Place each individual spool of thread in a baby food jar.
- Place all the baby food jars in a small box such as a shoebox and put the box in your lap.

Your thread stays separated and you don't have a tangled mess when finished with your project.

*Sharon Tartt,
Wilmington, North Carolina*

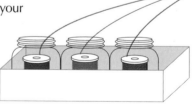

golf tee

Teed off

To keep bobbins together with their matching spools of thread, I use golf ball tees.

- Wind one or two bobbins of the same color.
- Insert the tee into the bobbins, and then on the matching spool of thread.

This keeps my thread together and ready to sew when I am – no more searching through drawers for bobbins.

*Toni Sawyer,
Cicero, Illinois*

Recently, I wanted a multicolor thread combination to use for couching on a denim vest. I could not find what I wanted, so I decided to make my own.

- Twist several colors of rayon thread together.
- Wrap the combined threads around an empty cone. (This will keep the thread feeding smoothly and prevent tangles while sewing.)
- Lay the twisted thread over the line to be stitched.
- Zigzag over the thread with matching or nylon thread, unwinding it from the cone as you go.

The combined colors of rayon thread couched on the denim vest looked great.

Martha Hickox, Amarillo, Texas

Just do the twist!

Note from
Nancy *Here's another way to create decorative cording that I've shown on Sewing With Nancy.*

- *Cut several lengths of decorative thread four times the length needed.*
- *Insert a short length of strong thread through the opening in a bobbin. Tie to form a lasso. Insert the decorative thread through the lasso; meet the cut ends.*
- *Attach the bobbin to the machine as if winding a bobbin. Hold the cut ends of the threads with one hand and pinch the threads at the bobbin with the other hand.*
- *Run the machine to tightly twist the threads. Meet the cut ends to the lasso and grasp the four strands together. Let go! The strands will automatically twist together.*

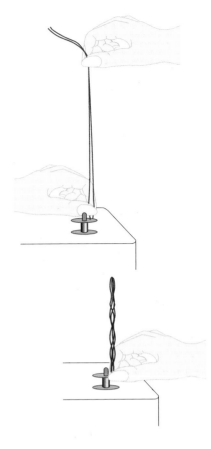

Fit to be tied

When hand sewing or quilting, I like to have my thread handy and easy to dispense as the work progresses. To keep track of a spool of thread:

- Run a length of ¼" or ⅛" wide ribbon through the hole in the spool of thread.
- Tie the ends in a bow, leaving space between the bow and the spool.
- Pin this to your project with a safety pin.

Sue Werkmeister, Maywood, Nebraska

B is for bobbin

Like many sewers, I had trouble determining exactly what type of thread was on a bobbin. Now I use Bobbin Buddies™ to label them.

- Write the name or type of thread on a Bobbin Buddy using a fine point permanent marker.
- Wipe off the writing easily with a dab of nail polish remover to change the label.
- Replace the Bobbin Buddy as soon as the bobbin is removed from the machine.

Linda Tague, Spencerport, New York

Using a permanent marking pen, I mark the color number of the thread on the bobbin. I use a lot of similar shades of thread and doing this makes it easy to match the bobbin thread color to the thread in the top of the machine.

Joni Kamfonik, Coos Bay, Oregon

These "booties" were made for serging

When serging using large Woolly Nylon® thread cones, the thread had a tendency to slip down and wind itself around the spindle. To solve this problem:

- Cut a 6" section from the leg of discarded pantyhose.
- Gather one end of the cut section together with your fingers, push it up inside the cone about halfway, and flip the other end up around the sides of the cone.
- Place the cone on the spindle.

The pantyhose will keep everything in place and the cone has a bootie!

*Alma Luckett,
Hamilton, Ontario, Canada*

nylon cover

A tisket a tasket, a static-cling-free basket!

When doing hand sewing, I keep a used dryer sheet in my sewing basket. It serves in many ways:

- After threading a needle, run it through the dryer sheet a few times, even if it is a specialty thread, like metallic thread – no knots, no kinks, and silky smooth sewing. (I do a lot of appliqué, cross stitch, and needlepoint with specialty fibers and this never fails for me.)
- Any dust that gets into the basket will be drawn to the dryer sheet instead of threads and fabrics.
- Using a scented sheet gives a nice smell to all your sewing. Since the sheet has been used, the smell is subtle, not overpowering.

Ila Nadeau, Springvale, Maine
Marjorie Stock,
Stratford, Ontario, Canada

Wipe out

To easily remove threads after ripping a seam:

- Hold the seam area flat against a firm surface such as your ironing board.
- Rub gently back and forth along the seamline using a clean eraser.
- If the threads don't come out immediately, turn the fabric over and "erase" from the other side, too.

Sheila Pour, Mechanicsville, Virginia

A spoolful of thread makes the medicine go down

When I travel I like to bring my stitching projects along, but my thread often gets tangled. To prevent this:

- Make a small hole in the lid of an old medicine bottle.
- Place a spool of thread in the bottle. Feed the thread through the hole and put the lid on.

This is very convenient for travel. The thread will not tangle and the bottle is easy to pack in my sewing bag.

Romona Reed, Elkhart, Indiana

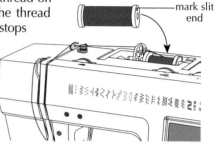

Machine threading that hits the spot!

The thread spindle on my machine is horizontal. When threading my machine, if I don't put the spool of thread on the spindle with the slit end first, the thread sometimes catches in the slit and stops the machine. Now I make a small dot with a permanent marker on the slit end so I'll be sure to slip it on first. This is a small hint, but it saves me time and frustration.

mark slit end

Opal Catron, Salem, Virginia

Send a care package

When I sew for my eight-year-old twin granddaughters, I send along matching thread for their mother's sewing basket. To identify the thread and prevent it from getting lost, I slip strips of the fabric I used through the spool and tie it. I also secure the threads with tape so they don't unravel.

June Stein, Brooklyn, New York

Pressing Matters

Having problems with your iron? Turn to these hints to relieve the "press"ure and smooth out the wrinkles.

Ironing board protection program

To remove fusible web from an ironing board cover, lightly rub a piece of sandpaper over the cover. This removes the fusible web and leaves the cover better than new!

Linda Fifer, Rio Linda, California

Keep a roll of paper towels near the ironing board at all times. When fusing web or interfacing, place several sheets of paper towels on the ironing board before fusing. If the fusible web sticks to the paper towels, simply throw them away.

Ruth Seeley-Abrams, Albuquerque, New Mexico

Prudent pressing cloth

When pressing fusible-backed appliqués onto garments, etc., there's often a small bit of the fusible sticking out here and there. Instead of using a press cloth, which gets gunked up with fusible backing, I use tissue paper. It's disposable and cheap.

Nancy Camp, Denver, Colorado

Trace without stopping for directions

When tracing designs onto fusible web, I usually trace the design onto the paper backing of fusible web and then iron the web onto the wrong side of fabric. However, this does not work on directional designs such as letters like R or F, or fish that I don't want swimming in the wrong direction! Normally, I had to retrace the design to create a reverse image before putting the design on the fusible web. My trick:

- Trace the design on the paper from the fusible web, making sure to use a dark marker.
- Carefully separate the paper from the fusible web.
- Flip the paper with the traced design to the other/wrong side. The design is now reversed.
- Iron the web on the wrong side of the fabric. When you cut out the design, it faces in the right direction.
- Make sure to carefully line up the paper and the fusible web before ironing so the glue from the web doesn't get on the iron. If this should happen, use a crumbled piece of waxed paper to clean the bottom of the iron.

Nancy Patchell, Tucson, Arizona

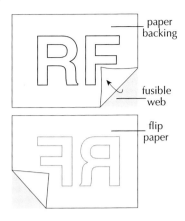

paper backing

fusible web

flip paper

Note from
Nancy

Another option is to trace the letter shape on the web side, flip the fusible web to the paper side, and retrace the outline from the web side to the paper side.

Curl up with a good tape

When I was expecting my first child I made a few receiving blankets for her using bias tape to finish the blanket edges. I cut my own strips using a matching fabric, but wasn't looking forward to being on my feet to iron under the edges. I discovered a trick that allowed me to sit while pressing the yards and yards of tape. I finger pressed the first few inches of tape, then clamped it in my hot curling iron. By slowly sliding it through, making sure the edges stayed straight, I had all of my fabric pressed in a matter of minutes, and I could sit with my feet up!

Sunny Allen, Bountiful, Utah

Roller derby

After wallpapering my bathroom, I accidentally left out my wooden wallpaper seam roller. I set the roller on my sewing machine to put away later.

Later when I sat down to sew for 10 minutes, I had one seam to press on a quilt block and did not want to heat my iron for one little seam. The light bulb went off in my head as I looked at the wallpaper roller. It worked wonderfully – I could sew now and iron later.

Using the wallpaper roller saved on my electricity bill and my sewing area stayed much cooler without having the iron on for a long period of time. The roller works like the small Wooden Iron, but it doesn't stretch the fabric. It works especially well on a bias seam.

Reva Reed, Krotz Spring, Louisiana

Behind the Scenes

Take 6

Timing the
– not quite –
half hour
TV show!

Each Sewing With Nancy half-hour program is timed to 26 minutes and 45 seconds. When planning for TV, I think, "Can I teach this in under 30 minutes?" Sometimes the answer is yes, other times no. When the answer is no, the project figuratively and literally gets "cut" from the lineup.

After planning the program or three-part series, I determine the length of each segment. For example, I may allocate 3:30 minutes at the demonstration table and another 4:00 at the sewing machine to detail a certain quilting project. My task is to allow enough time per project so that you can understand the technique!

The introductions or openings are the only portions of the shows that I script word for word. I write out the copy in advance and read it from the teleprompter. The openings (the name, in TV land) are 30 seconds when I present the show solo or 45 seconds when I have a guest. An interesting tidbit that I've learned over the years is that six and one half lines of typed copy equal exactly 30 seconds of TV. Little details like this make my life go more smoothly!

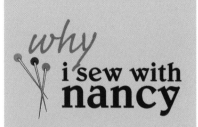

Leave them rolling in the aisles

Using leftover Teflon fabric, I made a small padded cover to use as an ironing "ham." I slipped two wooden cylinder building blocks from my children's old toys inside the Teflon case. The ham is great for pressing open small seams.

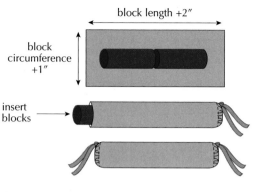

* Line the building blocks up as they will be placed in the ham; measure the length and circumference.
* Cut the Teflon 1" wider than the circumference and 2" longer.
* Fold the Teflon in half, right sides together, and stitch the lengthwise edge.
* Turn under ½" on the shorter ends to make casings. Stitch, leaving an opening to insert the cording.
* Turn the cover right side out.
* Insert ⅛" cording into one casing. Pull the cording tight and tie.
* Slip the building blocks into the cover.
* Insert the cording into a second casing. Pull the cording tight and tie.

Cathy Sisk, Arlington, Texas

My seam roll got lost in our last move. I have never replaced that much-needed tool, as I'd rather spend my money on fabric!

I made my own seam roll by rolling up cotton quilt batting very tightly and placing it in knee-high pantyhose. When the batting expanded it was just the right density. The seam roll is about 18" to 20" long and looks like a huge sausage! It works great!

Betty Edwards, Pineville, Louisiana

Note from Nancy

During college, I, too, made my own seam roll, using a tightly rolled magazine that I covered with wool. After many years of use, it became lopsided. Before tossing it, I took it apart and smiled as I reflected on the styles found in the 1971 issue of Vogue Patterns Magazine.

Iron out your problems

I use table salt to clean my iron. It sounds crazy, but it really works!
* Place a printed newspaper over the ironing board.
* Place a generous amount of ordinary table salt in the center.
* Turn the iron on and "iron" the salt in a circular motion.

Marge Axford, Rochester, Minnesota

To get rid of that "sticky goo" that so often clings to the bottom of an iron after applying iron-on interfacing, etc., run the hot iron in a circular motion several times over a piece of waxed paper. It works wonders!

Donna Steinhauer, Eau Claire, Wisconsin

When the soleplate on my iron gets "gunked up," I clean it with a cotton ball soaked in nail polish remover. It immediately cleans the soleplate, leaves a shine, and does not scratch. I then rinse the soleplate, dry it with a towel, and once again have an iron that performs smoothly.

Bettie Roth, Carmichael, California

Grab Bag of Notions

From corralling runaway pedals to using charcoal briquettes
to keep tools dry, these tips cover everything but the kitchen sink!

With this ring, I thee pin

Last year for Christmas, our quilt guild gave each member a miniature pincushion, worn on a finger like a ring, that was made out of a twist-off lid from a pop bottle.

- Make two slits in the lid.
- Measure your finger and cut a piece of elastic that length plus ½".
- Thread the elastic through the lid. Overlap the ends of the elastic and stitch.
- Fill the lid with batting or stuffing and cover it with a small piece of fabric. Ours had a small amount of lace around the edge.
- Glue the fabric in place. It will look like a fabric-covered cotton ball.

I find this pincushion great to wear at the sewing machine because my hand is holding or guiding the fabric and my little pincushion is already there. Just remember not to get the elastic too tight.

Debra Higgs, Andover, Kansas

batting

elastic

slits

Have appliqués will travel

I recently started to do appliqué, but had a difficult time keeping track of the many pieces. I tried pinning a few pieces to my pincushion but it wasn't big enough. To solve this dilemma, I turned a small canvas bag into a big pincushion.

- Buy a small canvas bag with handles and stuff it with fiberfill.
- Stitch the top of the bag closed.
- Separate and pin all the appliqué pieces to the big pincushion in the order you wish to appliqué them.
- Use long flower head pins to secure bobbins to the big pincushion and use little Bobbin Buddies to keep the bobbins from unwinding.
- Put a small pocket on the big pincushion to hold small scissors and extra needles.

This little bag goes with me to work, on trips, in waiting rooms, and in front of the TV. It has helped me a lot.

Becky Fischenich, Redding, California

Teaching old tools new tricks

While wallpapering my bathroom, I discovered that my 24" quilting ruler was the perfect size for getting a straight line on the wallpaper. I used an old rotary cutter blade and the back of my cutting mat to cut the wallpaper, and used a shorter ruler for cutting the border. Using the rotary cutter and ruler gave me a perfectly straight cut. I was able to match up the seams on the border with no problems!

Kathy Hovendick, Blair, Nebraska

When filling an opening of a pillow, doll, or stuffed animal with stuffing pellets, I use an empty serger thread cone as a funnel.

Michele Elliott, Coon Rapids, Minnesota

Because I have arthritis, it is difficult for me to get the thread out of the casters on my sewing chair. Here's my solution:

Don't throw away your old surgical seam ripper when it becomes dull – use it to cut the threads that become tangled around the wheels of a sewing chair. It does a wonderful job because it has a very thin blade. Then use serger tweezers that lock closed to pull out any stubborn threads.

Donna M. Stemnock,
Bethel Park, Pennsylvania

Put the pedal to the metal

When my grandchildren reach five or six years old, I teach them to sew. However, they are unable to reach the foot control of the sewing machine. There's also the age-old problem of the "creeping" foot control. To solve this problem:

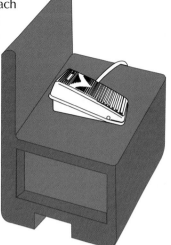

- Put the foot control in a booster seat that children use at the table.
- Place the booster seat on the floor facing the child and the foot control on the seat.
- The foot control is now high enough for even a five-year-old to reach, and it will never slide any farther than the back of the seat.

Elizabeth Zwicke, Waukegan, Illinois

I am teaching two granddaughters to sew. When first starting, they have trouble controlling the speed of the machine. I solve the problem by putting a makeshift "governor" on the pedals.

Slip two dish sponges under the lever part and hold them in place with a rubber band. The children can press down hard and the machine won't go fast. This way they can just concentrate on what their hands are doing.

Myra Karachy, Zeeland, Michigan

Rub-a-dub-dub; clean your mat with an eraser or scrub

After cutting quilt pieces with a rotary cutter and cutting mat, I take a large square of nylon net, wad it up, and rub the surface of the cutting mat. This removes any embedded threads and leaves the mat smooth without harming it.

*Leona Love,
Richmond, Missouri*

My cutting mat had lots of nicks with fabric stuck in them. I used a pencil eraser and just erased the fuzz away. The pieces of fabric came off cleanly and the eraser did not damage the mat.

Angel Moreno, Denver, Colorado

Note from Nancy

You can also use shower scrubbies to clean a cutting mat instead of wadded up nylon net.

Not just for grilling anymore

Because we live in an area with an abundance of rain and moisture, I need to keep my sewing desk and my husband's toolboxes and drawers dry. I place a charcoal briquette in a small container in the corners of the drawers or boxes, and the charcoal absorbs moisture.

Lee Gaber, Puyallup, Washington

While cleaning my sewing machine, I took off the throat plate to clean under it. I used a small vacuum cleaning attachment but still couldn't get one area free of lint because the attachment wouldn't go down into the small area. I finally thought of a solution:

- Wrap double-sided tape around the pointed end of a shish kabob stick and insert it into the small opening of the machine.
- Twirl the stick a little to collect as much lint as possible. The lint will accumulate on the sticky side of the tape.
- Extract the lint-loaded stick out of the opening.
- Remove the tape from the end of the stick, put another piece of tape around it, and repeat the process until all the lint is removed.

Wanda Starcher, Goshen, Ohio

Back to the drawing board

I love to make my own designs for quilts and machine embroidery. I have found that a dry erase board and marker are useful notions. The board is handy for making temporary notes about patterns because I can make changes as often as I like. When satisfied with a pattern, I copy it onto something permanent.

Brenda Taylor, Flat Rock, Indiana

Let there be light

While working on a project that needed a pattern traced, I didn't want to stand at a window to do the tracing. I used my grandson's Lite-Brite® along with a piece of translucent plastic on top – now I have a convenient light table.

Linda Basile, Akron, Ohio

Oh, what a tangled web we weave

When finishing edges of large amounts of lace or trim, I have difficulty because the lace becomes tangled as I serge. To remedy this, I invented a simple timesaving device.

- Wrap the lace around an empty paper towel roll.
- Insert a two to three foot length of ½" wooden doweling through the center of the tube.
- Attach two C-clamps to the front edge of the table in front of your serger. The C-clamps cradle the dowel rod, allowing the lace to easily unwind from the tube without any annoying tangles.

Lil Hopton, Lynchburg, Virginia

Look, but don't touch!

When my children were young, I had problems keeping them out of my sewing equipment. From my prized scissors to my simple serger tweezers, the children grabbed anything that met their needs, which usually involved the outdoors and animals of one sort or another.

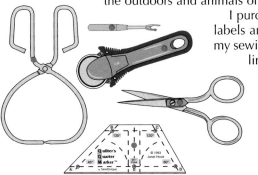

I purchased a box of ¼" round red labels and put them on everything in my sewing room that I considered off-limits. It worked great! To this day, my grown children know not to touch anything with a red dot on it.

Elaine Burchfield, French Camp, Mississippi

Beep! Beep! Time to play!

For about 18 years, I have enjoyed sewing as a hobby. However, my time for sewing is now limited with a three-year-old at home. I set my kitchen timer for 10 to 15 minutes. For that amount of time Matthew has to keep busy by himself. When the timer beeps, it is his time. I stop, even if in mid-seam. Then I set the timer again for 15 to 20 minutes, and spend that time playing or reading to him. When the timer beeps, I start the process all over again.

Tara Tarbet, Highland, Utah

Give scissors a facelift

While gathering items for a garage sale, I found several pair of good quality school scissors that my children (who are now teenagers) had used in elementary school. I sharpened the scissors and used them to trim patterns. I love using them! The small size makes maneuvering easy and the rounded tips keep me from accidentally poking holes in the fragile pattern paper.

Linda Barnhouse, Decatur, Alabama

A zipper here, a button there; watch your collection grow!

Before discarding old clothing, I cut off all the buttons and the zippers if they are in good shape. This way I acquire quite a collection and have a good supply when needed.

Eleanor Marek, Gassville, Arkansas

Behind the Scenes

Take 7

Whoever said that TV was *glamorous*?

At 7:00 a.m. on taping mornings, Donna, Pat, and I pack the van and drive to the studios of Wisconsin Public Television in Madison, Wisconsin. All of the supplies for the day usually fill the back of the van. Yet on occasion we have had to remove the bench seat to make room for everything.

It's an hour drive to our destination so we better make certain that we have all our samples, machines, and wardrobe changes. Only twice in 20 years have I forgotten wardrobe changes and samples . . . not too bad a record because those two days were nightmares!

Our first stop at the studio is at the unloading dock. This job quickly dispels the thought that taping a TV show is glamorous! All props, supplies, machines, and samples that were carefully loaded into the van, are now carefully transferred to a cart and wheeled into the studio.

Take cover!

To prevent losing pins from my round magnetic pincushion when I travel to workshops, I made a cover for it.

- Cut a circle of fabric with a diameter 3½" larger than the diameter of the magnet.
- Turn under the edge ½" and stitch close to the cut edge, leaving a small opening.
- Cut a piece of ¼" wide elastic the circumference of the magnet.
- Insert the elastic into the casing and stitch the opening closed.
- Slip the cover over the magnet.

I carry all my sewing supplies in a large basket. The covered magnet can go in at the last moment and I know that all my pins will remain on the magnet.

Jean Haynes, Muskogee, Oklahoma

wrong side

← insert elastic

What's your point?

All the pencil sharpeners I used to sharpen marking pencils made dull points or broke the writing point. I tape a double-sided emery board to my sewing table and rub the marking pencils lightly over it to make a nice sharp point.

Norma Roth, Bothell, Washington

Try a "baking soda spritzer"

I had a difficult time removing marks made by water-erasable marking pens from my fabric because my water is acidic. I add a couple of tablespoons of baking soda to a cold water spritzer. The marks come out every time and don't reappear. This also works on some marks that have reappeared on quilts because of the acidity of the water.

Rebecca Pressley, Superior, Colorado

Put a cork on it

When working with slippery fabrics such as lingerie, swimwear, blouse silks, and bridal fabrics, I was frustrated when the fabric slid around on my table. To eliminate this, I purchased ¼" thick rolled cork and glued it to the surface of my sewing table. (The cork does not snag the fabric.) It worked wonders! Not only does the fabric stay in place, but the pattern pieces do too.

If you don't want to glue the cork to a table, just use C-clamps to hold the cork in place while you're using the table, then roll it up and put it away when you're finished working.

Laurie Grade, Milwaukee, Wisconsin

Sit! Stay! Sew!

The foot pedal of my machine kept sliding around, and I was tired of chasing it all over the floor. Here's my solution:

- Buy a large plastic mat designed to help chairs roll easier on carpet.
- Determine the best location of the foot pedal on the mat.
- Put the hook side of a piece of Velcro on the mat and a piece of the loop side on the bottom of the pedal. (This worked so well that I did the same for my serger.)

Another advantage of using a mat under the machine: You don't have to worry about pins and needles getting caught in the carpet.

Cindy Moore, Bowling Green, Kentucky

Guest Spot

Sulky Thread's Joyce Drexler joined me in the 1980s on Sewing With Nancy *for a number of shows focusing on machine embroidery. Our shows were well received by our viewers, yet our first meeting – pre-cell phone era – didn't go quite as planned.*

"The first time I flew to Wisconsin, I was to arrive very late, and Nancy's husband Rich was to meet me at the airport.

"After landing, I soon realized Rich was nowhere to be found, and quickly became worried. I called Nancy from a pay phone. She said he had left for the airport long ago and should have been waiting for me when I arrived. Now we were both worried! Once Rich called Nancy, they quickly discovered our problem: Rich was 50 miles away at the Milwaukee airport, while I was at the one in Madison.

"Meanwhile, it was quickly approaching midnight, closing time at my airport. Nancy and I decided that I would wait for Rich at the Denny's restaurant.

"Alone in a strange town, I called myself a cab and waited. Soon the cab arrived, driven by a rather shabby looking man who said he knew a shortcut to town. That's when I got really scared. But my angel was with me, and I soon saw the glorious light of the Denny's sign.

"I walked in and the hostess asked me if I was Joyce Drexler. Wow, I thought, I haven't even taped a show yet and someone in Wisconsin knows who I am! As it turned out, Nancy had alerted them of my arrival. I was home safe."

Joyce Drexler

Joyce A. Drexler

"Sticky" Situations: Adhesives

Storing adhesives can sometimes be a gooey mess.
Stick with these viewer hints for everything you need to know about adhesives.

"Tails" from the sewing room

Here's a new use for basting spray: Picking up thread tails from the carpet.

Supplies:

- Standard size paint roller
- 1 empty paper towel cardboard tube
- 1 paper towel sheet

Instructions:

- Spray basting spray on the paper towel. Wrap the towel back around the cardboard tube.
- Slip the cardboard tube on the end of the paint roller.
- Spray the paper towel with basting spray, turning to coat all sides.
  - Roll this across the carpet to pick up thread tails.

  When you vacuum, this will prevent those annoying thread tails from wrapping around the beater bar of your vacuum cleaner.

Dianne Monk, Ozark, Alabama

paper towel   basting spray

There are a lot of threads scattered around my sewing room and hallway that clog the brushes on my vacuum. To prevent this:
- Purchase a vegetable brush, one with stiff bristles.
- Swipe it across the floor. It acts just like a lint brush but picks up all of those pesky little threads.

Judy Davis, Lake Mary, Florida

When working on a cut and press board or cotton-covered ironing surface, use a napped lint remover to easily clean up threads and small amounts of stabilizer.

Mary Ann Miller, Port Angeles, Washington

Bridging the gap

One morning as I was getting dressed in a new button-up sweater, I noticed some "gaposis." I needed a quick solution so I thought about all the little goodies in my sewing room and remembered the liquid basting glue (Glue Pins). I put a little dab on the problem areas. It worked great. I wasn't concerned because I knew it would wash out. I also carried the bottle in my purse in case I needed a "touch up."

Janet Lindstrom, Vilonia, Arkansas

Instead of pins or basting stitches, I use an ordinary glue stick for basting. It is especially useful when putting in a zipper.

Flora E. Merideth, Blossom, Texas
Elizabeth Burgenson, Phillipsburg, New Jersey

Just add water

I like to use Perfect Sew® liquid stabilizer because it leaves no residue on the back of my project, but I hate the mess of getting it spread evenly. I've discovered that if you put the stabilizer in a spray bottle with just enough water to allow the liquid to spray, it works great. It is so much easier to cover your fabric evenly, and you don't have to use nearly as much of the stabilizer. But the best part is that it's not nearly as messy. (Remember to mark the bottle so you know what's inside.)

Sherry Sasser, Kellyton, Alabama

A "chilling" storage idea

To store glue sticks, put them in a zip-closure plastic bag in the freezer. Whenever I need to use a glue stick, it is not dried out, it performs perfectly, and it seems to last much longer than when kept at room temperature.

Marion Farrenkopf, Durham, New York

Note from Nancy

It's perfectly acceptable to use a fabric or even paper glue stick on fabrics as a temporary basting method. Glue sticks work best on cotton fabrics, dry clear and crisp, and will not "gum" your sewing machine needle.

If using glue sticks on noncotton fabrics, test the glue on a scrap of fabric to check for possible change of color.

Notions – Small Useful Items!

If you look up the word "notion" in the dictionary, you'll initially find definitions including *theory, belief, whim,* and *idea,* with the last explanation listed as "a small useful item." As sewing and quilting enthusiasts, we most likely concur with the last definition. To be a true notion, the item must not only be useful, but also be purposeful and efficient to use. Not all sewing and quilting products that fit in the notion category are useful… those products I subconsciously put in the "gadget" category!

Many of the notions that you may use or have seen in stores, books, catalogs, and on TV were designed or developed by people who sew and quilt (or help their spouses) with the purpose of making a task easier. Here are a few of my favorite notions, along with a brief tale of the ingenious designers.

The Tailor® Board

For many years, June Kroenke of Hartland, Wisconsin, enjoyed sewing. I recall her saying, "I wanted to tell people I sewed instead of having my clothes say it first."

In November of 1960, June was constructing a red wool vest for her husband Roger to wear for Christmas, but was having trouble pressing the facings. She was frustrated that no tool in her sewing room could assist with her dilemma.

For six weeks, June worked practically night and day to design a product for pressing tricky seams flat. Once she had a drawing of her idea complete, she took it to a cabinetmaker to build. The first few prototypes were crude, but eventually she worked out the details and the Tailor Board was born.

From this, June started a mail order business, filed for a patent, sold the Tailor Board to stores, and demonstrated at sewing guilds, the state fair, and even on television. She also changed her name to June Tailor!

June was my mentor, kind friend, and one of the first guests on *Sewing With Nancy.* In November of 1993 she passed away, but the company continues on under the leadership of her daughter Meri and son-in-law Fran Yogerst.

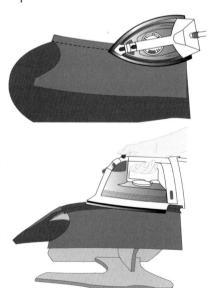

Here are a few ways I've used the Tailor Board. I hope they'll also help you!

Use the Tailor Board to press curves:
- Press curves over similar curves. Match the shape to be pressed to the same shape on the Tailor Board.
- Using a two-step pressing process, first press the seam flat, then press the curve open over the board. For details requiring sharp points and crisp edges, press on the board's wooden surface. When softer edges are desired with wool fabric and flannels, slip the custom-designed pads onto the board.

Press collars and pointed edges:
- Press the seam flat.
- Find the appropriate straight edge on the Tailor Board. Center the seam on the edge and press. Since the pressing surface is only 1" wide, the seam-cut edges will not leave an imprint on the right side.
- To press rounded edges, find the shape that resembles that of the sewn pieces. Press the seam open, then trim and grade the seam allowances.

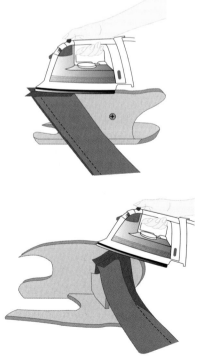

The Fasturn®

Emma Graham, an avid seamstress from Medford, Oregon, introduced me to the Fasturn product at a sewing show in Puyallup, Washington, in 1987.

When she opened the silver box containing long cylindrical tubes and separate wires that were designed to turn tubes right side out, I nodded my head and smiled, yet thought, "This might fit in the 'gadget' category." She explained that the tool had been designed out of frustration by her husband Don, who, after kindly turning tubes of fabric for her, first with a knitting needle and then with a safety pin, came up with this novel notion set.

Later, the contents inside the silver box piqued my curiosity. After a few minutes of testing, I found that Emma and Don really knew what they were talking about! Since then, the Fasturn has been a mainstay in my sewing room.

Here are a few tips I've learned over the years. I hope they'll also help you.

To easily turn fabric tubes:
- Determine the finished flat tube width; multiply by two. Add ½" for two ¼" seam allowances.
- Cut strips of woven fabrics on the bias; cut strips of knit fabrics on the crosswise grain.
- Stitch lengthwise edges together, using a ¼" seam, meeting right sides, and leaving both ends unstitched.
- Select a Fasturn cylinder that slips easily inside the fabric tube. Insert the cylinder inside the stitched tube; wrap and fold one end of the tube tightly over the end of the cylinder.

- Insert the wire into the cylinder from the handle end. Turn the hook clockwise so the pigtail goes through the fabric.
- Gently pull the wire back through the cylinder, turning the tube right side out. Do not turn the hook, or it may release from the fabric.
- When the turned tube reaches the lower opening in the cylinder, release the hook by turning it counterclockwise. Complete turning by pulling the fabric.

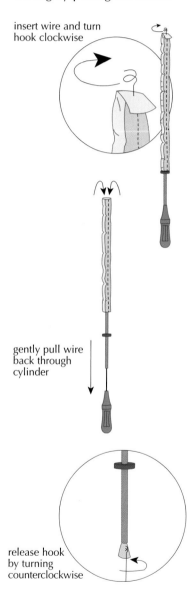

insert wire and turn hook clockwise

gently pull wire back through cylinder

release hook by turning counterclockwise

Add cording or fleece to tubes:
- Select cording that will fit inside the fabric tube. Or cut strips of polyester fleece the width of the original fabric strip.

- Cut, stitch, and thread the tube over the cylinder. Insert the hook and pull the first ½" of the fabric into the tube.

tape

fleece

- Tape the end of the cording to make insertion easier. With fleece, roll and tape the end to form a narrow point that will fit inside the tube.
- Insert the end of the cording/fleece into the end of the tube and gently pull on the hook. The cording/fleece will be drawn into the tube and automatically encased as the tube is turned.

insert rolled-up fleece into end of tube

pull gently to encase fleece

Turn longer tubes in two steps:
- If a fabric tube is too long to turn following the conventional method, stitch the tubes, leaving an opening in the middle of the tube.
- Thread half the fabric tube onto the appropriate Fasturn cylinder. Turn right side out. Repeat for the remaining half.
- Hand stitch the opening closed.

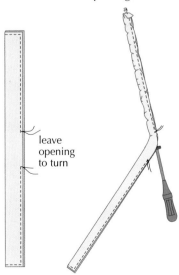

leave opening to turn

CHAPTER THREE

Spiffy *sewing* *solutions*

Basic sewing techniques may not seem like the subject of the spine-tingling thriller of the century, yet a working knowledge of the basics is necessary to complete any sewing project.

Sure, we all know how to stitch a straight seam and sew on a button, but be honest: Have you really mastered working with fleece and inserting zippers? Or do these seemingly innocent "everyday" sewing jobs never go as quickly as planned, eating up minutes if not hours of your valuable sewing time?

Take five from your busy schedule to brush up on the basics. From working with patterns all the way to adding finishing touches, these hints will have you on the edge of your seam.

Pattern Potpourri

Every project has to start somewhere; picking a pattern is often the first step. Take a page from *Sewing With Nancy* viewers and get the last word on using your patterns wisely.

Heads up!

I always cut off the head and hair of the pattern envelope model. Why? I often see a spectacular garment and think, "I've got to make that!" But later I am disappointed to find that in my own fabric choice, with my own coloring, size, and figure concerns, it doesn't look as well on me as I had expected. By cutting off the model's head and hair, I remove the person, and can focus exclusively on the pattern and finished garment.

In some cases, it helps to make a black and white photocopy of the garment to see if I like the garment or the fabric combinations. Some colors look gorgeous on a perfect-looking model, but never on me. It's a small tip, but it's helped me avoid investing time and money on worthless projects. It's amazing how different a simple long tank dress looks without the flawless face and coloring of a model.

LouAnn M. Kuzniar, Lyons, Illinois

Smooth operator

When making garments, I always iron my pattern pieces prior to cutting. Ironing the pattern pieces makes a huge difference in the accuracy of the fit and makes it easier to work with the patterns when pinning the pieces to the fabric.

Janice O'Malley, Wrentham, Massachusetts

"Gifted" patterns

If you have a pattern you are no longer going to use (maybe you've lost pieces or you just don't want to use it anymore), save the pattern pieces, iron them flat, and use them for tissue to wrap gifts. Stitching friends just love to open something that's been tucked into tissue paper that says, "bodice," "front," "sleeve," etc. It's fun, and it's recycling!

Judy Rowley, Ionia, Michigan

Survival of the fittest

To get great fitting pants, I use the same pattern over and over until the pattern becomes quite tattered. To preserve my pattern pieces, I make templates that I can simply trace around:

- Spray poster board lightly with spray adhesive.
- Gently apply the pattern piece and smooth it with a wallpaper brush.
- Use a craft knife to cut out all of the markings.

This method is also great for small craft projects. I recycle cereal boxes for the templates and store them in recycled manila envelopes with a photo of the project on the front. My pants template stays nice and flat under my dressmaker's board.

Karla Farnsworth, Blue Springs, Missouri

I can see clearly now!

When working with fabric that has an obvious design, I make clear pattern pieces so that I can position the fabric designs exactly where I want them to appear on a garment.

- Trace the pattern piece and markings on clear plastic (plastic type empty stuffing bags, clear trash bags, etc.) with a permanent marker.
- Lay the fabric out right side up in a single layer.
- Place the pattern piece over the fabric with the design. You will be able to see the placement of the design on the garment before you cut it out and sew it together.

Note: To cut a vest, hold it up against you and note the left and right side.

Note: If the pattern piece is cut on a fold, mark the center.

Lestine Bush, Williston, South Carolina

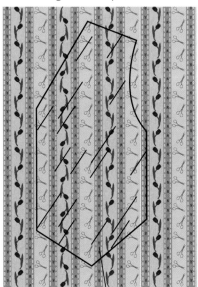

clear plastic

Making ends meet

I have tried many ways to cut the interfacing pattern piece. Many times, the piece I cut from the fashion fabric didn't match up with the shape cut from the interfacing. To make sure that the interfacing and fabric shapes are the same:

- Cut the pattern piece from the fashion fabric, transferring any marks to the fabric.
- Place the pattern piece wrong side down on the fusible side of the interfacing.
- Cover with a pressing cloth, and use the tip of a dry iron to "baste" the fabric piece to the interfacing in a few places.

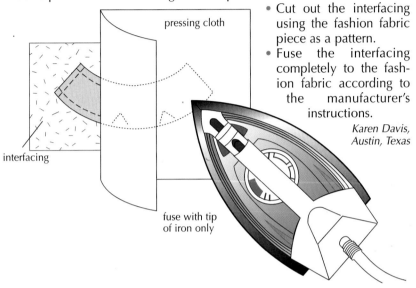

- Cut out the interfacing using the fashion fabric piece as a pattern.
- Fuse the interfacing completely to the fashion fabric according to the manufacturer's instructions.

Karen Davis,
Austin, Texas

Hit the sheets

My mother, an excellent seamstress, passed away several years ago. Just recently, while going through some fabric pieces I inherited, I discovered a very unique way she used to preserve pattern pieces. She duplicated the pattern pieces by tracing around them on an old bed sheet, then cut the pieces out and marked them. The sheet pattern piece I found was marked "child size 2" in permanent black marker. These pattern pieces are certainly washable and can be used over and over again for many years.

Jill S. Grundy, Prairie Village, Kansas

Blank canvas

When trying to decide what colors to use for tennis warm-up suits, I take the instruction sheet from the pattern that has black and white drawings, and paint or color it. This gives me an idea of how my finished project will look. I like to make copies and try several variations.

Pat Moore,
South Shore, Kentucky

The paper has two faces

Double-faced tracing paper is useful for transferring pattern markings. Lay the paper between the wrong sides of two pieces of fabric and trace the marks with a tracing wheel. Both sides are marked in one step.

Barb Silva, Rochester, New York

The highlight of the day

Sometimes it's easy to overlook even the simplest instructions. To make any special instructions – the number of pieces to be cut or whether a piece needs to be interfaced – easier to locate, I simply highlight them with colored felt pens, using a different color for each topic.

Jocille Kienlen, Arvada, Colorado

One size doesn't fit all

Sewing for two granddaughters requires me to use multi-size patterns. I trace the different sizes onto different colors of tissue paper. For example, I know that all the yellow pieces are size 2, and the blue ones are size 4. I store them all with the original pattern in a gallon zip-closure plastic bag.

Margaret Turza,
South Bend, Indiana

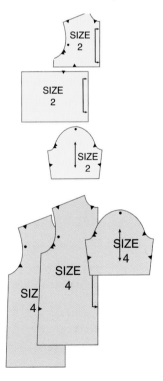

Making Connections

Over, under, in the ditch – the following hints make seams a cinch!
Sewing With Nancy viewers will help you sew great seams, no matter where they are!

Matchmaker, matchmaker, make me a match

To easily match plaids or prints, I use my blind hem foot and blind hem stitch.

- Press under the seam allowance on one of the fabric pieces.
- Meet the two pieces right sides together, placing the piece with the pressed seam allowance on top.
- Open up the seam by folding the top piece along the fold line so that both pieces are right side up. Align plaids or prints.
- Stitch, guiding the fabric fold along the guide on the blind hem foot along the right fabric, catching the left fabric every few stitches. This ensures that the two pieces are perfectly matched and secured.
- Sew the seam in the normal manner. When finished, remove the "hem" stitching.
  This method is quicker and easier than hand basting or taping.

Bonnie D. Marini, Tappan, New York

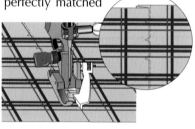

Sewing incognito

A pattern I was using recently called for bias binding around the armhole and neckline. On the wrong side, the bias was supposed to be hand stitched in place. That did not excite me! I thought about stitching in the ditch, but the stitching was still visible, so I used invisible thread. It worked great and was so easy! I have also used this technique in other places that call for similar hand stitching.

Vicki Vandever, Heyburn, Idaho

Note from
Nancy
I find it easier to use invisible thread, such as Monofil, in the needle and all-purpose thread in the bobbin. It's wise to have one visible thread in the seam!

A perfect match

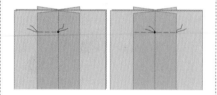

Sometimes I have trouble matching one seam to another, for example, matching the facing seam to the garment seam. When I follow these steps the seams do not shift and are perfectly matched:

- Match the two seams right sides together.
- Place the needle of the machine into the middle of the seam and sew three to four stitches one way, catching the seam allowance in the stitching.
- Rotate the piece. Place the needle into the seamline, and sew three to four stitches in the opposite direction.
- Finish sewing the seam without worry about the two seams getting out of alignment.

Shirley Simons, Louisville, Kentucky

Staying on top of things

Here's how I make a quick and easy flat felled seam. I serge the seams together, press the seam to the side indicated in the pattern, and topstitch with a double needle.

I sometimes use metallic threads for the topstitching to really set off the seam.

Sharon Herbert, Browns Mills, New Jersey

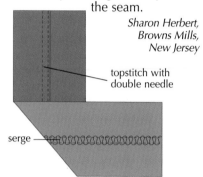

topstitch with double needle

serge

Topstitching on fabric that has an "optical illusion" (herringbone or twill) is hard on my vision. I place a plain piece of fabric or paper along the edge I am stitching. This helps define the edge, and quickens the task.

Dianne Zavatsky, Dallas, Texas

To determine where to stop to pivot at a corner when topstitching, I bisect the angle with a pin. It helps to use a long, fine pin. (Can you tell that I teach geometry?) When stitching, I stop and pivot when I reach the pin.

Jackie Yoshizu, Aiea, Hawaii

Note from
Nancy
To easily "bisect" the corner, fold the corner in half and crease the fabric. Place a pin along the crease mark.

Gather Together

Does creating gathers have you in a pinch? This collection of quick and easy hints will make you feel like you've got the world on a string.

Put your foot down!

When zigzagging over string to prepare for gathering, I use my five- or seven-hole multi-cord foot. I thread the string through the center hole and simply stitch a wide zigzag. Then I can guide the fabric knowing the string will remain in the center and not get caught in the stitching.

Cathy Gaupel, Eaton Rapids, Michigan

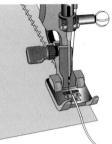

String your gathers along

Whenever I need to gather, I use Nancy's quick way of gathering using a zigzag stitch and a string. To enhance this technique, I mark the string the length of the finished gathers, leaving a few inches at either end. I pull the string as I am gathering so that when I reach the end, I have already achieved my gathers and all I have to do is distribute them. I use a pin at each end and secure the string by wrapping it in a figure eight.

Sofia Knight, Shrewsbury, Massachusetts

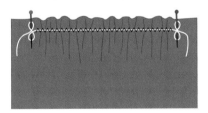

Note from Nancy

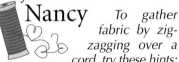

To gather fabric by zigzagging over a cord, try these hints:

- *Place the gathering cord on the wrong side of the fabric.*
- *Set a narrow zigzag stitch, wide enough to accommodate the cord. A wide zigzag will cause the fabric to pucker.*

Opposites attract

When basting or gathering, I slip in a bobbin with thread of a contrasting color. This makes removing the thread much easier and also uses up bobbins of leftover colors.

Anna May Tobelmann, Palm Coast, Florida

Skirting the issue

One of the best methods I've found for sewing a little girl's dress, especially when the skirt is very full, is to gather the front of the skirt and attach it to the front bodice, then do the same to the back. I also sew the sleeves in place before I sew the side seams. I then make one seam joining the sleeve, bodice, and skirt. That way everything goes into place very easily.

Esther Hering, Saylorsburg, Pennsylvania

Put your heads together

Whenever I have lots of fabric to gather, I use color headed pins.

- Fold the smaller piece into quarters, placing a black pin at the half and yellow pins at the quarters. Depending on the amount of fabric, place red pins at the eighths.
- Fold the ruffle, placing black pins at the half, yellow at the quarter fold, and red at the eighths.
- Pin the two layers together, matching the colored pins.

Charlotte Yearwood, Oshkosh, Wisconsin

Behind the Scenes

Take 8

A funny thing happened on the way to the studio!

We've had memorable trips to and from the studio, including a blizzard, icy roads, and a tornado warning. Yet the most momentous trip was on a sunny spring morning . . . the weather had nothing to do with the trip.

The topic of the series we were taping was "Bridal Gowns." Susan Andriks, bridal gown specialist and author of the Palmer/ Pletsch book by the same title, had been my guest the week before; this day we were finishing the details of the three shows.

As we were turning onto the street in front of our building to begin our journey, the hatchback of the van flipped open. Two wedding gowns, bridal veils, and all the samples for the day flew onto the street. After a collective scream, the car was very quickly pulled to the side of the road and the three of us moved faster than we thought possible to swoop the TV show contents from the pavement. There were scissors, thread, notions, and fabrics scattered in all directions. In fact, days afterward, I found wayward spools of thread along the side of the road.

Luckily the gowns and veils were in plastic garment bags. And most fortunate of all, there wasn't another car or truck in sight. What a way to start the day. This experience gave new meaning to the phrase, "Run Away Bride!"

Putting the Pieces Together

Sometimes, things like inserting a zipper or sewing a straight dart are enough to make any sewer cry. Whether you're sewing a hem, inserting a zipper, or making darts, dry your tears and let these hints guide you through every step of the garment construction process.

I have been sewing since I was 12 years old, and after 30 years I still find it rewarding, relaxing, and satisfying to my soul. Sewing is my creative outlet, I can escape the daily stress of the day, and all that I create is truly a labor of love.

Maria Cooper, San Antonio, Texas

I worked full-time B.K. (before kids) and still had time to sew my entire wardrobe. When the children came, I chose to change to part-time work and was able to watch daytime TV for the first time. I discovered that your show was broadcast during the time my children were napping so it became "my time!" I always felt like I was spending time with a friend who enjoyed sewing as much as I do.

As the years have passed, my job has dwindled to a mere ten hours per week, and of course I choose to work them around the timing of your show. Also, the decreased work week has given me time to pass on information that I have accumulated through the years by becoming a local sewing instructor. I started with six students and now have a mailing list of about 130.

Emily Carter, Pueblo, Colorado

Watching your show over the years has made me feel like I had a friend who also loved to sew. There are many, many sewers out there who don't have any friends who share their love of sewing, and shows like yours are a gift to us.

Bev Schoenbeck, St. Louis, Missouri

Dare to make darts

Sewing straight darts is no longer a problem for me with this technique:

- Press the fold of the marked dart.
- Place a piece of paper along the dart, matching the end points. Pin the paper in place.
- Stitch along the edge of the paper, being careful not to catch the paper in the stitching.

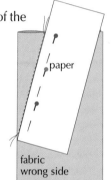

Helene Allen, Star, North Carolina

When a pattern has a dart, I use a paper punch to punch a hole at the top of the dart marking on the pattern. Then I can use a chalk or marking pencil to accurately mark the tip of the dart. This would also work well for marking other points (triangles and dots).

Mary Beth Renze, Pittsburgh, Pennsylvania

In the groove

While making a figure skating outfit that needed an invisible zipper for my granddaughter, I did not have an invisible zipper foot for my machine. Instead, I used my five-groove pintucking foot. I pressed the zipper tape, then placed the zipper coil under one of the grooves and aligned the needle position. It worked great.

Joan Kaak, Orillia, Ontario, Canada

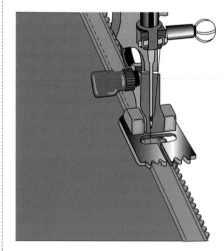

Strike a "cord"

When making a simple nylon jacket, I didn't want an exposed zipper, because I didn't want the overlaying fabric to get caught in the zipper teeth. I discovered this hint while studying my husband's casual jacket:

- Place narrow cording in the center front folds and stitch into place.
- Proceed with the usual steps to apply a separating zipper. The cording fills the fold, greatly reducing the chance of the zipper teeth catching the fabric.

Note: I've used only standard nylon or metal zippers, not outerwear zippers, for this application.

Evelyn Ibata, Cypress, California

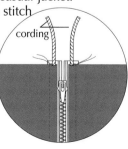

Now I lay me down to sleep

The zipper tab on my daughter's blanket sleeper did not always stay in the down position. When the zipper tab pushed upward, it poked her in the chin and made her cry. I fixed the problem in just minutes with a 1" x 4" piece of ribbon and about ¾" of hook and loop tape.

- Press under the short ends of the ribbon ¼". Stitch the loop side of the tape to one end of the wrong side of the ribbon.
- Meet the wrong side of the ribbon to the right side of the sleeper, center the ribbon over the zipper pull, and stitch the end of the ribbon without the loop tape to the sleeper.
- Center the hook side of the tape on the sleeper under the loop tape; stitch. It works like a charm – just zip, and stick down the ribbon.

Darleen Worm, Fond du Lac, Wisconsin

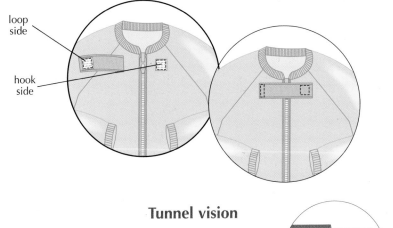

loop side
hook side

Tunnel vision

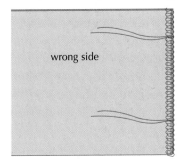

When inserting two elastics through a double casing, I do both simultaneously. This reduces problems trying to get the second one through.

Diane Nolterieke, Stuart, Florida

When pulling elastic through a casing I put a safety pin at each end of the elastic. If the elastic happens to get pulled too far, I just pull it back through the other end.

Elodie Eckenrode, Oregon, Ohio

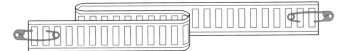

Pressing around the collar

One of the hardest parts of making shirts is pressing the collar seam open before turning the collar. After clipping to the seamline, it was hard not to burn my fingers when opening the seam to press it. I use the Little Wooden Iron to press open the seam first, and then quickly steam it with the iron. Voila! No more burned fingers, and the collar looks great.

Beverly Crane, Timonium, Maryland

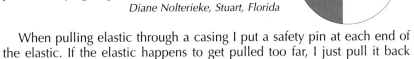

wrong side

Leave a paper trail

To prevent the stitches from puckering when sewing lightweight fabrics such as tricot, silk, or satin, I pin newsprint along all the seams before stitching them. The newsprint adds both weight and crispness to the fabric and makes the fabric easier to handle. When finished, I simply rip away the newsprint, and am left with perfect, even stitches.

Philip Plowman, Fort Worth, Texas

Tailing along

Recently I was sewing on a piece of suiting fabric that had the potential to ravel. I decided to serge the edges of the pieces before constructing the garment. Since I didn't want to eliminate all the clips and notches that were markings, I marked these places with thread. As I serged, I held a long, doubled piece of brightly colored thread at each marking point so that it was caught into the serged edge. This did the trick – sort of a serged-on tailor tack.

Janet Corzatt, Portland, Oregon

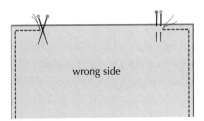

wrong side

On your mark! Get set! Sew!

To mark a point where I must stop stitching, such as at a skirt vent or the opening in a pillow cover, I insert two pins close together. Or I place two pins in a X. The pins keep me from stitching too far. This trick also alerts me to change stitch length where a zipper is to be inserted.

Katherine Anderson,
Murrells Inlet, South Carolina
Connie Macchione,
Vancouver, Washington

wrong side

Pick-Pockets

Patch, rounded, welt, and side, these hints will help you
make pockets with pride! Choose your pocket, as *Sewing With Nancy*
viewers share their tips for sewing pockets of all shapes and sizes.

Could I have my pocket on the side?

My favorite pair of slacks has sporty pockets that I love and wanted to duplicate. Here's the pocket technique I discovered when I took a pair of my favorite slacks apart to use as a pattern.

- Stitch the inside pocket to the garment front, right sides together. Clip to the corners; add Fray Check or double stitch.
- Turn the pocket to the inside and press. Topstitch the opening.
- Meet the back pocket to the front pocket, right sides together. Stitch around the outer edge of the pocket.
- Meet the garment back to the garment front, right sides together. Stitch the side seam, taking care to avoid catching the pocket edge.

Lucille Tuma, Columbus, Nebraska

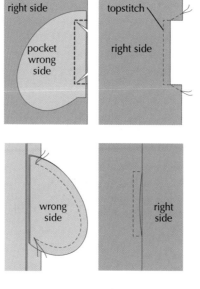

Assume the position!

Here's a way of getting accurate pocket markings on the right side of the fabric without having unsightly markings after the pocket is completed.

- Trace the pocket position on the wrong side of the fashion fabric.
- Stitch around the pocket outline with contrasting thread to transfer the marking to the right side of the fabric. Now it's easy to position the pocket and stitch it in place.
- Remove the contrasting stitching. No positioning marks are visible on the right side of the fabric.

If you don't like removing basting threads:

- Stitch around the pocket outline with fusible thread in the bobbin.
- Put the pocket in place and press. This holds the pocket in place for stitching. No basting threads to remove or markings to erase!

Marge Present, San Antonio, Texas
Sheri Myers, South Sioux City, Nebraska

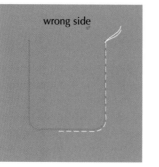

trace and stitch

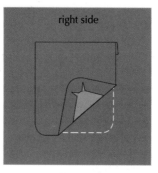

position pocket

Close the "gap"

When applying a patch pocket to a garment, especially one that will get heavy use, here's a tip so the pocket won't gap, yet will have room to be functional.

- Crumple a clean facial tissue, then gently open it without flattening it.
- Place the wrinkled tissue on the garment fabric inside the pocket markings, with the top of the tissue extending slightly above the top of the pocket area.
- Pin the pocket into position, being careful not to flatten the tissue as you pin.
- Stitch with the tissue in place, being careful not to catch the tissue in the stitching.
- After stitching, remove the tissue and notice that the top of the pocket is not tight against the fabric. This small amount of ease prevents the pocket from gapping, but still allows comfortable use of the pocket without straining the fabric or stitching.

Lynn Deitrick, Sarasota, Florida

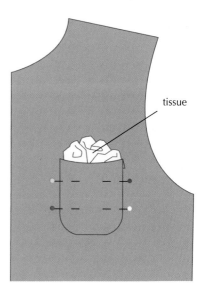

tissue

Frosty the pocket

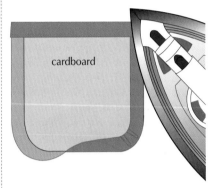

Here's how to press patch pockets to the perfect size without unwanted points or wrinkles.

- Cut a piece of freezer paper the size of the finished pocket.
- Pin the freezer paper, shiny side up, to the wrong side of the pocket.
- Adjust a dry iron for a medium temperature. Press the pocket seam allowances to the freezer paper with the tip of the iron. The heat of the iron makes the seam allowances adhere to the paper and shapes the pocket perfectly.
- Carefully remove the paper and press the pocket on the right side.
- Finish the pocket according to the pattern instructions and topstitch in place.

Norma Pisel, Kerrville, Texas
Sheila Jensen, Pocatello, Idaho

Easy does it!

To ease the seam allowance around the lower edge of a rounded pocket, I use my serger. I adjust the differential feed as I would for gathering and serge around the curved edge. The seam allowances easily shape to the pocket curve.

Donna Miller, Altoona, Wisconsin

She'll be comin' round the pocket

Here's how I make a nice edge on jacket pockets with round corners.

- Cut a piece of cardboard $\frac{5}{8}$" smaller than the pocket pattern piece.
- Cut the fabric out and place the cardboard on the wrong side of the fabric.
- Press the seam allowances over the edges of the cardboard. It makes a nice rounded corner.

Miriam Fowke, Lakeland, Florida

Guest Spot

Lois Ericson, teacher, pattern designer, and prolific author, has inspired many seamstresses with her extraordinarily creative ideas. She shared some of her inspiring ideas on the Sewing With Nancy *series "1st Class Sewing." Known for her trademark creative closures, Lois delights in finding new and exciting ways of working with fabric.*

Lois Ericson

"I don't know if there is any greater joy than being able to take an idea, no matter how vague or seemingly unimportant, to some kind of conclusion. I love to figure out how to make things work. We all know that there is nothing original – everything has already been done by someone in the past. We can put our own spin on an idea, our individual style can 'show through,' and our imaginations are the key."

Although Lois' talent was undoubtedly recognized before she was my guest on Sewing With Nancy, *I hope that her appearance will help her many fans put a face to her name.*

"I was in the Washington, D.C., area teaching at 'G' St. Fabrics. On my day off, my friend Sarah took me to lunch and then we stopped at a fabric shop where she had ordered something. I was wearing a vest that I had made and the woman in the store said, 'Nice vest, are you a Lois Ericson fan?' Sarah laughed hysterically and the woman was puzzled by the outburst. I said, 'Well actually, I am Lois Ericson.'

"She said she was embarrassed that she had not recognized me. I said, 'It's great to have your work recognized, even if you're not.'"

What big pockets you have!

Here's a way to simplify making pocket flaps without extra bulk.
- Place the upper edge of the flap on the fold of the fabric when you cut out the flap.
- With right sides together, stitch around the remaining edges, leaving an opening for turning.
- Turn the flap right side out and stitch the opening closed.
- Stitch the fold of the flap to the garment.

Margaret Thiessen, Pt. Roberts, Washington

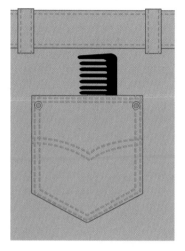

Inside tip for welt pockets

When I make a double welt pocket, I stitch a piece of the fashion fabric to the lower edge of the lining (approximately 3" deep and the width of the lining) before folding up that section to meet the upper edge of the lining. I finish the pocket as the instructions indicate. When I reach into the pocket, or if the pocket welts sag open, the fashion fabric shows behind the pocket instead of the lining.

Kimberly Schell, Fayetteville, North Carolina

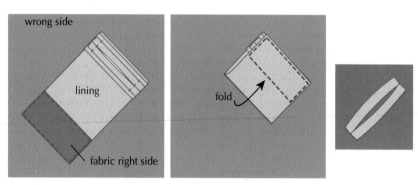

Don't pen me in

As a rancher, my husband is always calculating something and needs a pen. Since I make most of his Western shirts, I add a pen slot to the pocket flaps. When I followed traditional pattern instructions and left an opening for the pen, the raw edges at the slot opening started to fray after several wearings and launderings.

To prevent this, I modify the flap pattern, placing the upper edge of the flap on the fold and interfacing only one half of the flap. I stitch the folded edge of the completed flap to the shirt, leaving an opening for a pen and bar tacking on both sides of that opening. There's no bulk and no raw edges. In addition, I only need one row of stitching to attach the flap, rather than the three needed with conventional methods.

Donna Williams, Ignacio, Colorado

Burning a hole in your pocket

My son's jeans had a tear above the back pocket. Here is my creative way to hide the patch:
- Iron a patch on the back of the jeans.
- Draw the outline of a comb above the pocket using a pencil.
- Use a small brush and acrylic paint to fill in the outline.

David Neslony, Temple, Texas

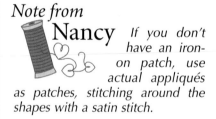

Note from Nancy

If you don't have an iron-on patch, use actual appliqués as patches, stitching around the shapes with a satin stitch.

Leftovers again?

When I purchase readymade clothing items, I often have to shorten them. I love to recycle sewing items and do not like to waste anything that can be put to good use. Recently I had to trim 6" to 7" from the hem of a full skirt. Since I love pockets, I used this scrap fabric to add pockets on both sides of my skirt, using a pocket pattern from another skirt.

Jennifer Tang, Sunnyvale, California

Button Bonanza

Does attaching a button or making a buttonhole leave you feeling like something is missing in your sewing life? Fill in the holes with these tips from *Sewing With Nancy* viewers.

Front and center

On blouses or shirts with vertical buttonholes, the right or left side sometimes shifts up or down, especially when the buttonholes are large. This creates a problem for keeping plaids, stripes, or a print design aligned, or for keeping the lapped edges of a neckline on a collarless blouse even.

To keep buttonholes centered underneath buttons, I sew the very bottom buttonhole horizontally or add what I call the "stabilizer" or anchor button:

- Find a small, flat, preferably clear button from your button box.
- Sew a small horizontal buttonhole between the bottom of the garment and the last vertical buttonhole.

No more shifting!

Mary Ann M. Badgett, Recovery, Ohio

anchor button

There's a hole in my button

Sewing buttonholes on black fabric was difficult for me because I could not see what I was doing. To remedy the problem, I threaded the top of the machine with white thread and stitched sample buttonholes on scraps of the black fabric until I achieved the length and stitch density I liked. Then I carefully switched back to black thread and stitched the buttonholes on my project.

Doris Gardner Baker, Springfield, Illinois

When sewing buttonholes, I place water-soluble stabilizer on the bottom of the fabric even though there is stabilizer between the layers. The buttonholes are crisp, sharp, and even every time.

Louise Lafontaine, Ottawa, Canada

The woman is always right

An easy way to remember which side the buttonholes go on a blouse is to think, "the woman is always right." This reminds me that a woman's blouse buttons right over left, so the buttonholes go on the right.

Lucy Felty, Henderson, Kentucky

"X" marks the spot

When marking button positions, it is difficult to make precise marks. Chalk markers do not make a precise line, and chalk pencils don't do much better once the point is worn down. My tip is to cross two pins to mark a point, or to use one pin under the fabric to mark a line. Then just run the chalk over the fabric for a sharp point or line.

Karen Kendler, Riverdale, New York

I've got it covered

To cover my own buttons, I spray the cutout fabric circles with Sulky® KK2000™, a temporary spray adhesive, then continue with the rest of the process. The spray holds the circles in place beautifully. The fabric curls into the shell almost automatically, and the adhesive disappears in a few days.

Pat Thompson, Sun City Center, Florida

Behind the Scenes

Take 9

Make-up anyone?

Applying make-up is not my forte! Yet the lighting on the set can play havoc with my everyday, Cover Girl-type of application. For the past eight years, I've had the opportunity to work with make-up artist Vicki Fischer. Vicki starts my taping days with style and humor. She knows what make-up works on TV and how to camouflage many of my imperfections.

My facial imperfections are my challenge. You've no doubt noticed that my face is not the standard fare for television. Many have asked, "Did you have a stroke or were you in an accident?" Actually, at the age of 18 months, an ear infection caused the nerve in the right side of my face to swell, creating a paralysis, termed Bell's Palsy. According to medical statistics, 94% of all people who get this malady recover, but I'm one of the unlucky 6%.

As a child and young adult, my slight handicap gave me great insecurities. Once I decided to accept my "packaging," others did too. I learned, thank heavens, that no matter how pretty the gift is wrapped, we care more about what's inside.

Knit Knack

Knits – ranging from interlocks to fleece – have personalities all their own. From clever ways of using scraps, to marking buttonholes, to lining a fleece jacket, the following hints will help you manage these versatile fabrics without leaving your comfort zone.

Feminine edgings

While I was trying to do a picot edge on the neckline of a lightweight jersey knit summer gown, the fabric stretched. I wanted to keep a light and feminine look and did not want a heavy neckline facing. I folded the neckline down ¼", inserted a ¼" piece of twill tape under the fold, and held it in place with basting glue. I then stitched the edge with a blind stitch and it stayed perfectly.

Alice Bowers, Las Vegas, Nevada

wrong side

twill tape

Woman on the verge of a breakdown

Working with mesh knit drives me crazy. It is like fighting with a bowl of wet noodles – very slinky, very heavy, and very stretchy on the crossgrain. Needless to say, when I started to hem the mesh, I really had problems. Whenever I tried to pin the fabric, the pins just fell out and the hem kept stretching.

I used the temporary spray adhesive that I use for machine embroidery. I sprayed this, very lightly, on the hem area of the shirt, waited the recommended 20 seconds, and I was amazed! The fabric handled as if it had been stabilized. I measured and folded up the hem, took it over to my machine, and sewed the hem, no problem at all. From now on, I will use this method for hemming all my stretch knits.

Karla Sutton, Alton, Illinois

You've got a hold on me

Tape, such as Tiger Tape™, used as a blanket stitch guide on fleece fabric can sometimes be too sticky and leave a mark or bits of tape behind when removed. Before I use tape, I simply adhere it to a piece of scrap fabric and pull it away. The tape picks up bits of lint, making it less sticky.

Tobey LaRoe, Tampa, Florida

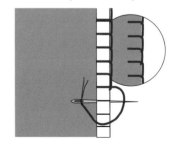

Note from Nancy

There are various widths of Tiger Tape. The ¼" wide tape marked at four lines per inch is a perfect guide for evenly spaced blanket stitches.

A"peel"ing marks

Marking the placement of buttonholes on a Polarfleece jacket was giving me problems. Water-soluble pens made a fuzzy line on the fabric, and I also wanted more stability so the buttonholes wouldn't lose their shape while I stitched them.

To solve this, I cut a 1" wide strip of iron-on tear-away stabilizer, pressed it onto the jacket front, and marked my buttonholes on the stabilizer with a water-soluble pen. After I made my buttonholes, the stabilizer peeled off easily. After a spritz of water, all the marks were gone.

Rose ChapdeLaine, Welch, Minnesota

tear-away stabilizer

Note from
Nancy

Test this idea on a sample of fleece. Make certain to use the tip of the iron to press, avoiding iron marks on the fleece. Also, use this idea on all types of knits, not just fleece.

Scrap-happy sewing

When working with fleece I always check machine tension prior to constructing the garment or project. This leaves me with a lot of long, serged pieces of fleece. Soft, stretchy, and strong, they are ideal for use as plant ties. I save them up during the winter and put them to good use during the late spring and summer.

Dorothy Winter, Wasilla, Alaska

When I have small amounts of Polarfleece left over, I cut ¼" wide strips and pull firmly. The strips become very good yarn to use for couching. They can be also crocheted or knit to use with whatever was originally made from the fleece.

Constance L.B. MacKinnon,
Courtenay, British Columbia, Canada

Purchased sleeve heads and polyester fleece only come in white, making them very conspicuous in colored garments. To remedy this problem I use remnants of fleece to color coordinate my jacket sleeve headers. I've even used plaid fleece in a red or navy jacket for an "inside surprise."

These sleeve heads also work well in dresses with droopy sleeves. I sewed a 1" wide strip in as a sleeve head and trimmed it until I got the effect I wanted. It looked great!

Lois Miskoe, Rocky River, Ohio
Kay Lancaster, Hillsboro, Oregon

Below the belt

When sewing a heavy Polarfleece robe, I found an easy way to make the belt carriers. I folded the two long cut edges of the strip to the wrong side and butted them at the center. Then I zigzagged over the cut edges, and the carriers were ready to be sewn in place.

Rosemary Cashin,
Cohoes, New York

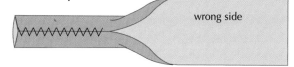

wrong side

Finishing seams in no time flat

When I make jackets with Polarfleece, I serge the seams, then use a double needle for topstitching. The bottom zigzag thread encloses and flattens the serged seam. With matching thread, the seam is almost invisible. It makes a really professional (or better) finish.

Sharry Russo, Deltona, Florida

Note from
Nancy

Use a 4.0 double needle for this top-stitching. This wider needle size will more easily accommodate the bulky seam.

Don't get cold feet

While watching your show on working with fleece, it occurred to me that I could salvage several pairs of my husband's and my socks by using scraps of fleece to line the bottoms. The fleece is soft, adds cushioning, and is easy to hand sew into the bottom of badly worn socks that would otherwise have to be discarded. I had some leftover waterproof Malden Mills double-sided fleece and after putting it onto my own socks, I couldn't feel the cold floor beneath my sewing table.

Janice Ewing, Providence, Rhode Island

Squeaky-clean fleece

I hate to waste any fabric so I was thrilled to discover that 8" x 11" pieces of fleece make good cloths for my Swiffer mop. I use them both dry and wet to clean my tiled floors and save money because I no longer buy the recommended disposable ones. Fleece washes beautifully and the fabric doesn't fray, so there are no edges to finish.

Yvonne Atkinson, Tampa, Florida

You've got something up your sleeve

I made a fleece coat with raglan sleeves that were too wide at the cuff. Rather than adding a ribbed cuff, I stitched pintucks ½" apart along the cuff edge on the wrong side of the fabric. I then hemmed the cuff.

This gives a lovely ribbed effect. I have always loved pintucks as a detail, ever since I started making my own clothes in the 1930s.

Ida Blackwell, Nepean, Ottawa, Canada

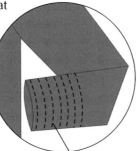

stitch pintucks ½" apart

Put a sock in it!

For my job as a nurse in a local doctor's office, I am required to wear a forest green lab jacket. Unfortunately, colored cuffs are very hard to find and white is not always the best color for my line of work. So I thought, why not use colored socks? Cutting the tops off about 3" to 4" makes a perfect cuff, and the color choices are endless.

Karen Krebs, Vancleave, Mississippi

My wife cut the tops from a pair of brown socks to replace the cuffs on my old leather jacket. The cuffs look just like new.

Clark Pearson, Tecumseh, Michigan

Doing double duty on a jacket lining

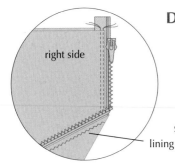

right side

lining

Recently, I put a sport zipper into a lined fleece jacket. To make certain that the layers were securely stitched, I topstitched with a 3.0 mm double needle. The two rows of stitching gave a decorative look on the front, and the lining was secured with the zigzag stitches of the bobbin thread.

Karen Stevens, Westminster, Colorado

Get in shape

Recently, while making fleece jackets, I modified the pocket to prevent stretching along the top edge.

- Cut one pocket out of cotton lining and another pocket out of the fashion fabric.
- Serge or overcast the top edges separately.
- Place both the lining and fashion fabric right sides together and fold down both pocket facings toward the lining (you will have four layers on top at this point).
- Pin, then serge or sew around the side and bottom edges, leaving the top edge open for turning.
- Trim, and turn right side out. Hand stitch the opening closed. The facing lining remains under the fashion fabric, giving the top edge the stability I want.

Barbara Rife, Greeley Hill, California

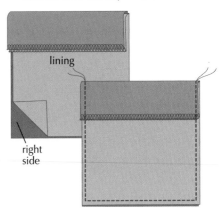

lining

right side

Guest Spot

Every time I have a guest on TV, I get to take a "class," a personalized class! I regret revealing this secret...my guests believe that they're teaching you, but first they're teaching me! Sandra Betzina, of "Power Sewing" fame, is a great teacher. When she finished writing her book on Fabric Savvy, I thought it would be a perfect time to get a personalized lesson from the pro. We developed a program highlighting specialty fabrics, and the type of needles, stitching techniques, interfacing guidelines, and the like, that these fabrics require.

Sandra's samples were beautiful and inspiring. Yet two of her simple pointers are what I remember most from my "class." Whenever I buy fabric, I remember Sandra saying, "Buy the best you can afford." My tendency is to gravitate to the sale table. I now try to buy less, buying quality and not quantity.

She also mentioned in passing that she was sewing two blouses at once. (I'm certain many of us have done that too.) Her solution for choosing thread color was to choose a compromise color – a thread that didn't match either fabric. Sandra recommended, of course, that when the final topstitching and/buttonholes are added, to change to a matching thread color.

Sometimes it's the simple hints that make a great difference. Thanks, Sandra, for making that difference.

Sandra Betzina

Sandra Betzina

Cuff 'em!

Does adding cuffs or ribbing to a garment make you feel like a prisoner?
Use these helpful hints to escape the bonds of cuff-related problems.

Every cuff has a silver lining

I adapted your technique for lining blazer sleeves when I made coats with ribbed cuffs for my children.

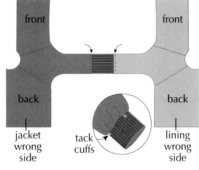

- Stitch the cuff end of the fashion fabric sleeve to one edge of the cuff ribbing, right sides together. (If desired, sew elastic into the seam at this time.)
- Stitch the cuff end of the sleeve lining to the opposite edge of the cuff ribbing, right sides together.
- Meet the jacket lining to the jacket, right sides together. Stitch the entire sleeve and side seam. Repeat with the second sleeve/side seam.
- As a final step, when the coat is completed, tuck the sleeve lining down into the cuff until it is positioned properly. Using short straight stitches, stitch in the ditch of the seam and the "valley" of the ribbing in several places around the cuff. When the ribbing relaxes, the stitches "disappear" and the cuffs look and feel no different than a traditionally stitched cuff. This adaptation also works on garments with raglan and kimono sleeves.

Linda McGee, Grand Ledge, Michigan

Cozy cuffs

Recently I used a pattern that called for a knit cuff on a quilted jacket sleeve. The cuff was too large, even though I made the cuff two sizes smaller than the pattern indicated. I decided to change the cuff, making it not only smaller, but also tighter at the lower edge. When I joined the ends of the cuff right sides together, I sewed a curve instead of a straight seam. This produced a snug cuff, and I didn't have to change the sleeve because the edges of the modified cuff remained the same dimension as the original cuff.

*Terri Gault,
Mount Vernon, Ohio*

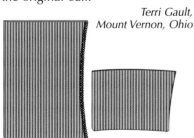

Neck and neck

When I make crew neck T-shirts, both the neckband ribbing and the neckline of the shirt have to be divided into quarters. I use pins with white heads to mark the neckband and shirt in quarters, and use pins with colored heads to pin the neckband in place. If I don't like the way the neckband is pinned, I remove the colored pins and start again, knowing that my garment and neckband are still quartered.

Carolyn Sippel, Renton, Washington

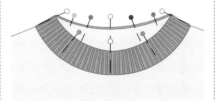

Joined at the wrist

When applying ribbing to a sleeve for a cuff, it looks much better if the bottom of the sleeve is gathered to match the dimension of the cuff before it is attached. Otherwise the sleeve flares out at the seamline and is less attractive.

- Cut a piece of ⅜" elastic the circumference of the cuff. (Allow a ½" tail for securing the elastic if desired.)
- Quarter both the sleeve edge and the elastic. Place the elastic on the wrong side of the sleeve and zigzag the two together on the seamline, matching the quarters and stretching the elastic to fit the sleeve. When the elastic relaxes, the sleeve is the same size as the cuff.

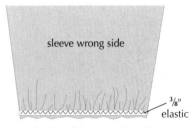

sleeve wrong side

⅜" elastic

- Stitch the ribbing to the sleeve in the usual manner, matching the quarter marks.

attach ribbing

- For a nice finishing touch, finger press the seam allowance toward the sleeve. Then topstitch along the seamline using a 4.0 mm double needle, with the needles straddling the seamline.

*Martha Schaefer,
West Columbia, South Carolina*

Finishing Touches

Don't let the hardest part of your projects be finishing.
To make your projects really shine, consider these hints the icing on the cake.

Kick up your heels

Making kick pleats on heavy wool and linen skirts was difficult for me. To solve the problem, I eliminated the kick pleat and stitched a rectangle of skirt fabric to the lining at the opening.

- Cut the kick pleat off the pattern, leaving a 1" hem to turn back on each side.
- Serge or finish the raw edges; fuse or hem in place.
- Cut a rectangle of skirt fabric 14" wide and 2" longer than the kick pleat length plus the hem depth.
- Clean finish the raw edges.
- Sew the rectangle to the side of the lining that faces the modified kick pleat opening and hem the skirt lining.

The pleat is always in place, even when I am sitting down.

Virginia Pflum, Arlington, Texas

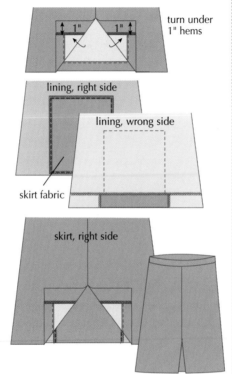

turn under 1" hems

1" 1"

lining, right side

lining, wrong side

skirt fabric

skirt, right side

Dances with chalk

When no one is around to help me mark a garment hem, I use this quick and easy trick.

- Liberally chalk a piece of string.
- Stretch and tape it between a doorway at the desired height from the floor. Make sure the string is parallel to the floor.
- Try on the garment, and turn around slowly, brushing against the string.
- Presto! The garment is ready to hem.

Marie Parisi, Selma, Alabama

Get the competitive edge

To finish the neckline of a basic shell blouse, instead of using a facing at the neck or making bias tape from the blouse fabric, I use a strip of spandex in a matching color in a "Hong Kong" finish at the neck. It puts a nice soft, comfortable fabric at my neckline.

Alice Wills, Soddy Daisy, Tennessee

When sewing silk, I often stabilize a bias edge to keep it from stretching. The pattern usually calls for stitching through seam tape to do this. I use a piece of the fashion fabric selvage instead. It is very stable, it's been pretreated the same as the fabric, and there is no possibility of a contrasting color showing through. And it's free!

Susan Bratt, Winona, Minnesota

Make a narrow escape

When a pattern requires turning under a narrow hem, such as on hems or facings, I machine stitch along the turning line with thread that matches the garment. I then press the hem under accurately without having to measure as I press. I remove the stitching later, or since I used matching thread, I can leave the stitching in place.

Lorraine Wallace, York, South Carolina

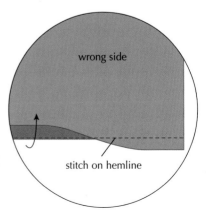

wrong side

stitch on hemline

Vested interest

This technique was adapted from a hint submitted by Laura Gayle Green of Kansas City, Missouri, who used silk organza strips instead of bias tape to edge the armholes of a lace vest. This technique gives the armhole a nicely finished look.

- Trim away the armhole seam allowance.
- Cut 1" wide bias strips of silk organza.
- Stitch the silk organza strip to the right side of the armhole, using a ¼" seam.
- Press the strip up, covering the seam.
- Fold the strip to the wrong side, wrapping the strip around the lace edge so that ¼" of the organza remains on the right side of the lace. Topstitch just below the first seamline for a narrow edge finish, barely noticeable from the right side.

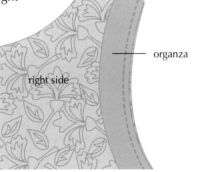

right side

organza

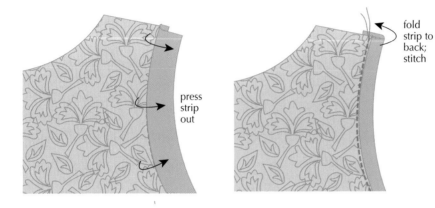

press strip out

fold strip to back; stitch

Don't ruffle your feathers

When sewing lace ruffles to collars or cuffs (or anyplace where the ruffle is sandwiched between two layers), I had a hard time keeping the lace ruffle from moving and getting caught in the seam. Pins didn't hold because they just slipped through the lace. I place Sewer's Fix-it Tape over the scrunched ruffles and then pin through the tape. Taping the ruffles together also works on fabric ruffles.

Jan Beitz, Fort Collins, Colorado

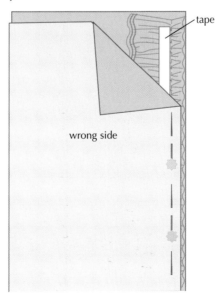

wrong side

tape

Behind the Scenes

Take 10

Literally, "Behind the Scenes"

While I'm having make-up applied, Donna lays out the samples on large tables in order according to the script. We generally store samples of each technique in large plastic bins or trays and then organize the samples by sequence on the tables. The tables are out of sight of the camera lens, but close by for accessibility.

The photo also shows that the walls of my set are "flats," four by eight foot plywood walls that are portable and propped into place when it's time to tape the program. These flats are made like most TV sets, with braces in the back that are anchored with heavy "bean-type bags."

The other elements of the set are very portable – even the chimney is made out of Styrofoam. It's comical to see a crew member of Wisconsin Public TV effortlessly carry the chimney off the set so that all the elements of my set can be condensed, enabling another program to be taped in the same studio.

Fixer Uppers

Not every sewing project starts from scratch. Whether it's a quick fix or a long-term solution you need, these hints will have your projects looking and feeling like new again.

Flower power

My favorite pink jersey turtleneck had ballpoint pen stains all over it. Washing did not take the stains out, so I embroidered over each stain with little flowers.

Another pullover shirt of mine had a hole in the sleeve, so I crocheted a pink rosette and sewed it over the hole. I sewed a matching rosette on at the neckline.

Adrienne Nevins, Tucson, Arizona

Here comes the bride

When doing bridal sewing, I often have to let out a dress, but the side seams are not large enough. When this happens, I let out the zipper by using a facing on the zipper flap side. The facing seam can be right at the edge of the fabric and the facing will be under the zipper flap. The other side of the zipper can also be let out to allow another inch of room.

Mary Bagby, Manchester, Iowa

Two sides to every story

When applying iron-on patches to clothing, for example to repair a hole in the knee of a pair of jeans, I apply two patches – one from the outside of the garment and one from the inside. This double patch serves two purposes: it doubles the amount of reinforcement over the hole, and it saves the wearer from scratches. Applying a patch to the inside of the jeans provides a smooth surface next to the skin.

Marybeth Stalp, Athens, Georgia

Read the label

It seems like the only times I tear my clothes are when I am away from home. Recently, when I was on vacation, I tore my windbreaker. Luckily, I had a travel sewing kit with me. To mend the tear until I got home, I used this quick fix method. It works on both men's and women's garments.
- Mend the tear the best you can, then rip the label out of the back of the garment.
- Place the label over the top of the tear and hand sew in place.

Kathleen Aukerman, Pitsburg, Ohio

Deep pockets

When my daughter went to France with her French class, I wanted a way for her to keep her personal papers and money safe. She didn't want to wear a fanny pack or a passport carrier around her neck. To solve the problem, I added two deep pockets on the inside of her leather jacket lining, one pocket for her passport and another for her money. The pockets were great – she didn't lose a thing.

Virginia Privara, Parma, Ohio

Chain reaction

When I use my serger with Woolly Nylon thread, I run off several extra 10" lengths of thread chain. I thread these chains into an embroidery needle and keep it in my sewing room or sewing kit for emergencies.

When I lose a button, I use this chain to sew on the button once through the button and tie a square knot on the underside of the garment. That is all that's needed to hold the button in place quickly and securely. I use this to attach buttons to my children's clothes and I have never had a button replaced in this manner fall off again. This is especially great for coat buttons. The Woolly Nylon gives extra strength and flex.

Terri McLaren, Lewiston, Idaho

An ultra hem

In the past, to shorten a pair of jeans, I would double fold the hem and stitch. Invariably, the machine needle would break due to the bulk of the fabric. Here's my solution:

- Cut a strip of synthetic suede, such as Ultrasuede, 1" wide and slightly longer than the jean leg width.
- Overlap and stitch the edges to form a circle the same circumference as the jean leg width.
- Place the suede circle on the jean leg ¼" below the hemline. Topstitch the suede band to the leg.
- Trim away the excess jean fabric, turn up the suede band, and topstitch.

No more heavy triple seams to sew through and they hang as nicely as if I had just finished a pair of dress slacks. I usually use tan suede since it looks good with jeans of any color!

Virginia Hays, Irving, Texas

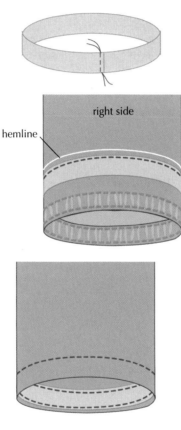

right side

hemline

Not quite ready-to-wear

While shopping the sale racks recently, I found several pairs of pants from the same fabric but no matching tops. I bought two pairs of pants and made a vest from one pair. If there is not enough fabric in the pants for the entire width of the vest, use coordinating fabric and make a patchwork vest.

Alice Borg, Tacoma, Washington

After some stitchin', pants become mittens

When my son wears out the knees in his sweatpants, I make them into mittens. I can get four pairs of mittens from one pair of pants. I cut one pair from each leg, using the existing elastic as the wrist elastic in the "new" mittens. I also can get two more pair from the waistband as well. The elastic is already there, and the sewing is easy.

Cheri Cole, Moscow, Idaho

Add-on pocket

My husband has received some nice shirts as gifts, but if the shirts don't have a pocket, he won't wear them. So I add a welt pocket. I use Ultrasuede, either the same color as the shirt or a contrasting color.

Belva Jensen, Scottsdale, Arizona

Spot be gone

A silk linen suit that I made got a spot on the front. I tried to remove the spot with "silk soap," but it left a faded spot. I took it to professional dry cleaners, but they could do nothing. So I took a scrap of the same silk linen fabric that I used for the suit, soaked it in water, laid it over the spot, pressed it with a steam iron, and it re-dyed the color into the faded area. It made the spot almost invisible. I was thrilled.

Naomi Franck, Canby, Oregon

"Clearly" a time saver!

In order to save time on last minute repairs when in a hurry, or to catch a seam or a piece of appliqué the needle missed, I keep a supply of bobbins with all colors of thread at hand. In the top thread I use invisible thread, already threaded at all times. All I do is change bobbins and I am ready to go.

Mollie W. Baron, Bethesda, Maryland

One, two, tie your shoe

While using Fray Check to repair regular shoelaces when the tips wore out, I discovered this use for the Fasturn: Make your own fashion shoelaces.

- Make tubes from fashion fabric and turn them using the Fasturn. To make the tips firm:
- Moisten about 1" of the ends with Fray Check.
- Roll with your fingers and let dry.
- After the tip has been formed, dip the ends into the Fray Check bottle. Hang to dry.
- Repeat the process until the ends are firm enough to lace through the eyelets of your shoes.

Blanche T. Tuxhorn,
St. Petersburg, Florida

Two Encore Favorites

Every year I present about six seminars around the country. If I were a betting person, I could bank on at least one person from each audience commenting that her favorite *Sewing With Nancy* technique is a "Wrapped Corner Collar." Another especially-liked technique is the "Professional Patch Pocket." I've no doubt taught these two techniques tens of times on television, since they're as akin to me as a creamy white sauce and fluffy meringue are to Julia Child. Yet, I know that not everyone has ventured to try these rather unconventional methods. So, if you haven't made a collar with wrapped corners or stitched a perfectly mitered pocket corner using tape, now's the time to give them a try!

Wrapped Corner Collars

To eliminate bulk from a collar, sew the outer edges in three steps. The technique is not a new idea! It is borrowed from pillowcase manufacturers; corners on these home décor basics are sewn with this simple technique.

The Wrapped Corner Collar technique can be applied to a two-piece collar with separate upper and under collar patterns as found on tailored shirts and jackets, as well as to casual-wear patterns where both upper and under collars are cut from the same pattern piece.

1. Cut out lightweight fusible interfacing the same size as both the upper and under collars. (Most guide sheet instructions call for interfacing only one collar layer, the under collar. Interfacing both collars adds body, preventing one collar from buckling under the weight of the other collar.)

2. Fuse the interfacing to the wrong sides of both collar pieces, following the manufacturer's instructions.

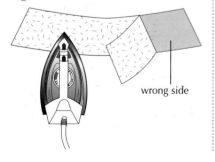

wrong side

3. With right sides together, pin the collars along the unnotched edges. Stitch the seam from end to end.

4. Press the seam flat, the way it was stitched. Then press the seam open.

5. Grade or layer the seam allowances, trimming the under collar seam allowance the smallest.

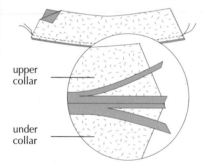

upper collar

under collar

6. Press the seam allowances toward the under collar and understitch the entire seam. Use a multi-zigzag stitch for understitching when using mid- to heavier-weight fabrics. A multi-zigzag has more stitches per inch, creating a crisper collar edge.

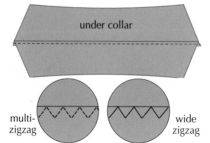

under collar

multi-zigzag   wide zigzag

7. Fold the collar along the seam with right sides together. Seam allowances will wrap toward the under collar. Stitch from the fold to the neckline edge on each end of the collar.

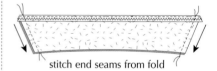

stitch end seams from fold

8. Grade the seam allowances and trim the corner allowances at an angle. Press the seam flat; then press the seam open.

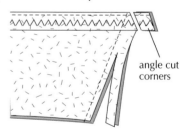

angle cut corners

9. Turn the collar right side out. Use a Bamboo Pointer and Creaser to help shape the point of the collar.

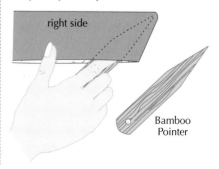

right side

Bamboo Pointer

Wrapped Corner Options

Wrapped Corner Options

- The Wrapped Corner technique is not limited to collars. Use this method when sewing cuffs, lapels, pocket flaps, and other details with corners. Rather than pivoting at a corner, stitch the corner in two steps as detailed on page 70.
- When serging with an overlock machine, it is impossible to pivot at corners in the traditional way. Adapting the Wrapped Corner technique allows fast, easy, and accurate corner seams. Use a 3/4-thread stitch. Instead of pivoting at a corner, serge off the edge. Fold the fabric along the needle stitching line and wrap the seam to the underside (i.e., under collar or under cuff). Serge the unsewn edge, and turn the fabric right side out.

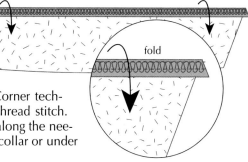
fold

Professional Patch Pocket

Here's a way to complete a patch pocket with perfectly mitered corners in minutes. The secret to success is tape – transparent or sewing tape!

1. Cut fusible interfacing the full size of the pocket. Cut the interfacing along the hem, dividing the interfacing into two pieces. Place the interfacing on the wrong side of the pocket, *slightly* separating the two pieces at the hemline. (This slight separation will encourage the pocket to accurately fold at this space.) Fuse, following the manufacturer's instructions.

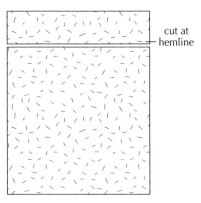
cut at hemline

2. Measure and mark 1¼" (twice the seam width) from each side of both lower pocket corners.

3. Place tape between the two marks on the wrong side of the fabric, extending the tape ends as shown.

4. With right sides together, fold the corner to a point, aligning the marks and the tape edges. Stitch next to the tape but not through it, forming the miter. Trim the seam to ¼". Repeat for the other corner.

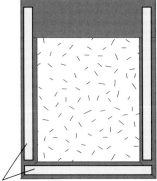
1¼" 1¼"

5. Stitch the side seams of the pocket hem. Press the seam flat; then press open. Grade the seams and trim the corners at an angle.

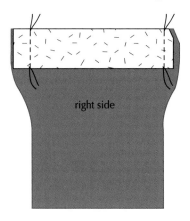
right side

6. Turn the pocket right side out. Press the seam allowances to the wrong side.

7. Cut ¼" wide strips of paper-backed fusible web, such as Wonder Under. Position the web strips on the seam allowances approximately ¼" inside the pocket edge. Press.

Wonder Under strips

8. Remove the paper backing from the web strips. Position the pocket on the garment. Cover with a press cloth and fuse to the garment. (The use of narrow web strips eliminates the need to topstitch over pins, which may cause uneven topstitching lines.)

9. On the right side of the pocket, edgestitch close to the side and lower pocket edges.

Optional: Use a blind hem foot, guiding the side bar of the foot along the fabric fold. Adjust the side bar to create the desired edgestitching distance from the pocket edges.

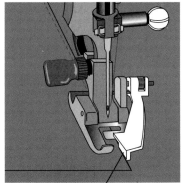
guide along fabric edge

CHAPTER FOUR

Enlightening *embellishment* ideas

The path to enlightened embellishments is not always easy. There are many obstacles along the way: fraying ribbon, boring buttons, and appliqués that just won't sit still.

Fortunately, this path need not be taken alone. In the following hints, *Sewing With Nancy* viewers offer sage advice on everything from making your own piping, to adding lace, to taking your serger to new creative heights.

There is a creative genius inside each of you just waiting to be discovered. So take a deep breath and relax, and use these hints to get in touch with your inner seamstress.

why i sew with nancy

Beautiful Buttons

Do you have a case of the button blahs?
The following hints from *Sewing With Nancy* viewers
will have you feeling better in a snap.

Separation anxiety

Here is my method for attaching beautiful buttons that must be removed before each laundering or dry cleaning. This is also a good way to recycle those old, boring plastic buttons that are too good to throw away, but are passed over time and time again.

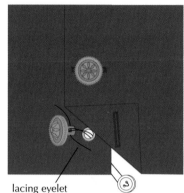

lacing eyelet

- Insert an eyelet where the button is to be placed.
- Remove the plastic or paper covering from a twist-tie so that only a thin piece of wire remains.
- Insert the wire into the holes of a flat button, and bend over ¼" of each wire end for safety.
- Position the flat button on the wrong side of the garment, behind the eyelet.
- Bring both ends of the wire through the eyelet.
- Thread one wire end through the shank of the decorative button; bring the second wire end through the shank from the opposite direction.
- Tug on each wire end and the buttons will slide together.
- Bring the ends of the wire back together and give them a slight twist.
- Wrap the wire ends around the decorative button shank and they almost disappear until it is time for removal!

If you have an expensive set of buttons, save money by using those same buttons on any number of outfits with this attachment method.

Wendy Samuelson, Bemus Point, New York

How does your garden grow?

A cute way to decorate children's clothing is to grow a button flower garden. I use green rickrack for grass and flower stems, and large colorful buttons for the flowers. Children love the gardens. They can be applied to quilts, dresses, t-shirts, bibs, curtains – the possibilities are endless.

Colleen Mitchell, Provo, Utah

Brace yourself

To support sewn-on embellishments such as buttons, I add fleece squares or strips on the wrong side of the garment as reinforcement. This adds strength when little fingers try to pull on the embellishments, and it also decreases the amount of waste for the trash can.

Kathleen Joslyn, Aumsville, Oregon

right side

fleece

wrong side

Limitless Lace

The addition of lace can take your project to a whole new dimension. Use the following hints from *Sewing With Nancy* viewers to go where no seamstress has gone before.

Feeling edgy

This method of applying lace to a neck or cuff edge encloses the rough edge of the lace. It works best on soft, lightweight knit fabrics.

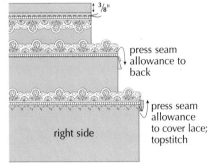

- Place the lace and fabric right sides together, positioning the straight edge of the lace ⅜" from the edge of the fabric. Machine baste.
- Press the seam allowance to the wrong side.
- Fold the seam allowances back over the straight edge of the lace, sandwiching the lace between the body of the fabric and the seam allowance.
- Topstitch from the right side, stitching through all layers with a serpentine, scallop, or wide decorative stitch.

Rebecca Martin, Madison, Wisconsin

Don't get caught!

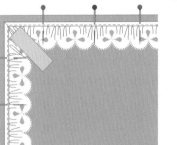

As the proud grandmother of a beautiful little girl, I am now sewing infant clothing after many years of working only with adult sizes. Recently, I encountered a challenge while working with a lace trimmed collar. The lace was catching in the seam at the corners.

My solution was to neatly fold the excess lace at the corners and secure it with tape.

It is also helpful when working with wider trims, to tape the lace to the collar at intervals along the outer edge of the collar. Since implementing these techniques, I have not had to rip out a seam to free the lace trim.

Debbie Kemp, Baton Rouge, Louisiana

Liberating lace

When a project requires gathered cotton eyelet lace, and the lace I have available is gathered eyelet edged with bias tape, I remove the bulk of the bias tape. With a zipper foot attached to my machine, I straight stitch close to the bias tape. The straight stitching stabilizes the gathers. To remove the bias tape, I release the stitching that holds the bias trim in place – this is often a chain stitch that removes easily. Once the bias tape is removed, I have a bulk-free trim ready to insert into my project.

Johanna Wawrzyniak, New Port Richey, Florida

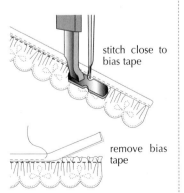

Ring around the hankie

While making handkerchiefs for my daughter-in-law, I had no problem serging around the edges to hem them. When I tried to sew lace around the handkerchiefs, I ran into problems – the lace kept slipping. I even tried using my zipper foot.

Then I tried my pintuck foot. Success! The serged edge fit under a groove in the foot. I positioned my needle and was able to neatly sew the lace in place.

Melba Coombs, Affton, Missouri

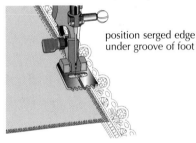

Trick or treat!

While making my niece's Halloween costume from lace, I wanted a rolled edge hem finish but couldn't get the stitch to hold on the lightweight fabric. To solve the problem, I placed ⅛" wide ribbon the same color as the lace along the fabric edge. I stitched the rolled hem over the ribbon and lace. It worked beautifully.

Rene Hongsermeier, Meridianville, Alabama

Release me!

I could not find the correct width of flat lace to trim a dress I was making for a wedding. I purchased a gathered lace in the correct width, removed the binding to release the gathers, and pressed the lace flat.

Finish the lace in the width of your choice by serging along the raw edge of the newly created flat lace.

Bettie Stanshery, Wharton, Ohio
Terri Peterson, Chesterfield, Missouri

Pipe Dreams

Have you been dreaming of an easy way to decorate curtains,
cushions, and clothing? With the following hints,
visions of piping will dance in your head.

She sews shells by the pipe edge

Here is an easy and very attractive way to decorate collars, cuffs, and yokes on dresses for little girls:

- Fold two bias strips in half lengthwise. Press.
- Insert fine cord in the fold of one bias strip to make piping.
- Stitch along the folded edge of the other bias strip with a shell stitch.
- Position the strip with the cording on top of the strip with shell stitching, placing the cording just below the shell stitches.
- Stitch both strips together using a zipper foot or cording foot.
- Position the strips along a garment edge, right sides together, meeting the cut edges.
- Stitch just below the cording.
- Fold the raw edges to the wrong side of the garment. Press.

Gail Bartlett,
Binbrook, Ontario, Canada

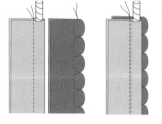

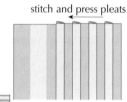

right side

fold raw edges to
wrong side

Earn your stripes

Ready-to-wear clothing can be very expensive, so I re-create it. Recently I was copying a striped dress with coordinating piping in a narrower stripe. To create the piping:

- From the wrong side, press the fabric along every other stripe, creating pleats.
- Straight stitch down the center of each stripe or pleat.
- Press the pleats in one direction. From the right side, the stripes are half the measurement of the original stripe.
- Cut bias strips and create piping.

I used the piping at the yoke and cuffs of the dress.

Lois Rossnagel, Ironwood, Michigan

stitch and press pleats

cut strips
on bias

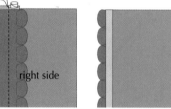

Pipe down!

Recently I made cushions for our outdoor furniture. Because I needed many yards of piping, I decided to make piping from clothesline rope. I covered the rope with fabric that matched the cushions. This worked very well and cost less than purchased piping. Also, you can buy different widths of rope depending on the size of the cushions.

Ingrid Dispenza, Voorheesville, New York

Puffed-up piping

While sewing curtains for my daughter's first apartment, I decided to add piping to a valance, but did not have cording on hand. As a substitute for the piping, I used quilt batting scraps.

- Cut the batting into 1" strips and the fashion fabric into 1½" strips.
- Insert the batting strips into the fabric, squishing the batting while stitching with a zipper foot.

This makes soft piping.

Diana Lindsley, Molalla, Oregon

batting

right side

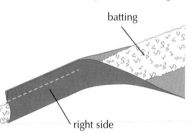

Yarn goods

To make piping, I use acrylic knitting yarn as the cord in my piping. Yarn is available in a variety of weights, it's inexpensive, looks great, and is a great way to use up yarn from previous projects. I can make thin piping for baby clothing, or use a rug weight yarn for larger garments. I keep a skein of black, white, and off-white on hand for my projects. For sheer fabrics, color coordinate the yarns with the fabric.

Debbie Bailey, Eagle River, Alaska
Mary Ann Stanley, Mobile, Alabama

Note from Nancy

Avoid heat and steam from an iron because they may affect the yarn.

Let the Ribbon Flow

Are all of your ideas for using ribbon dried up?
Shower yourself with these tips to bring your creative
drought to an end.

Sewing on the edge

Here's a technique I developed while trying to edge a ruffle with ribbon without all the bulk of a hem:

- Place the ribbon on the wrong side of the ruffle, extending the ribbon 1/8" beyond the fabric edge.
- Stitch the ribbon to the ruffle, sewing along the inner edge of the ribbon.
- Turn the ribbon to the right side of the ruffle; press.
- Stitch along the other side of the ribbon.

This method leaves a very tidy and nonbulky edge. It uses such a narrow hem that it works well on curved hemlines too.

wrong side

turn ribbon to right side

Cynthia Bickler, Waukesha, Wisconsin

I've been framed!

I was first introduced to silk ribbon embroidery at the Sewing Expo in Puyallup, Washington. I frame some of my work in small crafting frames, make sachets with the embroidery at Christmas time, and make greeting cards. To give the embroidery work extra support without the stiffness of fusible interfacing, I cover the back of the embroidery with nylon net or tulle.

Anne O'Brien, Seattle, Washington

tulle

Over the bobbin and through the hole

On your "Silk Ribbon Elegance" program, you suggested using a needle to thread the ribbon tail through the hole in the bobbin. As an alternate, I use a tool designed to fix snags on knits (Knit Picker). I use this tool to reach through the bobbin hole and grab the heavy threads or ribbon and pull them through.

Ginny Fischer,
White Salmon,
Washington

Sealed with a flame

The best way to keep the cut edge of ribbon, lace, belting, or a zipper from unraveling is to carefully singe the edge with a match or lighter.

- Cut the trim to the exact length.
- Slowly butt the cut ends up to the flame to melt and seal them.

This makes a clean, finished edge and reduces bulk.

Joanie Ludwig, New Albany, Indiana
Jodi Englehart, Toronto, Ontario, Canada

Behind the Scenes

Take 11

My Set: The "Sewing Room"

I've taped at seven different studios over the past 20 years and have been at Wisconsin Public TV since 1991. My current set is a hybrid of all my past Sewing With Nancy sets, giving me all the features that I need to teach sewing and quilting. I certainly didn't design the set; I only gave suggestions to set designer Shirwil Lukes. The L-shaped design features a bench area for the introductions, a desk for the "Mailbag" segment, a table for demonstrations, and of course, the sewing/serging area.

Shirwil designed my set and all others, by working with a mini-scale model. I was intrigued with her clay versions of cameras, mini-wooden tables, and sewing cabinets. This mini-version of the Sewing With Nancy set allowed the director to visually test the set before construction began and gave me the opportunity to see if I had all the elements needed to teach via TV.

It's So Easy to Appliqué

Do you like to show off? Or perhaps you have something to hide?
Either way, apply these hints to your project for guaranteed success.

I have to go powder my Ultrasuede

Recently, I was cutting an intricate pattern out of Ultrasuede. Since pinning is not advised for Ultrasuede and the color I was using was too dark to mark with a ballpoint pen, I had to brainstorm to find another method. My solution:

- Lay the pattern down on the wrong side of the Ultrasuede.
- Pat the edges of the pattern with a powder puff and face powder. The powder sticks to the fabric and provides a sharp line for cutting.
- Lift the pattern and cut.

Karen S. Kendler, Riverdale, New York

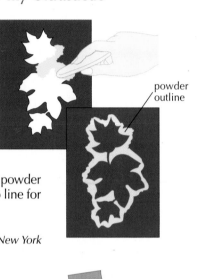

powder outline

Appliqué sandwich

Positioning appliqués on lapels can be very tricky. I was working on a project and got the right lapel's appliqué just the way I wanted, but the left one wasn't working out. Here's my solution:

- Peel the paper backing off the appliqués and place them right sides together.
- Position the appliqués on the right side of one of the lapels.
- Put the lapels right sides together, match up the edges, and press. It works great!

Kay Spears, Ironton, Ohio

right side

appliqué wrong side

Note from
Nancy
Press one side of the appliqué sandwich and then flip the fabrics. Press from the opposite side to completely fuse all appliqués.

Kids' Hint

Earn your sewing badge

When attaching patches on Cub Scout, Boy Scout, or any other uniform, I use masking tape. After I have the patch positioned where I want it, I tape it down with short strips. I set my machine at a narrow zigzag using clear quilting thread for the top and match the bobbin thread to the shirt. I then sew the patch on, removing the tape with a set of sewing tweezers as I come to it, being very careful not to zigzag over any tape.

Martha Shores, Snellville, Georgia

Just push pause

After making shorts and tops for my sons, I wanted to embellish them with cartoon characters. While watching a video with the cartoon characters, my husband and I paused the tape when the image we wanted was the correct size and traced the design onto paper. Then I used transparency film to create images with thicker lines to use as templates. This worked great.

Kathleen Geumlek, Norwalk, California

Note from
Nancy
It is okay to use images of cartoon characters for personal use, but not for sale, since the designs are copyrighted.

Never let them see you baste

When appliquéing an animal, doll, or flower on a baby quilt, I turn under all raw edges of the appliqué and machine baste with invisible thread. Then I use a decorative stitch and brightly colored thread to stitch around the appliqué to add depth and interest.

Elodie Eckenrode, Toledo, Ohio

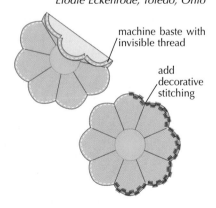

machine baste with invisible thread

add decorative stitching

Bouquet of fun

This is a pretty and easy way to add flower embellishments using fabric scraps.

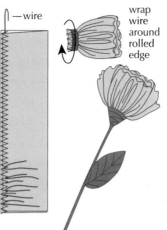

- Cut a scrap of fabric one yard long and 2" to 3" wide.
- Fold it in half with wrong sides together, meeting the long edges. Press.
- Place one yard of thin wire (like beading wire) along the raw (or selvage) edge.
- Zigzag with large stitches, attaching and holding the wire in place. After taking the first few zigzag stitches, bend the top of the wire down so that it doesn't pull loose from the stitching.
- After stitching, tightly gather the fabric along the wire and roll it together, forming a "flower."
- Wrap the extra wire around the rolled edge, holding it tightly in place.
- Wrap with green floral tape.

You can wire two or three flowers together. Attach green silk leaves, pearl stamens, or add a layer of lace to the folded fabric before zigzagging. Once you get the hang of it, these flowers are quick and easy to do, and each can be as original as your imagination allows! They can be attached (and easily removed) from a garment with a large safety pin. Or, permanently attach a "jewelry" pin to the back. For a child, you can attach these flowers to hair barrettes, making pretty bows to match her dresses.

Donna McGraw, Arlington, Texas

Crimp your style

When appliquéing small pieces that require turning the edges under ¼", I use the square end of my serger tweezers or my Little Wooden Iron to turn the edges while I press them in place. It helps prevent scorched and burned fingers and it makes the job progress much more quickly.

Jo Rick, Irma, Wisconsin

Get in line!

If your appliqué has a lot of detail with many pieces to arrange, or, if you need a little help placing your appliqué pieces accurately, this will make it easier.

- Take the pattern sheet (before cutting) to a copying service and have a transparency made.
- Place the appliqué pieces on your garment.
- Place the transparency over the appliqué pieces, check the placement of the pieces, and "nudge" them to fit into the placement as shown on the transparency.
- Use tape to hold the pieces in place. Press.

This works best with pieces backed by Wonder Under or a similar product, but will work on pieces without the bonded backing too.

Judy Eagleson, Vincennes, Indiana

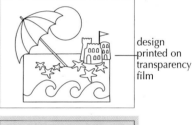

design printed on transparency film

place film over fabric pieces to check placement

 *Guest Spot*

Many viewers requested a series on heirloom cutwork. As this area was not a specialty of mine, I searched for an expert. Darlene Guillory, author of Traditional Cutwork Made Easy, was my choice, as I admired her work and style. With Darlene's technique I found out just how easy, and equally as important, how enjoyable cutwork can be.

Darlene Guillory

One of the tips that Darlene shared during the TV series was to use multiple layers of a water-soluble stabilizer instead of just one when stitching across the open or cut out areas – the stitches are called Richelieu bars. (This tip came prior to the era of heavyweight water-soluble stabilizers and has proven to be an invaluable tool.)

This adorable picture of Darlene's granddaughter showcases the Richelieu stitching in the cutwork sections. The stitches do not waver and are completely uniform. You can use Darlene's idea of stacking several layers of a water-soluble stabilizer on projects other than cutwork to give support to lightweight fabrics when embroidering or adding decorative stitches. Thanks, Darlene, for this and other very useful techniques!

Darlene Guillory

why i sew with nancy

I've lost touch with a lot of friends because I've moved a lot, but I know I'll be able to keep in touch with you by the click of a remote every Saturday.

Carolyn Armstrong, Houston, Texas

When I was in school, I dreamed of having a career involving sewing – I wanted to design. Then I got married and started having children, and neglected my sewing. When I found Nancy on TV she reignited my love of sewing, but the circumstances of my life kept me from pursuing my love. Watching Nancy, I could live my dream vicariously.

Tamara Densmore, Wadsworth, Ohio

I sew with Nancy because I have congestive heart failure and am often too fatigued to even get my sewing machine set up to use. I truly enjoy watching you and your friends sew such beautiful projects. I feel as though I am there sewing with you.

Carol B. Wojtaszek,
Lancaster, New York

I used to sew for weeks at a stretch, making a new school wardrobe for my daughter every year. It was a time of sharing for us, picking patterns and fabrics, fitting garments, and discussing embellishments as the garments came to completion.

Since I now work full-time, sewing is a way of relaxing, creating, and satisfying a basic need. Watching Sewing With Nancy keeps sewing in my life.

Gail Lewis, Peyton, Colorado

Soft touch

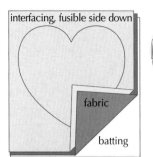

interfacing, fusible side down

fabric

batting

slash interfacing

For a nice padded appliqué, I face the appliqué with a fusible interfacing, adding a layer of fusible fleece under the wrong side of the fabric. The three layers are assembled as follows:

Bottom – layer of fleece batting.

Middle – appliqué fabric, right side up.

Top – fusible interfacing (with design drawn on it), fusible side down.

- Sew around the design with small stitches, stitching through all three layers.
- Trim, slash the fusible interfacing in the center, turn inside out, and baste the slash to close it again.
- Fuse the appliqué to the background fabric, then hand stitch around the edges. There will not be any wrinkles on the appliqué top.

Blanche Rehling, Millstadt, Illinois

Loosen up!

When I want the convenience of fusible web but not the ensuing stiffness, I use this technique:

- Trace the pattern on fusible web.
- Using an X-acto knife and the back of the cutting board, cut away all but 3/16" of the fusible web from the inside of the pattern.
- Proceed as usual. The result will be soft, yet accurate. This works well on large or small appliqués.

*Pamela Griffin,
Almonte, Ontario, Canada*

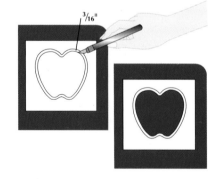

3/16"

Location, location, location

Here's a tip for plus sizes. Putting the appliqué off-center and higher up on the shoulder brings the viewer's eye away from areas we'd like to minimize.

Lou Jurek, Clearfield, Utah

No more tears

To cover small stains or tears on garments, I use "invisible" appliqués.

- Cut two identical appliqués, one from fashion fabric and one from interfacing.
- Meet the fusible side of the interfacing to the right side of the fashion fabric.
- Stitch along the edges.
- Carefully cut a small X in the interfacing layer, and turn the appliqué right side out.
- Fuse the appliqué to the garment.
- Zigzag or blind hem stitch the edges to the garment with monofilament thread.

Faith Jensen, Kuna, Indiana

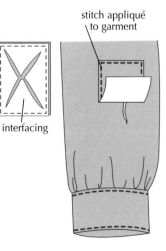

stitch appliqué to garment

interfacing

Bits and pieces

This technique saves a lot of time when an appliqué has lots of little pieces. Instead of going around all of the many edges with a satin stitch or blanket/buttonhole/blind hem stitch, I first temporarily attach the pieces with fusible web, then stipple to permanently hold everything in place.

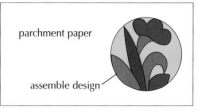
fusible web

I came up with this idea when I was in a hurry to finish a wall hanging as a Christmas gift. It was a snow scene, and I stippled with lingerie thread to give it a frosty look. In a later project I used a coppery metallic thread to add to the mood of an autumn wall hanging. I'd think twice before trusting this process on an item that needs to be laundered often, but for wall hangings it's a great way to save time and add interest.

Barb Wollenberg, New York, New York

stipple fused pieces in place

Pop goes the fabric

To easily remove the fusible web paper from the back of your fabric (I've seen people try to get between there with their fingernails), make a small fold along the edge of the fabric toward the paper. The paper folds and the fabric pops right up!

Robbin Corbett, Mission Viejo, California

It's all about connections

While working on an embellishment for a sweatshirt using Ultrasuede scraps, I wanted to connect 1" squares together without overlapping them. I first tried butting the squares together and sewing with a bridging stitch, but it was not tight enough. I did not want to add any bulk, like stabilizer, so I used Seams Great ⅝" bias cut tricot on a roll. I butted the two squares on the Seams Great and used a bridging stitch to connect them. I then trimmed all the excess Seams Great and achieved the look I wanted.

Janice Jackson, Saginaw, Michigan

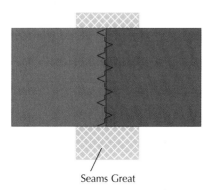
Seams Great

Autumn leaves

To decorate purchased fleece jackets, I attach Ultrasuede leaves, sewing down the center of smaller leaves with a satin stitch. I stitch three to five ribs on the larger leaves, as you would see on real leaves. In fact, I collect real leaves in my neighborhood, trace them onto stabilizer, then tape the stabilizer pattern onto the Ultrasuede with Sewer's Fix-it Tape, and cut around the shapes. The possibilities are endless. I would also consider using pink tulips, green leaves, spring flowers, etc.

Patrecia A. Ross, Riverview, Michigan

Put it all together

One of my favorite tips is something I recently discovered. When I do appliqué using fusible web, I use parchment paper to create the design on the sheet before I put it on my project. That way I only have one item to put on my project, instead of several small pieces. I also put it over the pieces to eliminate getting adhesive on my iron.

Phyllis Cholak, Batavia, Ohio

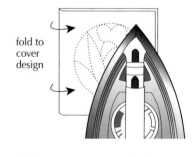
parchment paper
assemble design

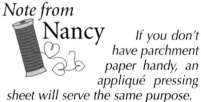
fold to cover design

Note from
Nancy

If you don't have parchment paper handy, an appliqué pressing sheet will serve the same purpose.

Appliqué in a bowl

Wanting to appliqué a frog on the back of a baby quilt, I looked everywhere for a motif that was just right. When fixing pasta one night, I found the perfect design in the bottom of my pasta bowl. I tried to trace it onto tissue paper, but the paper was too stiff and I could not see through it.

I grabbed a plastic baggie, cut it open, and had the perfect thing to trace that cute frog. The clear bag also worked as an overlay template when I positioned the frog pieces on the quilt. Just remember; do not iron the plastic, as it will melt.

Barbara Clinton, Anchorage, Alaska

Spectacular Stitching

Have you been limiting your sewing machine to straight stitching or zigzag?
Don't hold back any longer! Use these tips to unleash your machine's creative potential.

Picot perfection

Sewing kids' clothes is very enjoyable for me. I would like to share an idea for a creative trim:

- Cut continuous bias strips 2" wide or the desired width.
- Fold the edges in to meet at the center; press.
- Set your sewing machine for the blind hem stitch and attach the blind hem foot. Stitch along the fold and adjust the stitch width setting to create a picot edge.
- Apply trim using twin needles and stitching down the center. This catches the raw fabric edges. Or apply the trim using the cover stitch with decorative thread on the serger.

Because the trim is cut on the bias, it can be shaped to go around the neckline, hems, etc. and can be made from almost any woven or knit fabric.

Ruby Doe, Lauderhill, Florida

To add a finishing touch to a half-slip, I added a picot edge. After stitching with the blind hem stitch, the edge curled to the right side of the fabric. To prevent this, I stitched a row of decorative stitching just above the picot edge, then trimmed the hem allowance to the decorative stitching.

Loretta Fisher, Anacortes, Washington

Note from Nancy

When stitching on tricot or other lingerie fabric, be certain to use a "stretch" needle to avoid skipped stitches.

The envelope, please

Greeting card envelopes come in so many pretty colors that match fabric colors. I use the envelopes as stabilizer when I want to add scallops or other decorative stitches along an edge of collars, cuffs, etc. I match the envelope color to the fabric, and tear it away when I finish stitching. It's a good way to recycle the paper.

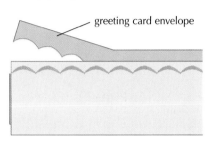

greeting card envelope

Thelma M. Ott, Albion, Indiana

Fill in the blanks

When making dresses for my granddaughters, I like to make scalloped collars. When the scallops were white stitching on white fabric, there was no problem. But when I wanted colored scallops, the white fabric showed through on the edge after I trimmed the scallops. I pur-

chased a package of fabric pens and used one to "color" the edge of the scallops after they were trimmed. Voila! The entire scallop was one color.

Marguerite Deaderick, Evinston, Florida

Towel off

Many of the fabrics I use for decorative stitching are delicate and need some sort of backing to stabilize the stitching. I found that any type of paper toweling works wonders. I add one or more sheets under the fabric as necessary. When I'm finished stitching, I just wet the toweling and the paper falls away on even the most intricate designs and the sheerest fabrics.

Linda Grana, Bergenfield, New Jersey

Check this out!

To add dimension to fabric, I like to stitch checks onto a plain fabric.

- Use twin needles in your sewing machine to stitch rows ¼" apart.
- Use the presser foot to space the tucks apart.
- *Optional:* Stitch diagonal rows, according to the design you want.

This embellishment would be nice on the cuff of a sleeve, for instance, or on a collar or a pocket – wherever you might want to highlight a feature.

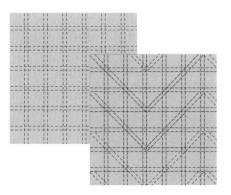

Josephine Harkness, Topeka, Kansas

Background check

Here is my solution for sewing a lettuce edge on a bridal veil. The first veil I attempted was difficult because I was unable to see the tulle on the sewing machine bed. It occurred to me to put a dark surface as a contrast background against the tulle. Electrical tape, cut to fit between the feed dogs, was the perfect solution. The improvement in viewing and quality of edging was dramatic.

Bette Nixon, Willits, California

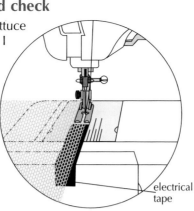

electrical tape

Leave your legacy in thread

Here's my tip for easy and even faggoting for heirloom projects.

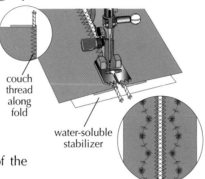

couch thread along fold

water-soluble stabilizer

- Fold under ½" on the edges of the two pieces of fabric.
- Attach an appliqué foot and couch a single strand of crochet thread directly on the fold of each fabric piece using a zigzag stitch with a 2.0 width and a 1.5 length, making sure the right swing of the needle goes off the edge of the fabric.
- Place a pintuck foot on the machine and place the two fabric pieces right side up over a piece of water-soluble stabilizer.
- Insert the fabric in the foot so one is in the groove to the left of the center groove and the other is in the groove to the right of the center groove. I use a "joining" stitch (as illustrated) to join the two pieces, sewing slowly and consistently and making sure the needle bites into the cording on the back of the hemmed edge.
- After the faggoting is completed, you can add more decorative stitching on either side if you wish.

Eunice Nicholson, Mantéca, California

Live wire

Using Nancy's method, I made fabric bows with strips of wire fused along the edges. It worked perfectly. I decided to take this method further and try embellishing.

- Apply ¾" wide strips of Wonder Under to the wrong side of the fabric along the long edges.
- Stitch a decorative stitch along each side about ½" from the edge. The paper backing works as a stabilizer and tears easily away after stitching.
- Fold under the long edge, using the edge of the stitching as a fold line.
- Insert a thin wire along the fold. Press.

Joan Roach, Port Alberni, British Columbia, Canada

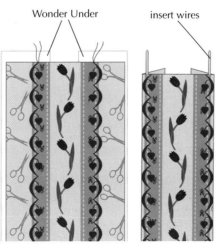

Wonder Under   insert wires

Behind the Scenes

Take 12

"I do my *worst sewing* on TV!"

That's right, the heading reads that I do my "worst" sewing on TV! Why? It all has to do with positioning. . . the positioning of the camera and, specifically, the sewing machine. In order for the camera behind my right shoulder to get a close-up view of the presser foot, the sewing machine is placed in the cabinet at a 30 degree angle, facing the camera. As I start a seam, I take time to look down at my work, but then look up at the camera and talk to you as I'm sewing. When I finish the sewing, I generally hold the sample up to the close-up camera on my left side. If you see my thumb full-screen, there's generally something underneath my thumb that I don't care for you to see. I've become a master at hiding my mistakes.

The next time you're sewing, cant your machine away from you, look up after you've started to sew, and talk as if you're teaching someone in the room. You'll get my point right away!

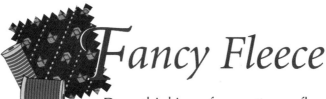

Fancy Fleece

Does thinking of ways to use fleece other than for blankets and jackets have you pulling out your hair? Relax – the following hints provide creative ways of using fleece that will make you stand up and cheer!

Standing ovation

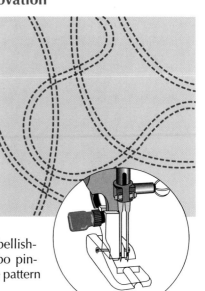

With the use of a 3.0 double needle and a five- or seven-groove pintuck foot, I made dainty sculptured pintucks on fleece (following the suggestions from Nancy Cornwell's book, *Adventures with Polarfleece®*).

For a more dramatic looking pintuck I use a 4.0 double needle and a Pearls 'N Piping Foot. This creates jumbo pintucks that really stand out and are easy to sew. I have used a random path design and crossed the jumbo pintucks with great results.

For a unique look, experiment with metallic or other decorative threads. As with other textured embellishments, I recommend creating the jumbo pintucks on a piece of fleece larger than the pattern piece before cutting out the pattern.

Ruth Nelson, Seattle, Washington

On the fringe

Because I love Polarfleece, I try to use it a lot. I have come up with a unique way to make fringe on Polarfleece.

- Lay your fabric on a large cutting mat.
- Place a smaller cutting mat on top of the fabric, leaving about 3" exposed. You will have a sandwich of the large mat, Polarfleece, and the second mat.
- Cut the exposed fleece with a rotary cutter, making ¼" slices along the exposed edge.

Your fringe will be even and the cutting will go very quickly.

Ginny Unger, Manchester, Missouri

sandwich fleece between cutting mats

Note from
Nancy

Using this technique, make a super-quick scarf by cutting fringe on the edges. Use a 12" x 60" (⅓ yard) piece of fleece. Use Ginny's technique to cut fringe on the short edges. I like to fringe 3" at each end of the scarf.

Spin your own yarn

When you are planning a project from fleece, don't let matching cuffs or ribbing be a problem. Make your own cuffs and ribbing with fleece yarn. Or use leftover fleece to create yarn for knitting, crocheting, making long tassels, or couching yarn.

To make fleece yarn:

• Trim off the selvages of the fleece.
• Cut crosswise strips of fleece. (The selvages have been trimmed off already.)
• Pull the fleece to stretch it out as much as you can. Now you have yarn.
• The strips, and ultimately the yarn, can be of various widths. Cut several 6" test strips at different widths: ¼", ⅜", and ½". Pull the yarn. Determine from the test strip the thickness to cut. If the yarn breaks when you pull it, it may be too narrow.

To make continuous yarn:

• Trim off the selvage edges. Cut strips as shown, stopping ¼" to ½" from the edge.
• Round off the squared cut edges for a nice smooth yarn.

A very small piece of fabric will make a very long length of yarn. You can cut a few rows, knit or sew, cut a few more rows, and continue sewing until you have the length you need, without wasting any fabric.

Alice Goetschius, Portland, Oregon
Laura Hess, Valparaiso, Indiana

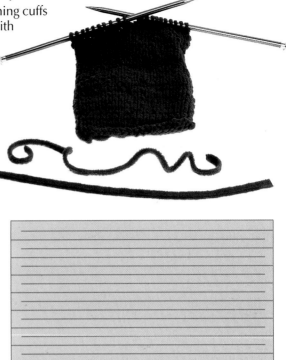

crossgrain = greatest stretch

Ding, dong, the witch has hair

In the process of making a witch doll this week, I needed something for her hair. I couldn't find anything in my stash of leftover yarns that would work. I had made camouflage jackets for fall and there were many scraps. After cutting the fleece in ½" strips, I pulled the fleece and sewed it down the middle to the doll head. It looks wonderful and curly also. Really witchy.

Pat Lutheran, Springfield, Missouri

Note from Nancy *Many of you submitted hints on making fleece yarn. It's impossible to list each one, so I've chosen to include the two hints on this page, as they're rather unique. Thanks to all who have told me about fleece yarn – it's a wonderful hint.*

Zip it!

I wanted to share with you an addition I have used in sewing the Self-Tying Scarf. I have been making the scarves as gifts for a couple of years since seeing the scarf in your book *Quick Gifts & Decor.*

• Once you have cut out the scarf pieces from fleece, cut one piece apart, approximately 5" from the 9" edge.
• Stitch a zipper between the two pieces, placing the topstitched edges along the zipper. (Of course, I hold the zipper in place with Sewer's Fix-it Tape as I learned on another of your series!)
• Continue with the scarf as the directions state.
• When the scarf is stitched together and turned right side out, stitch through all layers across the scarf about 1" to 2" above the zipper.

This creates a secure, zippered pocket in the scarf for holding a driver's license, a little cash, keys, or whatever the wearer wants to have handy without carrying a wallet. This addition has been especially popular with teens and with moms who spend time in ice arenas.

Linda Paine, Wheatley, Ontario, Canada

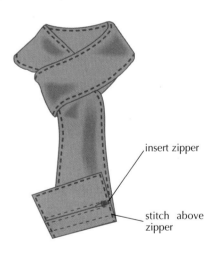

insert zipper

stitch above zipper

Note from Nancy *The basic instructions for the Self-Tying Scarf are on pages 92-93.*

Stunning Serging

Have you finally figured out how to thread your serger, only to ask,
"What now?" Get the scoop from these serger enthusiasts and shout out,
"Oh, the possibilities!"

Let's stay together

No matter how careful I am, it is difficult to cut a pattern piece twice for a reversible project, such as circular napkins, a circular tablecloth, etc., and have the edges align perfectly, even when they are both cut out at the same time. To solve this problem:

wrong side

- Cut one layer with the pattern tissue.
- Remove the pattern tissue and meet the cut fabric piece with the second fabric, wrong sides together.
- Glue the edges of the cut piece to the uncut fabric with a glue stick, by slightly raising the edges and dotting glue every inch or so around the entire cut piece.
- Allow the glue to dry completely (about five minutes).
- Cut the second fabric, using the first cut piece as the pattern. If serging the edges, you can do your decorative stitch and cut at the same time!

No pinning or basting is needed to hold the pieces together to prevent slippage because the fabric is glued together. The glue washes out when laundered the first time and will not harm the fabric. If using a conventional machine to bias bind the edges, this nicely holds the fabric together.

Belva Barrick, Glendale, Arizona

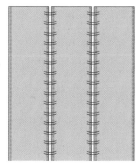

Brilliant braid

To create serger braid to apply to garments – around collars, sleeves, or pockets, or even on the edges of little girl's or doll dresses – I adjusted my serger for a three-thread overlock as follows:

- Use conventional serger thread in the needle, monofilament thread in the lower looper, and Pearl Crown Rayon in the upper looper.
- Set the stitch length and width at the maximum settings.
- Loosen the needle and lower the tensions slightly; remove the Pearl Crown Rayon from the upper looper tension by placing a piece of tape across the guide so the thread can't slide in there.
- Cut 1" strips of water-soluble stabilizer. Serge along the strips, allowing the serger to trim the edge.

To make a double trim:

- Turn the strip and serge a second row, trying to align the second needle stitching on top of the previous needle stitching.
- Thread a conventional sewing machine with the same thread used in the serger needle. Use a 1.5mm stitch width and a 2.0mm stitch length. Zigzag down the length of the trim, following the serger needle stitching. This stitching stabilizes the trim so it doesn't come apart when you dissolve the stabilizer.
- Stitch each edge of the trim to the garment, using monofilament thread and a small zigzag stitch. Spritz away the stabilizer with a spray of water.

Susan Smith, Pasadena, California

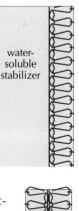

water-soluble stabilizer

Broaden your horizons

While making bridesmaid dresses, I discovered how difficult it is to locate wide satin ribbon (2" and 3") in colors other than black and white. I purchased readily available ⅞" ribbon and set up my serger for a two-thread flatlock. The flatlock gave the look of faggoting. I serged two strips together for a 2" finished ribbon and three strips for a 3" finished ribbon, etc. This gave me ribbon the width I needed and also added a little extra pizzazz.

Mary Ann Wendling,
New Richmond, Ohio

Smoothing out the edges

The serger cover hem stitch that can be found on some sergers creates a very useful and attractive hem. In the past, I had trouble covering the raw edge of the hem. As the hem is sewn on the right side, I couldn't see what was happening on the wrong side. To cover the raw edge:

- Press the hem to the wrong side.
- Baste the hem close to the raw edge with contrasting thread.
- Stitch the hem on the right side with your serger. The basting thread is visible and can easily be straddled by the two needles of the cover hem.
- Remove the basting thread. The raw edge on the wrong side will be covered.

Ilse Grant, Southbury, Connecticut

right side

basting thread

Piping incognito

I like the look of piping on yokes, cuffs, and between the tiers of full skirts, yet I do not like the trouble I sometimes have finding just the right color of piping or getting the piping in the seam correctly. So I make my own serged piping directly on the seamline of the garment, using decorative thread in the upper looper.

trim close to stitching

overlap seamline; stitch

- Use a water-soluble marker to mark the seamline on the right side of the fabric that will have the piped edge.
- To make it easier to serge a rolled hem over any garment seams in the piped section, trim those seams close to the stitching lines. Trim from the cut edge to slightly below the marked piping seamline, and seal the trimmed edge with a seam sealant.
- Serge a rolled hem along the marked seamline.
- Overlap the rolled hem piping onto the seamline of the adjoining fabric section, meeting the piping edge to the seamline of the second section. Use a conventional sewing machine and a topstitching foot to stitch along the inner edge of the rolled hem.

Sue Lis, Amarillo, Texas

Fusible thread to the rescue!

To make a beautiful braid, I serge over ¼" wide ribbon using decorative thread such as Pearl Cotton in the upper looper and fusible thread in the lower looper.

To attach the braid to your project, position the braid with the fusible thread next to the fabric, cover with a press cloth, and press. Permanently stitch in place with monofilament thread.

Cecilia A. Dean, Brandon, Vermont

Note from

Nancy   Fusible thread, such as ThreadFuse™, is a twisted polyester thread that contains a heat activated fusible nylon filament. When using it in the lower looper, I slightly tighten the tension of that looper, keeping the thread on the underside of the fabric (or in this instance, braid) and ultimately away from making contact with the iron surface.

Take 13

My *Magical* Table

I've received requests for the dimensions of my table by people who would like to have a duplicate of it in their home. Unfortunately for you, it was designed for the camera's eye, not for the sewing enthusiast.

This table includes adjustable elevations so that the tabletop can tilt toward the cameras. The angle that I position the tabletop depends on what I'm showing or the height of my guest!

To prevent pincushions, scissors, and other notions from rolling to the floor, we make "tape balls" from duct tape, attach them to the underside of the product, and "stick" the notions on the table. The photo shows that I hide other notions and samples under the propped-up area.

When I demonstrate, I place the samples facing the camera, away from me. Initially it felt as if I was working upside down, but after 20 years it's second nature. One late evening as I was sewing at home, I realized that I was positioning my pattern pieces on my cutting table as if I was teaching on TV. I decided it was time to go to bed!

Heirloom with a modern twist

I use my serger in tandem with my sewing machine to create heirloom projects. Here are three traditional heirloom techniques with a serger twist!

To add edging lace (lace with one straight edge and one decorative edge) **to the fabric:**

- Set the serger for a three-thread rolled hem stitch, lengthening the stitch to "3" and widening the width to "3." Using the traditional rolled hem short stitch length and narrow width creates a stiff seam. By lengthening the stitch, I get a softer seam more consistent with heirloom techniques.
- Attach a rolled hem foot.
- Thread the machine with cotton machine embroidery thread.
- Meet the edging lace to the fabric, right sides together. Serge along the edge.

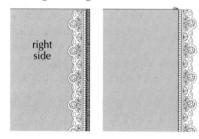

Note from Nancy

The traditional method of seaming lace to fabric is to overlap the lace on the right side of the fabric, zigzag along the straight edge, trim away the fabric from behind the lace, and add a second wider line of zigzagging over the first stitching. Using the modified rolled hem stitch, the seam can take place with just one row of stitching.

To add insertion lace (lace with two straight edges) **to the fabric:**

- Use the same settings as detailed at left. Meet the insertion lace to the fabric, right sides together. Serge along the edge. Repeat on the opposite side.
- Finish the insertion seam by topstitching with a conventional sewing machine. Insert a wing needle and set the machine for a zigzag or decorative heirloom stitch, also known as a pinstitch.

Note from Nancy

A winged needle has wide "wings" at the sides, designed to create large holes in the fabric – an heirloom decorative effect. To best create these decorative holes, spray starch the fabric and press to give the fabric crispness and stability.

Puffing strips, gathered sections of fabric, can be gathered and sewn to the project, again with a serger.

- Cut fabric strips the desired width and two times the needed length.

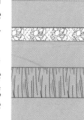

- Adjust the serger for a four-thread overlock stitch with the tension tightened to the tightest setting and the differential feed set at the highest "plus" setting.
- Serge along both long edges; the fabric will automatically gather.
- Attach the puffing strips to the fabric, following the insertion lace technique.

*Margaret Roy,
Prattville, Alabama*

Roll over!

While making skating dresses, I had trouble with the rolled edge on a chiffon skirt. The threads were pulling off the edge of the fabric. To prevent this, I used a strip of the chiffon fabric cut on the bias. I placed the bias strip on the wrong side along the edge, serged, and trimmed off the excess bias strip.

*Marg Rowbotham,
Stayner, Ontario, Canada*

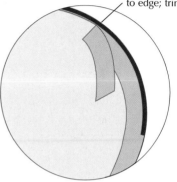

stitch bias strip to edge; trim

I recently made a vest with a serged (three-thread) rolled edge finish. I was not satisfied with the appearance of the fibers poking out of the stitch. I did not have Woolly Nylon on hand. To create density in the rolled edge, I used two threads in the upper looper instead of the usual one thread. I placed the extra serger cone on a cone thread stand, next to my serger, to feed alongside the upper looper thread. The results were stunning! No fibers showed through the rolled edge and there were no "whiskers." The quality looked like the finish on commercial napkins.

*Loretta Grunewald,
Shenandoah, Virginia*

Note from Nancy

Not only will two similar threads work well together in the upper looper, but also try combining decorative threads for a textured look. A combination I like is to thread metallic and Woolly Nylon through the same loop.

To prevent the threads from tangling, place spools on the spool pin so they unwind in opposite directions.

Mix & Match Fabrics

Are you an experienced sewer who needs an idea for some
leftover fabric, or are you a beginner who is not ready to tackle plaids?
Either way, look to the following hints for some imaginative solutions.

It's a plaid, plaid world

When making a pair of shorts for my toddler, I had quite a bit of fabric left over, but not enough to make a second pair. I used the leftover fabric to make a coordinated set.

- Cut off the sleeve portions from a white t-shirt.
- Use the cut-off sleeve portions as patterns, add a seam allowance and hem allowance, and cut out sleeves from the leftover shorts fabric.
- Add the new sleeves to the existing white t-shirt.

Elizabeth Rock, St. Francis, Minnesota

Start slow

My hint is for novice seamstresses. Many solid fabrics are sold with coordinating stripes, plaids, or one-way designs. If you aren't ready to tackle them but yearn to use them, buy ¼ yard to match your solid color fabric. Cover buttons with it. Sew a square and fold it as a hanky showing from a pocket. It gives a designer touch to an otherwise basic dress.

Pat Schawitsch, Salisbury, North Carolina

Kids' Hint

Hop to it!

My daughter purchased a preprinted panel of a frog to make a stuffed toy for my grandson. I made the frog, and then decided to appliqué the picture of the finished product included on the panel onto a shirt. I had two extra large t-shirts in complementary colors that no one was wearing. I cut the front from one of the shirts, and I cut the sleeves and the top of the shorts from the other shirt. I appliquéd the picture of the finished product onto the front of the shirt, and I appliquéd two fish from the border of the panel onto the lower part of the shorts. It made a cute outfit!

Gerry Conway, Franklin, North Carolina

Guest Spot

Philip Pepper, talented designer and educator for Pfaff, was my guest on two Sewing With Nancy series, "Sewing Spotlight" and "Stitching Strategies." His untimely passing in 2000 left us greatly saddened. Yet when recalling conversations and opportunities to work with him, I subconsciously "smile!"

Philip flew into Madison, Wisconsin, from Texas on a Sunday evening. By Monday morning 17" of new snow had fallen and was drifting higher by the minute. After two days of being marooned in his hotel room, I picked him up at the hotel. He was dressed in a suit with a scarf cavalierly flung around his neck. His comment, "I never knew it got so cold or the snow could get this high in December!" Needless to say, he traveled to the upper Midwest without an outer coat or gloves – two items he confessed that he didn't own, but soon purchased!

That trip, for Philip, was his first Sewing With Nancy appearance, but his second TV taping. He confessed that he was less nervous during this taping. During the first session in a studio, he over-gestured with his arms, causing the producer to literally tape his thumbs to the table to prevent the exaggerated movements. I never did figure out how he could demonstrate with duct tape getting the better of him!

Our second series on "Stitching Strategies" was eye opening for me. Philip taught us how to change the stitch setting on decorative stitches – something that I had never thought of doing. This idea allowed him to stack stitch, creating a lace look by combining several modified decorative stitches.

With fondness I look back on my time with Philip. I'm grateful that I had the opportunity to work with him so that many of you could learn of his sewing "magic."

Philip Pepper – With Fond Memories

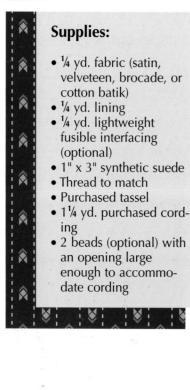Nancy's *favorite* techniques

Two Perfect Palettes for Creativity!

When I learn a new technique, I like to give it a *rehearsal* before starting a *big production*! I've chosen two projects, a scarf and an evening bag, that are perfect for rehearsing new embellishing techniques. Choose one or both projects to audition creative ideas that you learned in this chapter.

Creative Options Evening Bag

Create an elegant evening bag and enhance the fabric, using your favorite or newly learned embellishing technique. This easy-sew bag would be the perfect palette for serger braid (pages 86-87), an intricate Ultrasuede appliqué (page 78), decorative metallic stitches (pages 82-83), or elegant piping (page 76).

Supplies:

- ¼ yd. fabric (satin, velveteen, brocade, or cotton batik)
- ¼ yd. lining
- ¼ yd. lightweight fusible interfacing (optional)
- 1" x 3" synthetic suede
- Thread to match
- Purchased tassel
- 1¼ yd. purchased cording
- 2 beads (optional) with an opening large enough to accommodate cording

1. Create a pattern for the evening bag.

a. Draw a 3" x 8½" rectangle on pattern paper.

b. Write "place on fold" along one lengthwise edge.

c. Measure and mark 5½" down from the top on the other lengthwise edge.

d. Draw a line between the 5½" mark and the opposite bottom corner.

e. Draw carrier placement marks. On the 5½" edge, measure from the top and mark 1" and 2" down.

f. Draw in a ¼" seam allowance as shown.

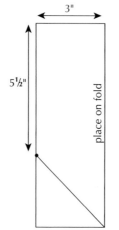

2. Cut the bag sections:

a. Cut two bag pieces from the fabric. If the fabric is lightweight, fuse interfacing to the wrong side.

b. Cut two bag pieces from the lining fabric.

c. Add an embellishment to the fabric pieces.

3. Position the tassel on the right side of one of the pieces, placing the knot at the cut edge of the point of the bag as shown. Baste in place.

4. Construct the bag, using a 1¼" seam allowance.

a. Prepare and position the cord carriers by cutting the synthetic suede piece in half to create two carriers, each 1" x 1½". Meet the 1" edges of each carrier. Position the carriers on the right side of one bag section at the pattern marking. Baste in place.

1" right side 1"

b. Meet the fabric pieces, right sides together. Stitch the sides and lower edges of the bag together. Turn the bag right side out.

c. Repeat, stitching the side and lower edges of the lining and leaving an opening for turning the bag. Pivot at the opening edges and stitch to the cut edges to make it easier to turn the bag and get sharp edges.

wrong side

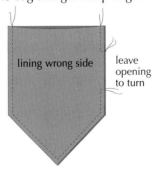

lining wrong side   leave opening to turn

d. Join the bag and the lining by slipping the bag inside the lining with right sides together. Pin and stitch the upper edge, matching the seams.

wrong side   stitch upper edge

Turn the pouch right side out. Hand stitch the opening closed. Tuck the lining inside the bag.

5. Attach the cord:

a. Thread each cord end through one of the carrier loops.

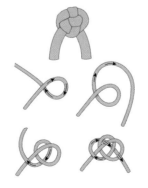

b. Decide on the final length of the strap and mark it with thread tacks in contrasting sewing thread.

c. On each end of the cord strap, make a Chinese ball button, shaping the button as illustrated, or thread a glass bead at each end of the strap, not the cord, and clip the tails. Alternately tighten the tails, then the loops.

d. Secure the cording ends together. Wrap the ends and clip the tails.

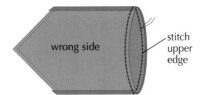

Behind the Scenes

Take 14

"3-2-1-Action!"

When I think about a Hollywood movie set, I picture a director who is wearing a dashing beret and yelling into a megaphone, "Quiet on the set!" followed by "3-2-1-action!" Sewing With Nancy is far from that scenario!

Unlike the "3-2-1-action!" phrase, my TV cues are much less dramatic. The floor director gives a hand and voice countdown from "10" down to "two." The "one" count and "action" signals are hand signals only to avoid the possibility of the floor director being heard on the tape.

During each segment, the floor director lets me know the time that's left by holding up time cards. After the one minute cue, I receive a 30 second cue card, a 15 second cue card, and then a hand signal countdown for the last 10 seconds. When I see the 30 second cue card, it's time to "wrap it up!" My goal and challenge is to stop speaking, plus end with a coherent thought when the floor director reaches the "one" count. My "crutch" ending phrase is "I hope you'll give it a try!"

Self-Tying Scarf

This project is an excerpt from the series that Gail Brown and I did together in the video and book, Quick Gifts and Décor. *It's been a favorite, and perfect for fleece accents such as embroidery (page 136) or pintuck stitching (page 84). Remember, use this pattern and add a zippered pocket as detailed on page 85. For a silky scarf, consider adding lace accents (page 75) or decorative stitching (pages 82-83).*

Supplies:

- ½ yd. Polarfleece or other high-loft fleece, OR
- ⅝ yd. of silky sheer, or drapeable fabric for a lightweight scarf
- Thread to match

Note: All seam allowances are ⅝" (1.5 cm).

1. Cut and mark the fabric.

a. Cut two 40" long pieces of Polarfleece. Taper them from 9" wide at one end to 5" wide at the other. Or, if using lighter weight fabric, increase the width dimensions to 11" x 7" as illustrated.

b. Working from the wrong side, place marks 8½" from the narrow end near the seam edges.

2. With right sides together, stitch the narrow ends.

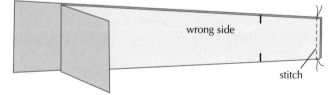

3. Clean finish the neckline area.

a. Machine stitch ⅝" from the edge between each mark.

b. Clip to the stitching line at each mark.

c. Fold the seam allowances to the wrong side between the marks. Topstitch along the fold, using the presser foot as your guide.

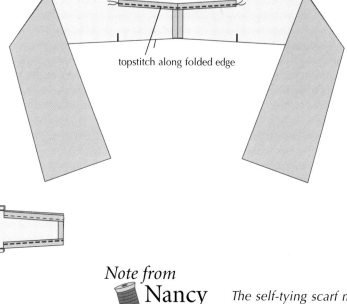

topstitch along folded edge

4. Fold the scarf, right sides together, aligning the 9" ends. Stitch from mark to mark, pivoting at the corners. Grade the seam allowances and trim the corners.

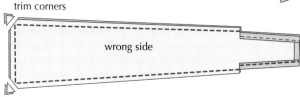

trim corners

wrong side

5. Turn the scarf right side out and press.

topstitch edges

6. When sewing with fleece, steam the fabric and finger press, as traditional pressing will leave an imprint on the fabric. Topstitch along the edge, using the presser foot as a guide and aligning this stitching with the topstitching in Step 3.

7. To wear the scarf, wrap it around your neck and pull the wide end through the loop.

Note from Nancy

The self-tying scarf makes a great gift, but did you know that it could also be used to make a difference in the lives of others in need?

Although the self-tying scarf comes from the book Quick Gifts and Décor, it also has ties to another book that Gail Brown and I did together – Creative Kindness. In that book, Gail and I share heartwarming stories of people who use their sewing skills to help others in need.

Gail and I encourage you to use this pattern and your leftover fleece fabrics to create warmth for others. Homeless shelters will welcome your gifts of kindness!

Guest Spot

To highlight my next Sewing With Nancy *guest, Gail Brown, in the space allotted, is like trying to read* War and Peace *during a weekend – it just can't be done! Gail, prolific author of topics such as home decorating, serging, and bridal, has appeared in 21 shows. Her first appearance on* Sewing With Nancy *was in 1984, my first guest!*

When Gail works on a series, she devotes her entire being to the project. From the time recorded on her e-mails, I know she works day and night.

During a series on "Instant Interiors," Gail asked us to be on the lookout for a shipment of samples that were on the way from her home in Hoquiam, Washington, to our offices in Wisconsin. Never did I expect to receive over 20 boxes filled with beautiful decorating ideas.

Gail was part of our first serging series; the sergers acted like two-year old children . . .throwing tantrums! Gail spent 45 minutes threading and re-threading one serger, only to appear in front of the camera as if nothing had happened. Yet we learned from this experience. The next serger series featured nine thread changes so we traveled to the studio with nine sergers all specifically threaded for each segment!

Gail's delivery on TV is with grace and warmth; her personality off camera is the same – she's a friend to all, and a blessing to me.

Gail Brown

CHAPTER FIVE

I came, I saw, I *quilted*

Making a quilt can sometimes feel like a quest with a few pitfalls along the way: fabrics that aren't the perfect match, rulers that slip, and bindings that get tangled, just to mention a few.

Never fear! Quilting doesn't have to be intimidating. You can express yourself however you like – large or small, bed or wall, appliqué or pieced – the possibilities are endless. In this chapter, you will benefit from the years of collective experience of *Sewing With Nancy* viewers. It's like having a quilting bee right in your own home!

Summon up your courage and prepare to take the quilting journey. With these hints at your side, you are sure to conquer your quilting fears and celebrate many triumphs along the way.

What's the Plan?

Roses are red, log cabins are tan;
it's a good idea to start a quilt with a plan. The following hints offer
colorful advice on designing, from choosing fabrics to looking at the big picture.

Front page news

When making a quilt where every block is different, I want to see how each block looks before I stitch it. My solution is to purchase a very large tablet from an office or art supply store (I have an 18" x 24" newsprint tablet), or to use an atlas.

- Place the tablet or atlas on your work surface and open it so the back cardboard piece is visible.
- Lay out one block as you want it. When you are happy with the placement, flip a page over it and start laying out another block.
- Continue until you have positioned all the blocks.

By laying each block on a page in the correct order, I am able to stitch each block in the order it is needed. If I am interrupted, I just close the book and put a weight on top to keep the pieces in place.

Lorrie Sjoquist, Bothell, Washington
Rosanna Williams, Fostoria, Ohio

Flag it down

When doing landscape quilting, I first decide what color scheme I want, then take out the pattern instructions. Using small sticky-note flags, I write a description and the amount of each fabric I need. For example: blue border, 1 yd.; black border, ½ yd.; tree #1, ¼ yd.; grass #1, ⅛ yd.

I take these flags with me to the fabric store. When I pick out the fabric I want, I place that sticky note on the bolt. Then when I get to the cutting counter I know by a glance how much of each I need without taking more time to remember which fabric I wanted for which piece. I leave the sticky notes on the piece of fabric until I get ready to use it. I may not sew it right away and I find this saves a lot of time trying to remember what I picked out for each project.

Linda Gray, Fort Peck, Montana

Playing with matches

When I have a fabric that's difficult to match, I use the wrong side of the fabric as the "matching fabric." This is especially useful when quilting.

Evelyn Gatt, Clearwater, Florida

You ought to be in pictures

When choosing fabrics for quilts, I've always had trouble judging which fabrics were light, medium, or dark values. I live too far from town to go to a copy machine to photocopy my fabric, and don't have time to take black and white pictures.

Then I discovered I could line up fabric possibilities for my quilt and look through the viewfinder of my video camera. This gives a black and white picture, and I can instantly decide what value my fabrics are and rearrange them if necessary. Using the batteries, I can even take my video camera to the fabric store.

Starr Eby, Lowell, Michigan

Quilting fabric to "dye" for

Recently, I made a quilt with fabric I custom-dyed. Here is the easy fabric dying method I used:

- Thoroughly wet five yards of white fabric until it is dripping wet.
- Spray it randomly with Spray Tumble Dyes in magenta, yellow, jade, and blueberry. The colors run together in a pleasing manner.

I used the fabric for portions of individual quilt block designs, as well as for framing quilt blocks and for borders. I didn't have to worry about finding matching fabrics because they all blended perfectly.

Blanche Rehling, Millstadt, Illinois

Photo finish

Recently, I made a quilt for my granddaughter using a modification of the log cabin pattern. Her bedroom is decorated with a cartoon character's theme and I used a twin sheet with that character on it for the quilt backing and cut the log cabin strips out of the remaining fabric. I transferred photographs that have special meaning for her onto white broadcloth and used those as alternate blocks.

These quilts have endless possibilities: a family tree quilt, a quilt incorporating photos of a fisherman's big catches, something with a sports theme for a sports enthusiast, etc.

Marlene Warren,
Chatham, Ontario, Canada

Note from

Nancy

There are many ways to transfer photographs to fabric. The most hassle-free way is to use 8½" x 11" sheets of fabric that are designed to be used with a photocopy machine. Gently tape photographs to a sheet of paper, place on the photocopy machine as to make a copy, manually feed the fabric sheets (such as Quick Fuse™ Inkjet Fabric Sheets) in the photocopier, and press "start!" The fabric is colorfast and washable, and ready for your quilt project.

It's hip to be square

Over the years, I spent many hours sewing clothes for my three daughters. Now that they are grown and have left home, I have the time to sort through my fabric scraps to cut squares for memory quilts. (I also cut squares from all their dresses and play clothes). I now have a grandson and have started sewing for him. Instead of waiting for him to grow up, I save a square from each outfit I make for him with the hopes to make him a memory quilt for his wedding day.

Debbie Crawford,
Union Mills, North Carolina

After I have completed a project, I always have leftover fabric. I cut as much as I can into 1½" wide strips and make log cabin squares. I use the squares to make quick gifts such as pillows and potholders.

Ellen Raupp, Reedsburg, Wisconsin

Cross my project with no guilt, stick a needle in my quilt

Over the years I have acquired several cross-stitch projects and wanted a new way to display them. I framed the pieces with fabric to make them a uniform size, then pieced them together to make a quilt top. I just love it! I made two of these quilt tops and hope they will become heirlooms, since there are interesting stories behind most of them.

Jewell Waits, Moulton, Alabama

Seeing the big picture

While completing a log cabin barn-raising pattern, I came up with a simple way of looking at the "big" picture to see if all the blocks were laid out correctly. I took a pair of binoculars and looked through them the opposite way (through the larger end of the eyepiece). Presto, the pattern was reduced and I could see the overall pattern most effectively – less eyestrain and headache!

Angie Anderson, Grey Eagle, Minnesota

Kids' Hint — It's raining scraps

When my children were small, they played under or near my sewing machine. They used the scraps that I let fall on the floor to make their own wall hangings. They sorted the colors and stuck them to poster board with a glue stick so there were no sharp scissors or needles to worry about. Their wall hangings were displayed right next to mine.

Ellen Ball, Crawfordsville, Indiana

Have your cake and eat it, too!

Like many quilters, I enjoy designing, planning, and giving quilts to friends and family. However, after the excitement of developing the design and the many hours spent completing the quilt, giving the quilt away is a bit like sending that first child off to college. Bittersweet! So, I've found a way to partially keep the quilts. I've started making one block for each quilt completed. Each block represents the quilt's central design and fabric choices. This becomes "My Quilt," a sampler, visually reminiscent of all my gift quilts. I thus give "my cake away" and get to "eat it, too."

Marion Dannert, Currituck, North Carolina

Note from
Nancy

Sampler quilts make wonderful memories. Due to the variety of colors and designs used in the individual blocks, choose a solid color fabric, perhaps a dark color such as navy, black, or forest green, to visually separate the blocks, providing a pleasing overall design.

*F*ollow the Yellow Grid Rule

Does your ruler veer off course the minute your rotary cutter touches the fabric? With the help of the following hints, you can keep your ruler in place and be off to cut some strips in no time.

Color me accurate

To mark my ruler when rotary cutting, I use a piece of see-through colored vinyl (sold in fabric/decorator stores in different colors). I cut a strip of the vinyl and line it up on the measurement I'm cutting. This way if I'm cutting 2½" strips, for example, I can glance where the vinyl is and I don't have to look for the measurement again – a great time saver and it decreases cutting mistakes. Also, the vinyl peels easily off the ruler – I don't have to worry about removing marks from the ruler, or about cleaning off sticky "goo."

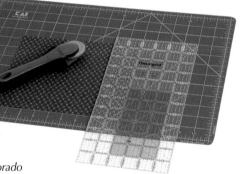

Sharon Stalp, Denver, Colorado

Flag on the play

Sticky-note flags are an invaluable tool in my sewing room. I use them to mark my quilting rulers. The flags give me immediate reference points; I don't have to constantly go back and forth between the instructions and the rulers. The flags can be used over and over again. I don't have to bother cleaning off the rulers, I just move the notes. They save me time, money, and frustration.

Allison C. Bayer, Richardson, Texas
Phyllis Salt, Miami, Florida

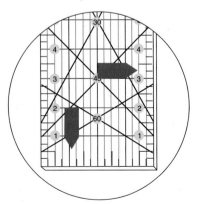

Who was that masked ruler?

While cutting out hundreds of same-size patches for a quilt, I came upon a method for dramatically improving speed and accuracy. Many of us know the tip to use masking tape on the top of an acrylic ruler to aid accuracy in cutting. This method, however, can make a shadow on the fabric, making it difficult to see when the fabric is exactly aligned with the tape. To greatly enhance speed, I stack two to three layers of masking tape to the underside of the clear ruler. This frame of tape provides a fast and accurate ledge to butt the fabric against, ensuring an accurate cut in much less time.

Margaret Ann Smith,
Orangevale, California

Treat yourself to a manicure

Here's a tip that helps me when I cut squares from fabric scraps. Before cutting the fabric, I mark my ruler along the appropriate lines using fingernail polish. After cutting, I remove the polish marks using nail polish remover, and re-mark the ruler whenever I cut squares of another size.

Eva Smith, Kimball, Minnesota

Seize the ruler

To make my rotary cutting easier and more accurate, I use fabric grippers, ½" sandpaper circles with an adhesive back, on my rulers. I hate covering up the cross marks, so I use a small hole paper punch to make a "donut" that leaves the lines visible. I use the centers on my solid and appliqué templates.

Nellie Switzer, Kingwood, Texas

As an alternative to purchasing commercial fabric grips to apply to my rulers, I made my own. I started with a self-adhesive sanding disk from my husband's woodworking shop and cut it into circles, squares, and strips. I attached those pieces to my rulers. The grips work great and save me money.

Jeannie Passmore, Sherwood, Michigan

To prevent quilting rulers from slipping and sliding while rotary cutting, I add "grippers" to the bottom of my rulers. I use my hot glue gun to make these little "feet."
- Drop a dab of glue about the size of a pea in several areas on the bottom of the ruler.
- Using a tile or the plastic pad intended for hot gluing, press the dot flat and let it cool.
- Peel away the tile or pad and, voila! The glue dot is stuck to the bottom of the ruler and the ruler stays in place while you're cutting.

Sharon Schnese, Appleton, Wisconsin

Square dance

Cutting squares into half-square triangles is very time consuming, especially when I have over 200 to cut. I found a way to cut those triangles in a third of the time.

- Working with three squares at a time, align the diagonals of the squares along one of the grid lines of your cutting mat.
- Gently line up the edge of the quilting ruler with the diagonal line of the squares.
- Cut all three squares in one motion with a rotary cutter.

Nina Garesché, Worthington, Ohio

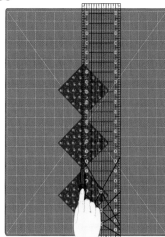

Lasting Im-"press"-ions

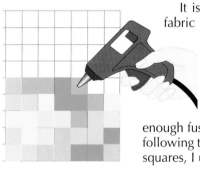

If you can't take the heat, stay away from the ironing board. Or, use the following tips to stand up to the pressure and keep your cool when your iron gets hot.

This is a stick up!

It is difficult to arrange and fuse 1" or 2" fabric squares to a printed 1" fusible grid while holding a heavy iron. To make this step easier I use my small hot glue gun (after making sure there is no glue in the nozzle), and touch it to each square in a few spots. It works great! It is just enough fusing to hold the squares in place while following the pattern. After I have arranged all my squares, I use my iron to do the full fuse.

Dorothy Neault, Proctor, Minnesota

Let your finger do the pressing

When finger pressing quilt blocks, I wear a metal thimble on my middle finger. I can do all the work while wearing it and when it comes time to finger press, I simply use my thimble! I use a rotating circular motion and the end of the thimble against a hard surface like a tabletop. This works great and saves time – I don't have to pick up a separate tool each time I need to finger press.

Carlene Walker, Yellville, Arkansas

Grace under pressure

When pressing seams on the tiny pieces used in making miniature quilts, I had problems because my regular iron was too big and clumsy. I borrowed the hobby iron my husband and son use when making model airplanes, and I was pleased with the results. You can find these irons at hobby shops; they're sometimes called "heat sealing tools." These small irons would also be helpful when making doll clothes and little collars and cuffs, etc. on baby clothes.

Shirley Phillips, Troy, Michigan

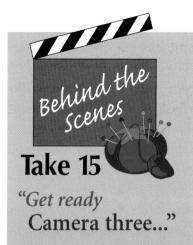

Behind the Scenes

Take 15

"Get ready Camera three..."

The Control Room couldn't be more appropriately named. The director, Laurie Gorman (in the navy jacket), has been with my show for over 10 years. She directs the staff members in charge of lighting, sound, cameras, timing, and videotapes to make certain that all the variables come together. During the taping, she looks at multiple monitors, pictured below with the Sewing With Nancy logo. Each monitor features a different camera angle; she chooses the best view.

After years of working together, Laurie instinctively knows when to switch from one camera to another, giving direction to the crew over the head sets, such as, "Get ready camera three, take to three."

A bonus for me is that Laurie knows how to sew, creating gifts and unique costumes for her kids. This skill makes my job during production go smoothly. That wasn't always the case. Years ago I remember a director calling out, "Cut" in the middle of a segment, because he couldn't find the "finger press!"

Let There Be Light Tables

One quilter's spring-arm lamp and flowerpot are another quilter's light table. After reading these hints, you'll see things in a whole new light.

Spring fever

Many of us have a spring-arm lamp in our sewing or craft areas. Here's how I converted mine into a light table.
- Extend the arm and turn the light upside down at a comfortable level, with the bottom (now the top) edge on the level.
- Cover the lamp with an 8" x 10" piece of glass from an old picture frame.

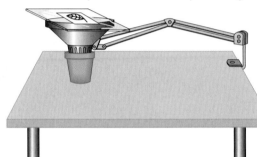

- Turn on the light, and trace on the glass surface. The on/off switch on my lamp is on the top end, so I place the inverted lamp in a small flowerpot, cup, or whatever fits the light so it doesn't turn off when I press down to trace.

Eleanore Lindemann, Golden Valley, North Dakota

The light at the end of the table

After using my friend's light table, I loved it so much that I decided to make my own.

Supplies:
- 12" x 16" picture frame (flat on both sides)
- Four 2½" dowel rods for the legs
- 12" x 16" piece of clear Plexiglas™
- Plug-in kitchen cabinet light

Instructions:
- Attach the legs to the front of the picture frame with screws.
- Place the Plexiglas in the notch made for the original glass.
- Paint the whole table white for maximum light reflection.

Liz Kelly, San Antonio, Texas

The case of the homemade light table

When I was preparing to attend a quilting weekend, one of the suggestions was to bring a light box. I do not have one, and didn't want to have to carry anything extra. Here's what I did:

My sewing machine is one of the newer models, and most of these cases are similar in that they have no bottom (that's essential). I turned the case upside down, inserted an extension cord through the opening on the bottom, and attached a small fluorescent light bulb to the extension cord. The inside of the carrying case is white, so it makes a good reflector. I used my 12" ruler for the top. It worked very well, and I didn't need to bring anything extra.

Gerry Shelhamer, Sun Prairie, Wisconsin

Paper or Plastic?

What do breakfast cereal, a bakery, and poster board have in common? Read the following tips for the answer; they'll help you make templates that will be the model of good quilting behavior.

Diamonds are a quilter's best friend

While making a throw for my sister's living room in an oversized baby block diamond-shaped pattern from scraps of tapestry and heavy cotton velvet, I could not find a pre-made ruler big enough to allow me to cut individual pieces from the slippery fabric. Lining up the 60° lines on my ruler to the edge of the fabric was very slow. My solution was to create a supersized template. Here's how:
- Cut a diamond shape out of Bristol Board the size of the quilt diamond block.
- Tape it to your ruler, lining up the edge of the diamond with the edge of the ruler, being careful to keep the edge of the Bristol Board just inside the edge of the ruler to prevent dulling your rotary cutter blade.
- After cutting the fabric into strips the appropriate width, lay your ruler on the fabric, lining up two parallel edges of the diamond on the edges of the cut fabric strips.
- Cut along the ruler edge, moving the ruler after each cut and realigning the three sides of the diamond shape.

Karen Nevin,
Gander, Newfoundland, Canada

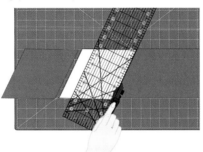

The butcher, the baker, the quilt template maker

To make templates for quilting, I use clear plastic food containers that come from packaged bakery goods. I just trace my pattern with a permanent black marker and cut it out with an older pair of scissors. I find that the edges of these plastic patterns do not wear down and lose their shape like cardboard patterns do.

Rose Edwards, Torrance, California

Stiff as a board

When cutting pieces for a quilt with templates, I prewash the fabrics, then go to the ironing board. With a professional weight spray starch, I spray my fabrics three times each, pressing after each spraying. This makes a stiff surface for transferring template markings and makes cutting easy.

Kathy Pipkorn, Phillips, Wisconsin

I'll pencil you in

Here is a trick to easily add a ¼" seam allowance to pattern edges.
- Stand two newly sharpened pencils point down on the table.
- Holding them with the points even, tape them together at two places to keep them from slipping.
- Draw two lines exactly ¼" apart. Most pencils will work, but measure the lines before use because some pencils may be larger in diameter.

Hypatia Walsh,
Tucson, Arizona

¼"

Board meeting

Here is my method for making quilting templates:
- Make a photocopy of the paper template from a pattern or magazine.
- Iron paper-backed fusible web onto the back of the copy, peel off the paper backing, and fuse it to poster board.
- Cut out the new template using a rotary cutter with old blades.

With my template, I don't have to trace the markings or worry about forgetting a dot. It is all there on the paper template I have fused to the poster board.

Janice Blumberg, Madera, California

Breakfast of champions

To make quilting templates, I recycle cereal boxes:
- Trace pattern outlines and all other information printed on the pattern onto tracing paper.
- Glue the traced pattern to the wrong side of the cereal box.
- Carefully cut out the template, cutting through both the paper and the cereal box.

Roxanne White, Cumberland, Wisconsin

Come in from the cold

Recently I came across this idea by accident when I found myself too close to a deadline to do things the usual way! I belong to a monthly friendship block exchange in my quilt guild. That month the block involved 12 templates and I knew that I didn't have the time to make proper templates. So I took the page of templates and ironed freezer paper to the back and front. The seam allowance lines were still visible. When cut out, the paper was stiff enough to trace around it once or twice.

Pat Bartels, Appleton, Wisconsin

Quicksilver Quilting

Do problems with quilting make you feel like you're sinking in quicksand? Whether you're stitching a seam, tying with yarn, or quilting by hand or machine, these hints will get you back on solid ground and quilting as swiftly as ever.

1/4 is your lucky number!

Recently I taught a series of classes on the basic feet that come with a sewing machine. Using the blind hem foot, I demonstrated not only how to blind hem stitch but also how to topstitch and make ¼" tucks. Then a light went on in my head. If I could use the blind hem foot to make ¼" tucks, why not ¼" seams? I adjusted the guide on the foot and my needle position to give me exactly the seam I wanted.

At age 72, it is exciting to think of new ways to use basic sewing feet!

Virginia Blanton, Memphis, Tennessee

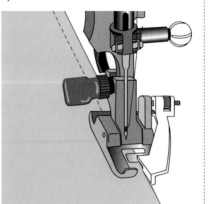

It's a hit!

When several seams meet in the center of a quilt block or elsewhere, there seems to be an extra thickness there, even if I fan out the seam. I lay the block (or finished quilt top) on a breadboard, with the seams laying in the correct direction, and hit it with a hammer from the wrong side. It flattens out the lump nicely.

Marcie Stilen, Shiocton, Wisconsin

Quilting with an edge

For stitching in the ditch, I find it helpful to use an edge joining foot. I can position the metal piece right in the seamline, and the stitches will be straight and true.

Also, I lengthen my stitch length when I machine quilt. I find a longer stitch works better because of the thickness of the fabric layers.

Sandy Snow,
Glendive, Montana

Thumbnail sketch

Quarter inch tape has often been used as a guide for accurate ¼" quilting, but I have found another way to use it. I put a ¼" piece of tape on my left or right thumbnail and use it to measure accurate seams when piecing. I don't have to hunt for my measuring tape since the tape is always right there on my finger.

Joan Wise, Hagerman, Idaho

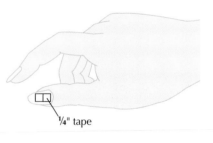

¼" tape

Getting from point A to point B

When matching exact points on a quilt, I baste them with double-sided basting tape. I place the ¼" wide tape on one seam, remove the paper backing, and stick the seams together. I can easily reposition if necessary. I have found this tip to be extremely helpful when accuracy is crucial.

Joan Loomis, Watertown, Wisconsin

Seal the deal

When I tie a quilt, I touch each knot with a tiny dab of seam sealant. That way, my knots do not work loose so I don't need to retie them.

Ann Kempen, Kaukauna, Wisconsin

Baby shower

For years I have been tying baby quilts to give as gifts, and have always used a fabric or patterns that had guides for where to position the knots. Recently I chose a quilt fabric that had no such pattern. Rather than measuring and pinning, I found a way to make my own guide.

- Using a plain white plastic shower curtain, cut a piece about 24" square and draw a 2½" grid on it. (The grid can be any size you want.)
- Fold each intersection to form a point and cut off the tip to end up with little holes every 2½" all over the guide.
- Pin the guide over the quilt and easily tie through the openings. By overlapping the last row of tied knots, it is easy to move the guide to other portions of the quilt.

Irene Marshall, Sherwood, Arkansas

cut off tips

fold

fold

Stop, drop, and re-roll

When I ran out of bobbin thread while machine quilting, I used to have difficulties finding just where I had left off. Now I keep a small safety pin with a short length of bright ribbon tied to it by my machine. When I need to stop to replace the empty bobbin, I pin the safety pin to the spot on the quilt top where I stopped, replace the bobbin, and spot the pin easily when I resume machine quilting.

Helen Thompson, Groton, New York

I've got rhythm

When doing stipple/meandering quilting, I develop a rhythm and pattern as I get into it, but this seems to take about 10 or 15 minutes. I always have some place mats ready to be quilted and quilt one of those first so when I start on the quilt, the stitching will be consistent.

Dotty Patterson, Victor, Montana

Guest Spot

Natalie Sewell, fiber artist, taught me the art of landscape designing in 1997; I've been smitten ever since! We first worked together on TV, presenting a series on "Trees and Flowers – Landscape Quilts." Due to the popularity of the topic, Natalie returned to the show to inspire us with "Flower Garden Quilts." Most recently, we collaborated on a book on landscape quilting and presented a third series, concentrating on sky and water scenes. Like so many of my guests, Natalie is a genuine friend, mentor, and collaborator.

When I asked Natalie for an anecdote from one of the taping days, she reminded me of the difficulty we had keeping our samples in order! This is the part of the show you never get to see.

Natalie Sewell

"In the middle of taping the second segment of our second series, 'Flower Garden Quilts,' Nancy and I were placing about 300 tiny pieces of fabric of leaves and flowers gracefully over a wooden picket fence. Normally we would glue all these little pieces down, but we were trying to save some time, and the pieces seemed to stick well to the fabric. The studio was very warm, so Nancy asked for a fan. As soon as it was turned on – you guessed it – the little leaves and flowers flew everywhere. The camera crew loved it, but they also helped us collect all the bits and pieces and we started all over again, this time with glue."

Natalie Sewell

Blue plate special

When I have a quilt on a frame for hand quilting, I use a baby's divided plate to keep needles, threads, and scissors close by. The small plate rests lightly on the quilt and the dividers keep things from rolling to the center of the plate. For snipping threads, I use a child's round tip scissors. I don't have to worry about a sharp scissors poking a hole through my quilt.

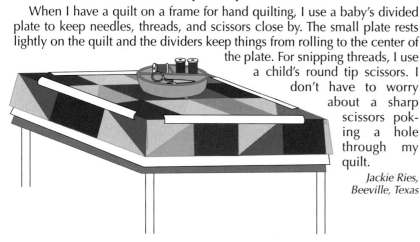

Jackie Ries,
Beeville, Texas

Sink your teeth into hand quilting

I love to hand quilt but hate to drag around a spool of thread. As sure as I'm sitting there quilting, that spool is rolling around and ends up all tangled, not to mention dirty. Here is my solution:
• Fill a clear plastic bobbin on your machine with quilting thread.
• Pop the bobbin into an empty dental floss container.
• Work your thread through the hole in the top of the container.
• Use the built-in cutter to cut off the length of thread you need.
  There you go – no muss, no fuss.

Angela Monyak, North Bend, Oregon

Fits like a glove

When doing free-motion machine quilting, I have found that if I wear latex examination gloves, I can rest my hands lightly on the "quilt sandwich" at each side of the presser foot to easily guide it where I want it to go. The gloves "grip" the fabric and make it easy to move the quilt in any direction.

Clara Stoll, Bellevue, Washington
Rose Nickel, Fond du Lac, Wisconsin

Sometimes I have trouble pulling a needle through fabric because the stitches are tight and the needle becomes slippery. I cut the fingers off a pair of inexpensive household rubber gloves, about 1" from the tips. I wear one tip on my thumb and another on my index finger when I quilt. With these fingertips, I can easily grip a needle, I don't have to put the tips down and pick them up repeatedly, and they are very comfortable, even in hot weather.

Donna Huffman,
Antigonish, Nova Scotia, Canada
Dorothy Patton,
Ellerhouse, Nova Scotia, Canada
Linda Petre, McMurray, Pennsylvania

This is only a test

When marking a quilting pattern on a finished quilt top, I am often tempted to skip testing to make certain the markings will come out of the fabric. I've developed a simple solution. Before prewashing the fabric, I mark the fabric with the same type of fabric pencil I will use for marking the quilting patterns. I mark each piece of fabric in the same corner of the selvage so I always know at a glance if the pencil or marker will come out.

Mrg Simon, Pierre, South Dakota

Lap of luxury

When doing hand quilting in my lap, I use a sheet of Plexiglas cut to a comfortable size. I place the Plexiglas across my lap and use it as a working surface. This prevents me from sticking needles or pins into my leg.

Linda L. Malenich,
McDonald, Pennsylvania

Hold on tight and don't let go

When machine quilting, I tried office-type rubber fingers but found I had to take them off every time I repositioned the quilt or they would fly off. Instead, I use round, rubber jar lid openers. I place them on my quilt under my hands. They grip the fabric, keep my hands from slipping, and yet are easily moved out of the way.

Kay Barrow, Cumming, Georgia

Head of the class

After teaching quilting and machine quilting for many years, I've come across many helpful tips. One tip that has seemed especially helpful to my students is for rolling up a quilt in preparation for machine quilting. I roll the left side toward the front of the quilt and the right side toward the back of the quilt. This eliminates any bubbles on top of the quilt that could be created by rolling both sides toward the quilt top.

Hella Wagner,
Austin, Texas

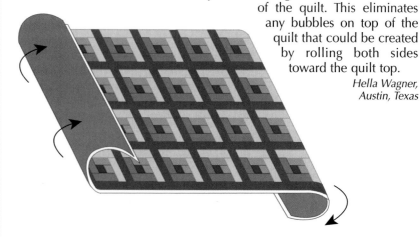

Shrimp cocktail

As a handy quilting aid, I use "Seafood Peelers." These rubber fingers were originally designed to prevent wear and tear on fingers when preparing crawfish tails. However, they also make it much easier to pull a needle in and out through quilt seams. The peelers have several advantages: they're tough against needle pricks, they don't fall off, they don't lose their shape, they give me the ability to have a permanent and strong grip, and I have no thumb strain when I use them.

Annette Lewis, Crowville, Louisiana

Drop anchor

When you're quilting and you come to the end of your thread, the usual procedure is to make a knot and pull it through the top, burying the thread in the batting. Sometimes the thread breaks just above the knot, too short to rethread the needle and pull the knot through. Often, there isn't enough thread left to do a couple of backstitches to anchor the thread. This leaves the area very weak, and the stitches are likely to loosen in the laundry. Here's my solution:

- Insert the wire end of your needle threader into the fabric about ¼" away from where the thread has come through the top.

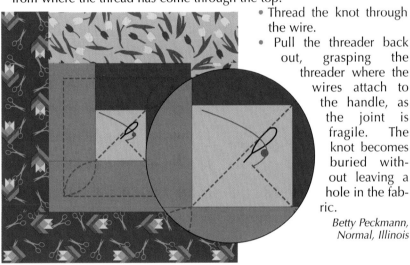

- Thread the knot through the wire.
- Pull the threader back out, grasping the threader where the wires attach to the handle, as the joint is fragile. The knot becomes buried without leaving a hole in the fabric.

Betty Peckmann, Normal, Illinois

In the slick of things

When machine quilting, I place a vinyl tablecloth on my sewing surface. This makes my work surface slick so the quilt moves easier. Also, I have tables and ironing boards of different heights around my machine to extend my workspace, and the vinyl tablecloth helps to smooth out the differences.

Lynette Fulton, Guasti, California

Kids' Hint

Let's start at the very beginning

When teaching my granddaughter the basics of quilting, I first had her make individual blocks using the sewing machine. Then, instead of joining them in the traditional manner, I had her put them right sides together and serge them on the wrong side. This taught her how to use the sewing machine and introduced her to the serger, too.

Fran Looney, Brooklyn, Michigan

Take 16

Next, the *Mail Bag!*

For 16 of the 20 years that Sewing With Nancy *has been on TV, PBS has been my network. The first years you could find my show on the Satellite Program Network, and then Tempo Television, two defunct national, cable networks. It was a start!*

For two years, my show was on PBS and cable. It was costly to produce two formats: one for cable with six minutes of commercial time and the PBS format without commercials. To economize, we taped only one program, but added a six-minute segment at the end of the PBS version known as the "Mail Bag." During this segment, I passed along hints and showed snapshots of projects viewers created. We liked the Mail Bag segment so much we've kept it – even though we haven't done cable for years. I ask you to send hints to me, giving mail and e-mail addresses at the end of each program.

I'll let you in on a secret! When formatting the program for that first year on PBS, we didn't have hints. My staff and I fabricated letters, assigning names and addresses of relatives and friends. Now we have hundreds of hints to choose from, including many of those listed in this book!

All I Want for Christmas Is a Flannel Board

Flannel boards make the design process very merry indeed. If you didn't get what you wanted under the tree this year, check out these hints for ways to make your own flannel board.

Making a flannel board is two, two easy

Having always had trouble keeping track of pattern pieces, I made a flannel design board.
- Cut a square of heavy cardboard. (I cut mine approximately 2 ft., but the square could be larger or smaller.)
- Cover the cardboard with a scrap of flannel, felt, or wool.
- Hang the covered board on the wall.
- Pin instructions and/or pattern pieces to it for handy reference.
- Take it down and lay it flat for jobs like laying out quilt pieces or appliqué patterns.

I often see quilters using more sophisticated (and no doubt more expensive) flannel boards, but this one cost me nothing and does the job just fine.

Bonnie McGee, Bonne Terre, Missouri

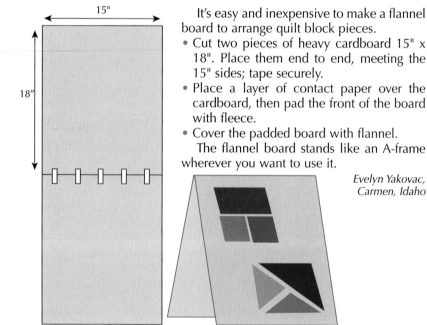

It's easy and inexpensive to make a flannel board to arrange quilt block pieces.
- Cut two pieces of heavy cardboard 15" x 18". Place them end to end, meeting the 15" sides; tape securely.
- Place a layer of contact paper over the cardboard, then pad the front of the board with fleece.
- Cover the padded board with flannel.

The flannel board stands like an A-frame wherever you want to use it.

Evelyn Yakovac, Carmen, Idaho

Be my guest

As a substitute for a flannel board, I place a flannel sheet on a twin bed mattress and place the mattress up against a wall. I very quickly have a flannel board that can go back on the bed in an instant for an unexpected guest. If need be, I safety pin my quilt pieces to the flannel sheet, roll it up, and I'm ready to resume work the next time I'm sewing.

Aileen Margulis, Jericho, New York

Hook, line, and flannel

Here is how I made an easy design wall using flannel and inexpensive wreath hangers.

- Buy two wreath hangers that fit over a door.
- Hang them on the door about 1" or so from each of the top corners of the door.
- Lay a wooden dowel in the hook part of the hangers.
- Measure the distance between the two hooks. Cut a piece of flannel 1" less than that width measurement, and the desired length.
- Make a casing on one short end of the flannel big enough to accommodate the dowel.
- Slide the dowel through the flannel and hang it on the hooks. Or, just fold the flannel over the dowel and let it hang.

Voila – a very portable design wall!

Jean Laino, Amherst, Massachusetts

measure between hooks; cut flannel 1" less

casing

Music to your ears

I love to quilt but have had a difficult time keeping small pieces of my quilt block in one area until they are sewn together. I use a flannel board that is a piece of heavy corrugated cardboard covered with flannel. The only problem with using this is where to put it in my small sewing space.

To solve the problem, I took my son's unused metal sheet music stand that folds quite compact when not in use. I placed the stand beside my sewing machine and set the flannel board on it. It works wonderfully, and I have recycled an unused stand that was just taking up space in our house! The stand even has little metal arms that help hold the flannel board tightly to the stand.

Carol Kemp, Duke Center, Pennsylvania

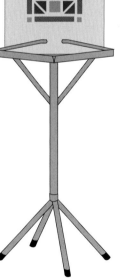

Falling to pieces

When I work on a quilt pattern, I place the pieces on a flannel board. The only problem with that is if there is a ceiling fan in the room or if people are walking by, the pieces fall from the flannel board. To avoid this, I pin a sheet of tissue paper over the pieces I am working on. This way they are stabilized and will not be blown from the board.

Doris Mayes, Fort Worth, Texas

Burning desire

Years ago, while using my June Tailor Quilter's Cut 'N Press™ board, I had to quickly leave my sewing room for five minutes or so to deal with an emergency with one of my children. Everything turned out fine, but I had accidentally left my iron face down on the pressing surface of the board. As you might imagine, it was irreparably scorched. I bought another one, but for some reason didn't throw out the one I ruined.

Several days later an idea came to me – I cut a piece of white flannel 2" larger than the board. I carefully pried away the edges of the pressing surface and applied a thread of glue. I then used a bamboo skewer to stuff the flannel around and secure it to the edges, smoothing the surface as I proceeded.

The result is a portable flannel board that I hang in my sewing room and take with me when working on projects elsewhere. I have used it since then and love it! One of my friends also did this with her board that had gotten gunky and old from being used so much.

Kristina Strom, Glendale, Ohio

Up against a wall

As a design wall for laying out a quilt top, I use a flannel-backed vinyl tablecloth. It can be tacked up anywhere with the flannel side out and quilt pieces will stick to it. Once the quilt pieces are laid out, I roll up the entire arrangement. Everything remains in place because the quilt pieces do not stick to the vinyl, but remain exactly in place on the flannel side.

Also, because the tablecloth is made from lightweight fabric, it makes moving the project very easy. This is great for when I am interrupted and need to put a quilt top away or when I want to lay out a quilt before going to class. I just roll it up and take it with me intact.

Marlene Cameron,
Chilliwack, British Columbia, Canada
Lorene Arnette, Florence, South Carolina

Assembly Required

It takes three layers to make a quilt, and a lot of pins to hold them together. Gain some insight into your quilt's inner workings with batting, layering, and pinning tips from *Sewing With Nancy* viewers.

Pull yourself together

As a home decorator, I need a fast method of holding the layers of a quilt together without pins or frames that get in the way while machine quilting. After a few experiments, I now use fusible web to save many hours of work time.

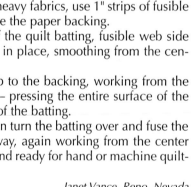

paper-backed fusible web

wrong side

right side

fuse with tip of iron

- Press 1" squares of paper-backed fusible web to the wrong side of both the quilt top and backing in a grid pattern, about 6" to 8" apart, over the entire piece. (For very heavy fabrics, use 1" strips of fusible web instead of small squares.) Remove the paper backing.
- Place the prepared backing on top of the quilt batting, fusible web side against the batting. Temporarily pin it in place, smoothing from the center out to avoid puckers.
- Use the tip of an iron to fuse the web to the backing, working from the center out. Press only the web spots – pressing the entire surface of the fabric will eliminate some of the loft of the batting.
- Allow the batting/backing to cool. Then turn the batting over and fuse the quilt top to the batting in the same way, again working from the center out. The quilt is now tacked together and ready for hand or machine quilting – without pins or a frame.

Janet Vance, Reno, Nevada

One plus one equals one

For quilting, I most often use 100% cotton batting, like Warm and Natural. I usually have lots of leftovers, so I piece some of the smaller pieces together to make a piece of batting big enough to use in another project.

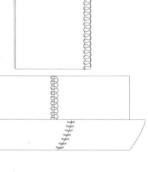

- Lay two pieces of batting together and rotary cut a straight edge.
- Serge that edge using a flatlock stitch.
- Open the batting and lay it flat. You now have a flat piece of batting with no overlapping lump.

You can now use the batting to quilt, and can't even tell where the seam is when you're done.

Debra Hardman, Anchorage, Alaska

Note from

Nancy

Check your serger's owner's manual for tension changes to create a flatlock stitch. Generally, the needle tension is loosened to a "0" setting to allow the seam to lie flat. This is a great hint!

Case closed

On your show, you mentioned using safety pins to baste the three layers of a quilt together and pinning from the center out. This is also how I pin my quilts, but I noticed that you closed each pin as you put it in the quilt. I have found that closing the pins each time you insert one can distort the fabric and cause shifting.

Instead, I have found that if you insert all the pins first, without closing them, the fabric stays in place better. Once all the pins are in place, go back and close them. It won't matter if the fabric shifts at this point because everything is pinned in place.

Jan Merkel, North Wales, Pennsylvania

Stuff it!

When I have a project that needs just a small amount of stuffing, such as a mini-quilt, place mats, or Christmas ornaments, I incorporate a piece of cotton or polyester batting as I stitch the item.

- Place the top and backing, right sides together, over a similar-sized piece of batting.
- Sew, trim, and turn as usual.

Robbi Courtaway, St. Louis, Missouri

In top form

One use I've found for batting scraps is pillow forms:

- Cut two layers of batting 1" larger than the desired pillow.
- Serge three sides, then fill with batting scraps.
- When the pillow form is the desired firmness, simply serge the fourth side.
- For a round or oval pillow, just serge most of the outer edges, stuff, and finish.

I can't believe I used to pay for pillow forms, while my closet held bags of batting scraps!

Lee Ebs, New York, New York

Could I See Some ID?

Don't let your quilts be caught without proper identification. The following hints offer some inventive ideas for noteworthy quilt labels.

Pocket change

When I quilt a wall hanging, I put my label information – name of quilt, my name, date, etc. – on the rod pocket to eliminate sewing on a separate label. I simply write or embroider the information on the rod pocket before stitching it to the quilt.

Karen Sweeney, Hartwell, Georgia

Quilted by Kate Bashynski

Let the record show

To add my name, date, and other information to my quilt backing fabric, I use machine embroidery. I like this method of identifying a quilt because it cannot be removed (as a separate label could). And personally, I don't like using marking pens on quilts. My method is permanent, and I also get to use the embroidery capabilities of my sewing machine.

Wanda Young, Springfield, Missouri

Hard copy

After one of your viewers suggested using a computer to make a quilt label, I was thoroughly intrigued with this idea and decided to try it myself. However, instead of starching the muslin before feeding it through the printer, I fused paper-backed fusible web to the fabric. This made the fabric stiff and it fed through the printer without a problem. The labels were then ready to be fused to the quilt with no sewing.

Nellie Mueller, Arlington, Texas

Note from Nancy

One caution: Not all computer printers are able to handle fabric. Check your owner's manual or contact your dealer to be sure you don't damage your printer.

New kid on the block

When I make a quilt or wall hanging I make an extra block to use for my label. It always matches the item! Sometimes when I make a baby quilt, I include the baby's name, birth date, weight, and length on the label, plus my name and the year the quilt was made. I could also add a special message on the label. It's easy when my machine does all the lettering.

Voni Lindgren, Frankfort, Illinois

stitch label block to wrong side

Picture perfect

To label the scores of quilts my mother-in-law made for her children and grandchildren, I created a quilt label. She lived to be 103, and one winter she designed, hand cut, and hand pieced 38 quilt tops and also quilted many of them!

I took a photo of her on her 101st birthday, made color copies, and applied them to fabric using photo transfer paper. I applied fusible web to the back and cut the labels with pinking shears. I made 100 labels and sent them to all the people she gave quilts to over the years, asking them to fuse and/or stitch the labels to the quilts.

Jean Smith, Rupert, Idaho

When I inherited three quilts made by my great-grandmother, I noticed that they had no labels. I made a label for each quilt as follows:
- Reduce a photo of the person who made the quilt using a color copier, in black and white format.
- Create appropriate text using a computer.
- Paste up the combined text and photo; heat transfer it onto fabric.

I had my great grandmother's label transferred on muslin to coordinate with the quilts. I turned under ¼" hems and hand stitched the label onto the quilt. This gives the quilt even more personality. I plan to use the same method to make labels for quilts I make so future generations can have an idea of what "old grandma so-and so" was like. I also plan to sign my labels with a permanent pen.

Sharon Davis, Redmond, Washington

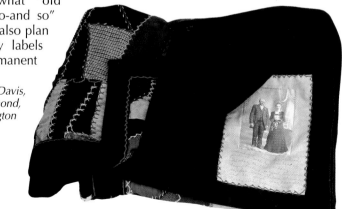

In a Bind

Does making and attaching binding have you tied up in knots?
Use the following hints to free yourself from the restraints of feeling
tangled up in binding.

Tying up loose ends

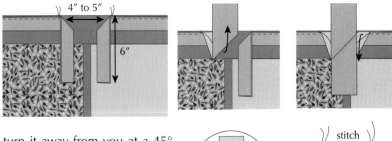

stitch along
crease

stitch

Making quilts is one of my passions. Here's how I finish my bindings so the quilt has a very professional look.

- Sew the binding to the quilt edge, leaving 6" of binding free at the beginning and end. Stop stitching about 4" to 5" before the starting point.
- Secure the quilt to an ironing board with pins.
- Open the binding on the left side and turn it away from you at a 45° angle. Pin it in place and press.
- Open the right side and turn it toward you at a 45° angle, just touching the left fold. Pin it in place and press.
- Meeting right sides together, pin exactly on the ironed creases. Stitch along the crease and trim away the excess fabric.
- Attach the remaining edge of the binding to the quilt.

Mary Bernower, Alliance, Ohio

Pass the bar

While making an item that required bias tubing, I discovered a way to use my Celtic Bias Bars to keep the tubing a uniform width.

- Fold the tube fabric in half, right sides together.
  - Insert the Bias Bar between the two layers, butting it against the fold.
  - Attach a zipper foot, positioning it so the foot guides along the bar.
    - As you stitch, slide the bar inside the tube to advance it.
      - Turn the tube right side out and reinsert the Bias Bar in the tube to help press it.

Marsha Holmberg, Gainesville, Florida

Celtic Bias Bar

Note from Nancy

Celtic Bias Bars, metal 12" strips of aluminum that range in width from ⅛" to ¾", are used to press narrow bias tubes, generally used for stained-glass quilting projects. I've always used the bars during the pressing step, but never in the stitching process to achieve a consistent seam width. This is an excellent tip!

Going pro

When making bias tape with a tape maker, I find it very helpful to lightly spray starch the fabric before putting it through the tape maker and pressing. The spray starch gives the fabric body and really speeds up the process. This gives a very professional looking finished product.

Anna Overland, San Antonio, Texas
Liz Barefoot, Bonifay, Florida

I'm stuffed

One of my specialties is making quilts to use as bedspreads. I like a corded look on the edges of my quilts.

- Cut 3" to 4" wide fabric strips for the binding.
- Fold the strips in half and sew the cut edges to the edge of the quilt.
- Stuff the binding with long strips of cotton purchased at a beauty supply house. (Cosmetologists use binding strips when they give permanents.)
- Fold the binding over the cotton strip, meeting the fabric fold to the first stitching line, and hand stitch the fold in place.

Marijune Long, Lima, Ohio

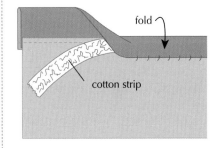

fold

cotton strip

Wrinkle, wrinkle, little tape; here are three ways to stay in shape

To keep bias tape flat and wrinkle free after pressing:
- Roll the tape onto an empty paper tube.
- Place the tube on a cone thread holder to stabilize the tube and prevent it from rolling.

I just "spool" off lengths of the tape and stitch them to my quilt whenever I have time, and my tape stays beautifully pressed.

Laura Stiehl, West Salem, Wisconsin
Helen Petree, Tipton, Missouri

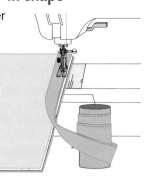

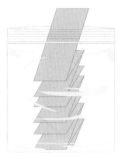

When applying binding to blankets, quilts, or smaller articles, I always seemed to have the entire strip of binding twisted and knotted on the floor, under my feet, etc. I solved the problem by taping a plastic bag to the table in front of my machine. I fan-folded the binding into the bag and began sewing. This technique works well with lace, too.

Mrs. Omer Sylvestre, Redvers, Saskatchewan, Canada

Keeping 15 yards of long strips for borders or binding can be a real hassle. I pin my strips to a safety pin at about one yard intervals. It's easy, and there are no more tangles, because I remove one loop at a time from the pin.

Lillian Stutheit, Turner, Oregon

Little quilt on the prairie

Here is my method for making prairie points:
- Cut a fabric strip double the width of the block size plus ⅛" to allow for the folding of the fabric. (For example, if you normally use 4" blocks, cut the strip 8⅛" wide.)
- Fold the strip in half lengthwise; press.
- Open the strip and mark perpendicular to the fold at 2" intervals.
- Cut from one cut edge to the fold line at 4" intervals as shown.
- On the opposite edge, cut on the alternate marks from the cut edge to the fold as shown.
- Fold and press the cut flaps in half diagonally, meeting the side cut edge to the fold line.
- Fold the triangles in half; press.
- Fold the bottom points up along the first fold line.
- Lift the loose triangle points from the bottom row over the folded edge of the points from the top row.
- Stitch along the fold to make it easier to handle the strip.

Moira Gilmer, Brockville, Ontario, Canada

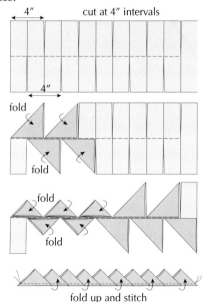

4" cut at 4" intervals

4"

fold

fold

fold

fold

fold up and stitch

Behind the Scenes

Take 17

"You're much *better looking* in person"

Since I'm a frequent visitor via TV in many homes, many of you think of me as your friend, for which I'm honored! Unfortunately, I don't get to see you on those occasions. When taping the program, this snapshot shows how you look to me! All I see is a camera lens and a dark room.

Several times each year, I have the occasion to present seminars at conventions, guilds, or PBS functions. One of the first comments I tell every group is, "You're much better looking in person!"

It took me years to address the television camera in a conversational manner. (Yes, the camera people are there, but they're really not interested in what I'm saying. They're focusing on their job and listening via their head set to the director.) I practice my delivery by talking in front of the large mirror in my bedroom...with the door closed! I know I still have room for improvement and could use a professional coach. But unless I get offered a spot on the Today Show, I'll keep practicing in front of my bedroom mirror.

Showing Your Wares

Mirror, mirror, on the wall: Should I display my quilt in the living room, bedroom, or hall? With the following hints as your guide, look into your quilt's future for tips on hanging, repair, and storage.

Don't leave me hanging

When I made a single sleeve for the back of wall quilts, I found it difficult to hang the quilt. I needed two hooks, or I needed to have a ribbon or string from the ends of the dowel to hang over one hook. I found that if I made two sleeves, each one about 1" less than half the width of the quilt, I could hang the quilt on one hanger. I insert a dowel into the sleeves and hang the quilt from the point where the dowel is exposed between the two sleeves.

Jan Bechler, Corvallis, Oregon

place hook here

quilt back

Quilt dreams

Whenever I make a quilt I always buy one yard more of my favorite color or print for that quilt. When my new quilt is completed I then make a pillowcase out of the extra yard of fabric that I purchased for that special quilt. When I am not using the quilt, I store it in the pillowcase. I have many quilts, and this makes it easy for me to know which quilt is in which pillowcase.

Cindy Schwing, Dewey, Illinois

Knock on wood

Using two old wooden spools and a dowel, I make an inexpensive quilt hanger. With large spools I use a ⅜" dowel, and with smaller spools I use a ¼" dowel.

- Glue embroidery floss or yarn onto the spool.
- Insert the dowel through the quilt rod pocket or hanging tabs.
- Place a spool at each end of the dowel.

That's all there is to it! I support the rod and the quilt by screwing cup hooks into the wall.

Janet Gildner, Grayling, Michigan

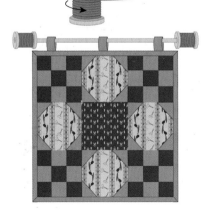

Keep your quilts in suspense

To hang mini quilts, I use a slat from a mini blind in the sleeve/rod pocket. The slats are flat, lightweight, and you can cut them to the desired length with a utility scissors.

Sheri Davis, Botwood, Newfoundland, Canada

Break the mold

While watching your program on landscape quilts, I decided to send in this tip for hanging them.

- Instead of a yardstick, buy a stick of screen molding. (This is shaped almost like a yardstick but has rounded edges on the front side.)
- Cut the molding about 6" longer than the quilt you're hanging and paint it the color of your wall.
- Insert two screws in the wall where you will hang the quilt. Leave them sticking out about ¼".
- Drill a hole in each end of the molding for the screw to slip through.
- Slide the molding through the casing of the quilt.
- Slip the holes in the molding over the screws, and push against the wall. The molding will settle on the narrow part of the screw, and the head will hold it on.
- Dot the head of each screw with the paint used to paint the molding.

You will have a hanging that is easy to change and almost invisible, and your quilt will lie flat on the wall.

Winifred Smith, Liberty, Texas

slip molding over screws

When you care enough to repair the very best

With each quilt I complete, I create a quilt "care packet" so that if the quilt is ever damaged, it can easily be repaired.

- After completing a quilt, cut a piece of backing fabric approximately 6½" square.
- Press under ¼" on each side. Appliqué three sides to the back of the quilt near one of the bottom corners.
- Cut a small sample (3" x 6") of each fabric used in the quilt and a completed square if possible and baste them together into a small packet.
- Insert the packet into the pocket and stitch the fourth side closed. The packet is basted together to keep it from bunching together when laundered.

Linda Anthony, Clearfield, Pennsylvania
Jackie Bradley, Kingman, Arizona

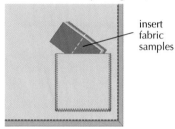

insert fabric samples

Long sleeve quilt

Whenever I make a quilt or wall hanging, I always include a sleeve on the back. Even if the recipient does not hang the quilt right away, she can do so in the future.

Instead of sewing on a separate sleeve, here's my method:

- Plan the backing 8" or so longer than needed.
- Position this extra length at the top of the quilt.
- Cut out a 1" x 8" section from each corner of the extra backing fabric, as shown.
- Cut a 1" slit on each side of the backing fabric, as shown.
- With the quilt top facing up, fold in the ends of the sleeve about 1" on each side. Stitch.
- After the piece is quilted, fold the extra fabric in half, fold the sleeve to the back of the quilt, and line it up with the top of the quilt.
- Secure the top edge of the sleeve when you stitch the binding.
- Hand sew the bottom edge of the sleeve to the backing.

This way the sleeve matches the backing and is completely invisible.

Cheryl Brown, Tampa, Florida

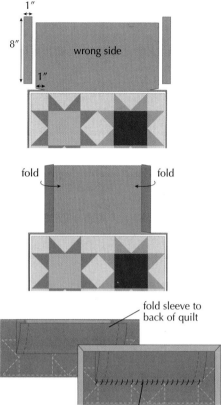

1"
8"
wrong side
1"

fold   fold

fold sleeve to back of quilt

hand sew edge to backing

Guest Spot

Gretchen Hudock, quilt designer and author as well as Nancy's Notions quilting consultant, is a master of quilting. Gretchen appeared with me on the Sewing With Nancy *series "Pictorial Quilting," and has recently authored her own book,* Quick Quilts *using Quick Bias. Gretchen is also a dedicated teacher and gives her students confidence. Here's one of her phrases of wisdom that we all can appreciate!*

"I like teaching beginners because we all were beginners once. When my students are too meticulous in their projects, I like to share this advice from a friend. Ask yourself, 'Can you see it from the road?' This puts the learning process into perspective and helps us learn from 'unplanned' sewing designs. Your 'mistake' may turn out to be something wonderful!"

Although Gretchen is a gifted teacher, she remains a child at heart. Her appearance on my show enables her to "visit" her parents without traveling.

"Even as grown-ups, we want our parents to be proud of our achievements. My parents were thrilled about my appearing on the show. They recently moved to Florida and discovered that their neighbor faithfully watches Nancy every day. The neighbor lady was excited when mom mentioned that I appeared on the show. She keeps my mom informed when it will air so that mom and dad can watch me. I never know when the show is airing so I often get a call saying, 'We saw you on TV this morning!' Through the magic of television, my parents and I can still connect."

Gretchen Hudock

Gretchen K. Hudock

Quick Trapunto & Stippling

Trapunto and stippling are two of my favorite machine quilting techniques. Trapunto refers to a raised quilting design padded from the underside, while stippling is free-motion stitching distinguished by meandering wavy lines. Both techniques add depth and dimension to a quilt. You can add stippling to a quilt without having a trapunto design. If you prefer to learn stippling by itself, start with Step #2 and end with Step #4.

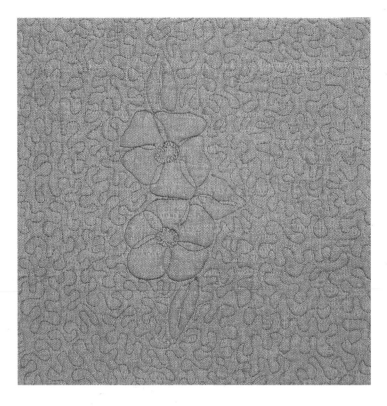

Trapunto designs can be as simple or as complex as you like, ranging from basic shapes to intricate flowers. The quilt block pictured here features both trapunto and stippling. Although you can add stippling to a quilt without a trapunto design, this quilt block shows how combining the two enhances the texture and overall appearance.

The instructions that follow use a simpler heart motif as the trapunto design. When you first start to do trapunto, it's best to start with a simple shape. After you have more experience, consider using a more artistic design. It is a great technique to have in your stitching repertoire to create stunning quilts.

1. Layer and stitch the trapunto design.

a. Cut the trapunto design from Grid Works™ or other wax-coated paper, creating a template. Press the template to the right side of the fabric.

b. Cut a piece of high-loft batting slightly larger than the trapunto design. Pin the batting to the wrong side of the fabric behind the area that includes the trapunto design, pinning from the fabric right side.

c. Straight stitch around the trapunto design. Match the bobbin thread to the fabric. Sewing from the right side of the fabric, stitch following the trapunto template. If the design is detailed or intricate, making it difficult to stitch with a presser foot, use free-motion techniques as detailed for stippling.

Optional: Use Wash-A-Way™ Basting Thread in the needle. This thread dissolves with moisture, so it can be easily removed after the final quilting is completed. Or, use a needle thread similar to that used for the remainder of the quilting project.

batting

d. Remove the pins and trim away the batting that extends beyond the trapunto area. Use appliqué scissors to trim close to the stitching. Or use a conventional shears, beveling it so the blades are parallel to the fabric to avoid cutting the base fabric.

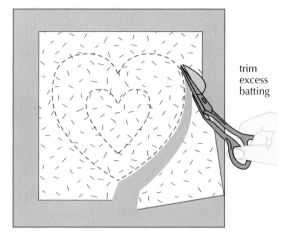

trim
excess
batting

2. Layer the quilt using a two-step process to secure the three quilt layers. It's easier than trying to work with three layers at the same time.

a. Join the top and the batting. Place the batting on a flat surface, such as a tabletop or the floor. Cover the batting with the wrong side of the quilt top. Pin the layers together with pins, starting at the center and working outward. (This is a temporary pinning step.) Gently roll the layers and set aside.

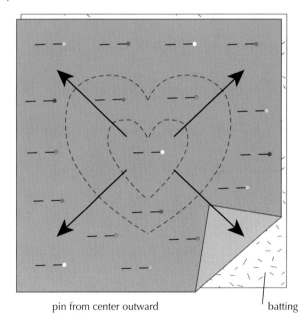

pin from center outward   batting

b. Cut the backing at least 3" larger on each side than the quilt top. Place the backing on a hard surface, right side down. Tape all four edges to the surface.

c. Place the top/batting layer over the backing fabric. Pin the layers together with curved safety pins. Remove the straight pins.

d. After pinning, release the tape and roll one edge of the quilt to the center. If the quilt top is large, secure with quilt clips. Repeat, rolling the opposite edge toward the center and leaving space in the center for quilting.

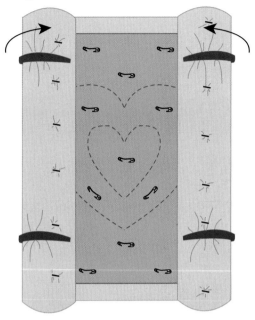

3. Set up the machine for stippling.

a. Lower or cover the feed dogs. Rather than having the feed dogs guide the fabric through the machine, you control the motion of the fabric with your hands.

b. Replace the conventional presser foot with a darning foot or Big Foot. Since stitching is free-motion, these feet provide good surface contact with the quilt fabric and keep the fabric close to the bed of the machine, improving stitch quality. Because these feet are transparent, they allow you to clearly see the stitching.

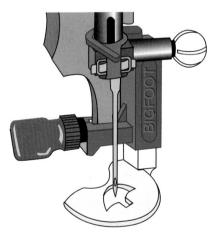

c. Use a cotton or rayon embroidery thread for both the bobbin and the needle, matching the color to the fabric. If you want the stitching to blend with the background fabric, use monofilament thread in the needle and cotton or polyester thread matched to the backing fabric in the bobbin.

d. Choose a needle suited to the thread. With rayon threads, use a machine embroidery needle. With cotton threads, select a machine quilting needle. With monofilament thread, choose a Metafil needle.

e. Adjust the tension based on thread usage. If the same thread is used in both the top of the machine and the bobbin, use a balanced tension. If the top thread is different than that in the bobbin, loosen the top tension by two numbers or notches to prevent the bobbin thread from being drawn to the top of the fabric.

4. Stipple.

a. Start in the center of the quilt at the edge of the trapunto stitching.

b. Lower the presser bar. Lowering the presser bar is really important! Unless you lower the bar, there is no tension on the thread. If you forget, you'll end up with a tangled mass of threads on the underside of the fabric.

c. Draw up the bobbin thread. Sew in place two or three stitches to fasten the threads; then clip the thread tails.

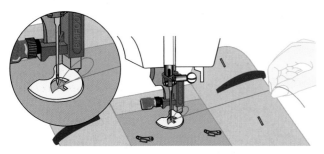

pull up bobbin thread

d. Secure the layers. Position your hands on both sides of the presser foot to hold the fabrics in place and guide them during stitching. Or simplify that task by using Quilt Sew Easy. This flexible hoop has foam pads on the underside that gently grip the fabric so it doesn't slip. Hold the hoop's handles with your index fingers and thumbs, and quilt. When the stitching gets too close to the edge of the hoop, stop. Then lift and reposition the hoop.

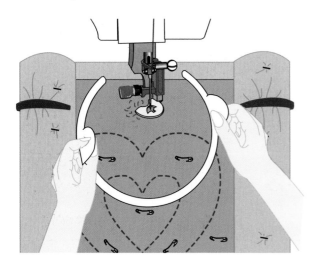

e. Stitch in small 1" to 2" box-like sections, creating clusters of "waves" or "puzzle ends." Practice on scraps before working on your project, using the same combination of top fabric, batting, and backing as in the actual project.

Stitch one or two waves in one direction. Move the fabric by moving the hoop. Look in front of the needle to anticipate where the next stitching will be, rather than looking at the needle.

Change the direction of the stitching and sew another pair of waves. Stitches can be as close together or as far apart as you wish. Practice at being consistent.

Repeat, filling the entire 1" to 2" section before moving to another area.

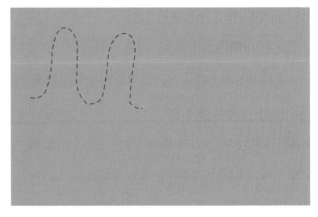

After stitching one section, repeat the process to fill another area. Continue until the entire quilt is stippled. By working in small sections, the fabric is easier to handle and the quilt layers don't shift.

5. Restitch around the outline of the trapunto area, using the same thread as for the stippling. Although the original trapunto stitching went through only the top and batting layers, this line of stitching goes through all three layers, so the design looks similar on both the top and bottom of the fabric.

6. Remove any Wash-A-Way thread used for the first trapunto stitching by spritzing the thread with water. The needle thread dissolves, releasing the bobbin thread. If you used conventional thread for the first stitching, two rows of stitching are visible on the front of the fabric, with only one on the backing side.

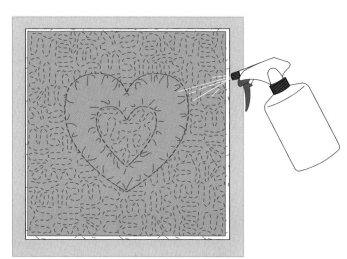

You can stipple almost anything – from baby quilts to art quilts and anything in between. For example, this landscape art quilt, titled "It Could Be October," features stippling, which gives the quilt texture and personality. The close-up of the quilt shows the stippling in detail.

Guest Spot

Donna Fenske, designer and vice president of TV production, has been working with me since 1984. Besides the vital role that Donna plays off camera for Sewing With Nancy, *she has also appeared as my guest for two three-part shows, "Gifts in Minutes II" and "Chalk It Up!" Whether behind the camera or in front of it, Donna is an important part of* Sewing With Nancy; *I couldn't do this show without her!*

Donna Fenske

"I enjoy the process of planning a TV program and preparing the step-by-step samples of the projects. We plan each show months in advance, yet sometimes changes are made to a sample after Nancy completes a run-through (rehearsal) of a segment at the studio. I make certain that extra fabrics and a full line of notions are always close at hand to accommodate any last minute revisions. You'd be amazed at the number of products and supplies that we store at our studio!

"Taping days are long and demanding, but we still like to have fun. Every afternoon of a taping day, Nancy takes time out for a blonde joke. These joke breaks give us all some comic relief. It is an unwritten rule that the jokes must be rated 'PG-13,' and only blondes are allowed to tell the jokes. The studio crew even collected blonde jokes and organized them in a three-ring binder to keep the supply plentiful. Since I too am blonde, I get to join in the fun!"

Donna Fenske

embroidery
as easy as
ABC

Welcome to Embroidery 101: a world of endless possibilities. With so many creative options, getting started is as exciting and as scary as the first day of school. To help get you on your way, we've assembled the best teachers we could find – *Sewing With Nancy* viewers!

- **H** is for the hoop that keeps fabric where it belongs.
- **I** is for these great ideas that will not steer you wrong.
- **N** is for the needles that stitch but do not break.
- **T** is for the thread that runs through every project you make.

So hit the books and study this chapter well. After applying these hints to your embroidery projects, you're sure to move to the head of the class in no time!

Project Progress Report

Is your current project just not making the grade, or do you need a fresh burst of inspiration? Buckle down with the following hints that get an A+ for inventiveness!

Happy holidays!

Instead of making two sets of place mats for the holidays, one for Thanksgiving and one for Christmas, I made one set of reversible holiday place mats. I use one side for Thanksgiving, then simply flip them over, and I'm ready for Christmas.

- Use one yard each of two fabrics at least 54" wide, to make a set of eight place mats. Use a fabric with enough body to support dense stitching. Thinner fabrics do not work well.
- Cut the place mats 17¾" x 13¼" (this includes seam allowances).
- Add embroidery in the lower left hand corners of the place mat pieces. (I embroidered a turkey for Thanksgiving and a Santa and sleigh for Christmas, so they serve two holiday seasons.)
- Place the two embroidered fabrics, right sides together, with a piece of thin polyester batting on top.
- Sew all the layers together, leaving an opening at one side for turning. Turn the place mat right side out, press, and slipstitch the opening shut.
- Using a ruler and chalk pencil, place dots on one side of the place mat at 2" intervals.
- Use a decorative stitch like a snowflake on the Christmas side, with bobbin thread to match the fabric of the Thanksgiving side. The snowflakes are stitched at each marking to "quilt" the layers together.
- Use a decorative stitch like a scallop to stitch around the border of the place mat.

Evelyn Reynolds, Iuka, Mississippi

Time for a change

Just before I nearly threw away an old tole painted clock I was tired of, I came up with this idea:

- Take the "works" out of the old clock. Measure the placement of the hours on a piece of fabric.
- Use an embroidery machine to stitch the numbers.
- Decoupage the embroidered fabric on the old face and replace the clock works.

Joyce Miller, Chillicothe, Ohio

Name that clothing

After my father was moved to a nursing home, I realized that it was necessary to label all personal items and every article of clothing with his name. So I turned to my sewing machine (a Christmas gift from my father) to find a solution for labeling his dark clothing. Laundry markers work on light colored items, but the dark ones were a big problem.

I took white grosgrain ribbon, placed it row after row on a sheet of Wonder Under, and pressed it. Then I programmed my machine with my dad's name with enough spacing to cut them apart. I just sewed his name over and over, cut the labels apart, and ironed them on the *outside* of his shirts, pajamas, robes, and sweaters.

This not only identified them as his property, but it also made it easy for the many nurses and others on staff at the nursing home to always call him by name, which made him feel more at home.

Sue Jones, Oklahoma City, Oklahoma

Try your hand at counted cross-stitch

Although I really like the look of counted cross-stitch, I find it very time consuming. I experimented with the machine embroidery unit on my sewing machine and found some cross-stitch type motifs on the embroidery card. I tried the stitches on several different fabrics before trying them on aida cloth. I was very pleased with the hand-stitched look accomplished with machine embroidery speed. I plan to use the idea for nametags for gifts and apparel as well as jar lid covers.

Betty Gray, Wingo, Kentucky

Wall to wall embroidery designs

To embroider the covers of six dining room chairs (18 pieces - one seat, two backs each) was a daunting task. To do all 18 pieces in the same pattern would bog me down in boredom, but to come up with 18 new designs was very taxing for my creative juices. I solved the problem by using an old wallpaper sample book from the local paint store. The designs and colorings were already done. It worked out well.

Dana E. Moore, Jacksonville, Florida

Lay your cards on the table

I'm originally from India, and thanks to my mother, I have been sewing since I was 11 and I love it. Even back in India, I always made my own greeting cards for holidays and other occasions. The designs on my cards and notes were painted or glued-on fabric, paper, and trim appliqués. Here in the U.S., even when I purchased cards on rare occasions, I found myself choosing cards with faux embroidery designs. So now with my sewing machine, metallic thread, and just a couple of minutes, I embroider an outline design on my cards, stationery, gift tags, and notes. Then I fill in the designs with colored pencils. The possibilities are endless, and I make most of the gift tags from recycled beautiful junk mail. I get lots of compliments from the recipients.

Zohra Arastu, Columbia, South Carolina

Painting without the shadow of a doubt

Here is an easy way to achieve the look of shadow embroidery using an embroidery machine and fabric paint.

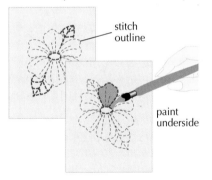

stitch outline

paint underside

- Choose a design that is only an outline or that you can select only the outline to be stitched.
- After the design is stitched, "paint" the underside of the fabric with a fabric paint color similar to the color of the thread.

Here are a few helpful hints for successful machine shadow work:
- Paint with a light hand and a lightly loaded brush. Too much paint can bleed through to the right side of the fabric and you will lose the shadow look.
- Stabilizing the fabric with a heavy starch works best. Tear-away stabilizers will leave behind little fibers that paint will adhere to. Be sure to rinse or wash the starch out of your design before you paint, because the starch will prevent the paint from adhering to the fabric.
- I only use this technique on sheer fabrics such as linen or batiste.

Dolores Skowronek,
Milwaukee, Wisconsin

Baa, baa black sheep, have you any buttonholes?

Here is a cute way to substitute embroidery for buttons and buttonholes. I made dresses for my granddaughters with this technique, and my daughter is delighted because it saves time in dressing the girls.

Using the smallest animal designs on my embroidery machine, I stitched them where the buttons would normally be spaced and sewed snaps underneath the designs. Next time I may use letters or numbers in place of the animals. A fancy stitch, flowers, leaves, or silk ribbon work with rosebuds and leaves are other ways to accent the opening.

Elizabeth (Liz) Rumsey,
Oak Harbor,
Washington

why i sew with nancy

I learned how to sew 36 years ago from my mother, who was also a 4-H leader. Although I learned how to sew well, it didn't excite me way back then. When I started watching Sewing With Nancy *on PBS, I began to realize that I could have fun with sewing and channel my creativity toward it. There are so many techniques to learn and so many new gadgets to explore! Thanks to your show and the others that have come along since, I had the motivation to change careers and become a professional seamstress. It's the most fun I've ever had, and I look forward to sitting at my sewing machine every day.*

Susan Waterman,
West Warwick, Rhode Island

I have watched Sewing With Nancy *(for more years than I can remember) because Nancy's voice and instructions are excellent and clear. (I remember the episode when you showed us your bloopers and your early lack of ease, and how times and presentations had changed.) I have notes from your instructions, so old; my DH (Dear/darn hubby) raises his eyebrows when he sees how yellow the paper is.*

Mimi Ceizyk, Tucson, Arizona

It's a pleasure to have my morning coffee with Nancy. I keep a notebook handy and take notes of the programs I find especially helpful. And of course, it's always a pleasure when she has guests, especially Gail Brown with her serger hints and Mary Mulari with her appliqué ideas.

Fran Looney, Brooklyn, Michigan

Around the world in 80 stitches

Some time ago I made an "around the world" pillow as a birthday gift for a friend of mine. Before quilting it, I embroidered my friend's name, "Happy Birthday," and the date in the solid colored side borders. The embroidery made the pillow a special and more memorable gift.

Karen Lorck, Sun City West, Arizona

Take the edge off

Many embroidery designs have black outlines around the edges. Often, I like to use a different color thread for the outline, such as grey, brown, or navy. I find that using these colors makes the edges less harsh and softens the design.

Laura Schwengel, Hartford, Wisconsin

Let your embroidery shine!

Do you need a coordinating lamp, but can't find a shade that matches the theme and colors of your room? It's simple!
- Start with a basic white shade.
- Cut a piece of fabric the correct size to cover the shade.
- Embroider designs on the fabric.
- Attach the fabric to the shade with a glue gun.
  Voila – you can match any decor or theme!

Lynn Isaacson, Mt. Iron, Minnesota

Note from
 Nancy   *An even easier and faster way to make your own lampshade is to use a self-adhesive lampshade. These shades are available in a variety of different sizes to accessorize your home.*

Make a name for yourself

Recently, a newly formed group of seniors were scheduled to meet at my home. I knew that as in most cases, the verbal name introductions would likely escape everyone's memory in a matter of minutes. To avoid this, I made attractive nametags.

- Using purchased 3" x 5" index cards, cut each card in half so you have two 2½" x 3" rectangles.
- Embroider a pretty border around the cards.
- Cut 4" lengths of purchased seam binding in coordinating colors.
- Fold the seam tape in half and position the cut ends along one 3" edge of the card, overlapping the ends approximately ½". Tack in place.
- Use a permanent marker to write each person's name.
- Use a straight pin or a safety pin to attach the nametag to each person's clothing.

The seniors were very pleased with their identity tags, and new friendships were formed. I have also made table place cards using this technique.

Irma Madden, Ocala, Florida

Oh! The places you'll embroider

Early one morning I was working on a Polarfleece vest while watching an episode of *Sewing With Nancy* I had taped the day before. One of your easy projects was a scarf made from Polarfleece. I had enough fleece leftover from the vest, so I immediately cut out two 40" pieces and made a scarf.

I then used my embroidery machine to embroider the same motif on the scarf as I had used on the pockets of the vest. I have made four of these scarves and have given away two of them to two very happy people!

Catherine Ruff, Longmont, Colorado

Note from Nancy

Instructions for the Self-Tying Scarf, which Catherine used as a palette for embroidery, are on pages 92–93.

Back to square one

Whenever I sew an outfit for a baby or toddler, I sew an 8" square of the same fabric and back it with soft fabric, such as flannel or fleece. I pin the square to the outfit with an animal diaper pin. This way, I can always wipe the child's nose without hunting for a tissue. I embroider a cute design on the square and wash it along with the outfit.

Anne Henry, Bellingham, Washington

"Illusions" of grandeur

My passion is machine embroidery, and since I retired I have learned to create a pretty nice piece of clothing. This year, while making a fleece jacket with a snow scene, I was disappointed in the flatness of the snow. I experimented and found that if I use two threads in the needle – white and iridescent – it gives the "snow" an absolutely breathtaking sheen.

I was having so much fun and enjoying my beautiful results that I couldn't stop there! I embroidered a sun with yellow thread and then circled the area where there would be shade from the sun, the side of a tree, in front of the snowman, etc. To stitch the shaded areas, I switched the thread to metallic palest blue and white. I was very pleased with the illusions created.

Kallie Johnson, Carson City, Nevada

Get carried away

To match or coordinate the colors of my living room furniture when I shop for accessories, I carry spools of embroidery thread that best match the furniture so I can check color coordination. When I get caught up with all my "have-to" chores, I'll stitch out a sample with the threads.

Carol Hoak, Tampa, Florida

Support Staff

No seamstress is an island; everyone could benefit from a little help once in awhile. With the support of these hints on stabilizers and adhesive sprays, you and your stitching will stand tall and proud.

Keeping stabilizers under wraps

There are so many different stabilizers on the market, and each one is a little different. I had my stabilizers stored hit-and-miss in plastic bags or whatever they came in, and it was always a job finding the one I needed. Here's my way of organizing them:

- Place each type or brand in a zip-closure plastic bag.
- Label the bag to indicate exactly what stabilizer is inside, and whether it's a tear-away, iron-on, etc.
- Keep the instruction sheet in the bag also. Now there is no guessing, and my stabilizers are much neater.

Azalee Watson, Kaysville, Utah

SOS: Save Our Stabilizer

When I accidentally leave my water-soluble stabilizer out in the air too long and it becomes brittle, it can be "re-moisturized."

- Place a wet paper towel in one end of a sealing plastic bag and the folded, brittle stabilizer in the other end, making sure to keep the wet toweling from actually touching the stabilizer.
- Place a pin through the plastic bag to prevent the two from touching.

There is still enough open area for the towel's moisture to reach the brittle stabilizer, and it will be as good as new.

Lois Baumunk, Milan, Illinois

Wash that tape right out of your fabric

While completing a gift of embroidered napkins late one evening, I ran out of adhesive spray, as well as adhesive and iron-on stabilizers. To finish the napkin set, I used a wash-away basting tape to affix one corner of the napkin to the stabilizer. I hooped the napkin/stabilizer combo, positioning the napkin corner in the embroidery area. The tape held the corner taut, while the hoop held the other two sides and the stabilizer. The tape easily released without any damage to the fabric.

This was not my preferred method of stabilizing, but it worked out fine in a pinch!

Susan Jost, Washington, New Jersey

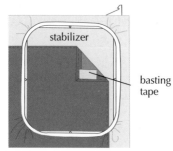

Waste not; want not

When doing machine embroidery, I never cut my stabilizer to fit the hoop. I just fold the end if I want a double layer or start at the edge of the stabilizer and place it in my hoop, leaving the balance of the folded piece loose. If I am cutting stabilizer from rolls, I cut long pieces rather than hoop size pieces. Then as I finish embroidering a project I can place the next piece in the hoop using the unused section of the stabilizer that was previously in the hoop but not stitched on. It wastes less stabilizer that way.

Also, the piece between two embroidery designs is often large enough to make a second layer of stabilizer on a double layer section when doing the third embroidery design. I just keep moving my sheet of stabilizer along, maximizing every inch.

Mary Ann Miller,
Port Angeles, Washington

Machine embroidery is one of my favorite pastimes. Here's a way to reduce the amount of stabilizer you need to use.

- Instead of putting the stabilizer in the hoop, cut two squares of stabilizer (or as many layers as you want to use) at least ½" larger on all four sides than the total area of the design you wish to sew.
- Layer the two stabilizer squares on the back of the fabric, lining up the center of the square with the center of your design.
- Hand baste with large stitches around all four sides of the stabilizer to hold it in place.

It takes only about a minute, and you've saved the excess stabilizer that you would have had to use in a hoop.

Janis Elspas,
Lomita, California

We interrupt this stitching for a stabilizer update

When doing hooped machine embroidery I sometimes find I have insufficient stabilization, or I've forgotten the stabilizer altogether. Rather than breaking the stitching, inserting the stabilizer, and starting over, here's what I do:

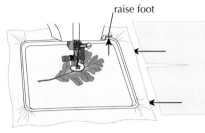

raise foot

slip stabilizer under embroidery

- Cut a piece of stabilizer large enough for the project.
- Cut a slit in from the side of the stabilizer.
- Raise the presser foot, slip the stabilizer under the embroidery, and slide the threads in through the slit.

Marj Kilian, Richmond, British Columbia, Canada

In the thick of things

When inserting some fabrics and stabilizer in a hoop, the hoop does not hold well because there is too much thickness in the corners. Here's a way to stabilize with the heavyweight cut-away stabilizer that worked great for me:

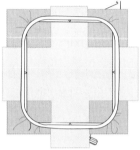

- If one sheet of stabilizer is needed, I cut the corners out of the square of stabilizer.
- If two sheets of stabilizer are needed, add a second strip of stabilizer under the other sheet of stabilizer, not in the hoop.

Or, use two strips in a criss-cross fashion, holding them together with spray adhesive.

Nancy Weiler, Sun City, Arizona

Give me all the details

When doing very detailed designs, sometimes it is difficult to get all of the water-soluble stabilizer off without completely drenching the project and waiting for it to dry. To simplify the process, I spray the design with a water bottle, then place a scrap of water-soluble stabilizer on top. The scrap of stabilizer works like a piece of tape and gently removes the excess stabilizer.

Shannon Durecki, Fairbanks, Alaska

Seal of approval

After making a vest from washable felt, I added an embroidered design using a cutwork design card and my computerized sewing machine. Part of the design didn't have fabric behind it, and I didn't want to pull off the stitches when I removed the stabilizer. I went around all the stitches with a seam sealant. As it reinforced the stitches, the seam sealant also dissolved the stabilizer so it peeled away easily.

Treeva Ramsey, Valdese, North Carolina

stabilizer   seam sealant

Comments from the peanut gallery

Not all white peanuts used for packing material are plastic. If you can compress the peanuts between your thumb and finger, they are made of starch, not plastic. You can use them to make a rather thick solution:

- Dissolve about 30 peanuts in ½ cup water. Or vary the amount of water or peanuts to your preference.
- Immerse the fabric you plan to embroider that would ordinarily require a stabilizer.

When the fabric dries, it will be very stiff and require no further stabilizer.

Carol Douglas, Phoenix, Arizona

Behind the Scenes

Take 18

Pintucking in the afternoon

I receive many cards, letters, and packages in the mail. But when I opened a package and found a romance novel featuring a shirtless, sweaty guy on the cover, I was puzzled. The novel, entitled Keeper, *published by Silhouette Publishers* had a note attached to it. A Sewing With Nancy viewer sent me the book and directed me to page 171. Out of curiosity, I turned to the page and found this interesting copy.*

"Um-hmm…What else did you do today besides doodle?" He'd caught just a glimpse of the doodle; L.J. in a skimpy hospital gown.

She wrinkled her nose, "Mostly slept and watched TV. The highlight of my day was learning how to do pintucking on *Sewing With Nancy*." She shook her head gravely. "It was pretty much down hill after that. Radar went home on one channel, Henry Blake got shot down on another, and Miss Kitty left Dodge."

The rest of the page got a little too steamy to reprint in a sewing book. You'll have to buy the book to find out the ending. Or perhaps you already know!

* Excerpt taken from Keeper, *by Patricia Gardner Evans, published by Silhouette Books, New York, New York.*

why i sew with nancy

It is encouraging to hear Nancy admit to a few sewing mistakes now and then. If the "expert" can recover from a sewing mishap, then surely the rest of can too.
Vicki Heckman, College Park, Maryland

I truly love to sew and create; it is an outlet for me. I work full-time in a highly technical career and it's great to be able to unwind and watch the show for new and exciting information.
Barbara Plassman, Delta, Ohio

It's hard to believe it's been 20 years. When you first started airing on PBS, I was in the eighth grade, taking a sewing course in home ec class. Every Saturday morning I watched Sewing With Nancy, *taking in everything I could on the subject of sewing.*

I am still an avid sewer. I don't have children of my own, but I have a four-year-old niece. For her birthday I got her a Singer kids' machine. I took the needle out and gave her some fabric scraps and kids' scissors. She sits for hours running fabric through the needle-less machine. She loves it. I tape your show, then when she comes to stay with me we watch it together.
Marion Parrott, Jellico, Tennessee

As styles and fabrics change, your show brings me up to date. It is more interesting to see you and your guests actually doing a project step-by-step than reading about it in a magazine. I don't mind an annual contribution to public television to keep informative, wholesome programming available.
Martha Walters, Blooming Prairie, Minnesota

Come out, come out, wherever you are

When I have used cut-away stabilizer and my embroidery is completed and still in the hoop, here is how I easily remove the stabilizer:
- Turn the hoop over to the wrong side.
- Gently insert the pointed end of a seam ripper into the stabilizer, making a small slit in the stabilizer only.
- Remove the seam ripper, insert the ball end into the slit, and "zip" around the outside edge of the embroidery. It is much quicker and you don't risk damaging your garment with a snip of a scissors.

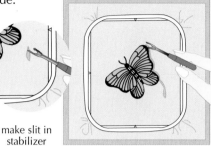

make slit in stabilizer

"zip" around design

Elizabeth Falzone, Geneva, Ohio

When I use water-soluble stabilizer, I keep a cotton swab and a glass of water beside my machine. Before I unhoop my completed design I simply wet the swab and run it over the stabilizer and wait for a moment. The stabilizer releases easily, and I can reuse the smaller, unused section of stabilizer in a smaller hoop.

Cissy Roseberry, Centreville, Maryland

When working on my first project using a tear-away stabilizer, I found it difficult to tear the stabilizer away from the fabric. To solve the problem, I used the tweezers to puncture the stabilizer and then used the tweezers in those narrow corners to grip the remnants of the stabilizer to tear it away.

Amy Snavely, Whitney Point, New York

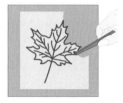

Come on in, the water's fine!

Making lace with an embroidery machine is easy by hooping several layers of water-soluble stabilizer and stitching a lace pattern. To easily remove the stabilizer:
- Heat a cup of water for one to two minutes.
- Drop the stabilizer into the hot water.

The stabilizer dissolves in no time.

Fran Johnstonbaugh, Oklahoma City, Oklahoma

Note from Nancy

You might consider adding a layer of netting or bridal illusion (tulle) between the layers of the water-soluble stabilizer to give a base to the lace. The netting will not be noticeable after trimming close to the stitching.

Save up for a rainy day

Since I do a lot of machine embroidery, I use "tons" of water-soluble stabilizer. As you have always said, save your small pieces to use on smaller projects. I use my small pieces to make one large piece:
- Place a machine hoop on a table or flat working surface.
- Lay the small pieces of the stabilizer over the hoop one at a time.
- Put just a dab of water on your fingertip and place it on the pieces as you layer them. The pieces stick to each other and remain together without moving around.
- Put your project over the stabilizer and hoop, place the other hoop on, and you're set to go.

Susan Drago, Baker, Louisiana

Milk your carton for all it's worth

When spraying fabric adhesive on a stabilizer, I cut the bottom and top off of a gallon milk container. It fits inside my embroidery hoop. I just spray inside the carton, and it keeps my hoop from becoming sticky.

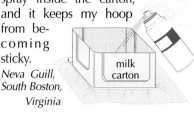

Neva Guill, South Boston, Virginia

Sticky when wet

After using a water-soluble stabilizer for an embroidery project, I save all the small pieces that I tear away that are too small for another project in a separate airtight bag. When I have enough, I dissolve them in a bottle with water. I now have a liquid stabilizer that works wonders!

Darcie Hardy, Bismarck, North Dakota
Millie Heisler, Hot Springs Village, Arkansas

All washed up

To hold my fabric in the hoop for machine embroidery, I've been using a temporary spray adhesive. I've tried several products to remove the glue from the hoop, but I've found a better, quicker, and more inexpensive way to remove the temporary adhesive – rubbing alcohol.

- Remove the screw from the embroidery hoop.
- Place the hoop in a square glass baking dish.
- Fill the dish with rubbing alcohol until it covers the hoop.
- Let it soak for a few minutes.
- Remove the remainder of the rubbing alcohol with a paper towel and rinse with cold water.

I was surprised at how quickly it worked. I poured the remainder of the rubbing alcohol back in the bottle and marked the bottle "for glue removal only."

Linda De Feo, New Port Richey, Florida

Now you see it, now you don't

Sometimes when I do machine embroidery, the fabric shows through, especially if it is a bold pattern and I use rayon thread. To prevent this, I place the tear-away stabilizer on the right side of the fabric instead of on the back. After I finish the embroidery I simply tear away the stabilizer. It works as a lining that you can't see through. The machine needle also helps perforate the stabilizer so it tears away easily. If it doesn't all come off, a pair of tweezers or sharp scissors finishes the job nicely.

Mary Ellen Colucy, Syracuse, New York

Note from Nancy

Keep in mind that tear-away stabilizer is available in white and black. Coordinate the stabilizer color with the fabric.

Jumping Through Hoops

Hooping is one of the most important parts of machine embroidery, but it doesn't also have to be one of the most frustrating. With the help of these hints, you'll see how simple it can be – the proof is in the hooping.

You've got a screw loose

The small circle rubber grippers or finger grippers that are so wonderful for pulling needles through fabric are also wonderful for loosening and tightening the screws on embroidery hoops. My specialty is machine embroidery and I was happy to discover this little trick.

Noreen Bruns, Denver, Colorado

To tighten the screw on my embroidery hoop, I use pencil cap erasers. They are cheap and can be thrown away when worn out. They work like a breeze.

Shirley Hornung, Harrisburg, Pennsylvania

Let your hair down and keep your fabric up!

When doing machine embroidery, I keep excess fabric away from the hoop area by rolling the fabric up and securing it with a large jaw-style hair clip.

Grace McBride, Largo, Florida

Note from Nancy

Another good habit to adopt is to always check that no fabric layers have become folded underneath the embroidery area. One quick check before stitching could save you hours of ripping.

Not a creature was stirring, not even a hoop

In the newer large embroidery hoops, I have found that fabrics slip more easily. To solve this problem, I use 220 grit adhesive backed sandpaper cut into strips narrower than the sides of the inner hoop. I adhere the strips to the outside edge of the inner hoop. This grips the fabric more securely.

Janice Graves, Lake Stevens, Washington

sandpaper strips

Hanging By a Thread

Does keeping track of the many different types and colors of thread have you in a snag? The following hints will help you move past all of your thread hang-ups and have you stitching smoothly in no time.

Put a lid on it!

When sewing with slippery threads, such as rayon or metallics, the threads sometimes spring off the spool and get tangled around the spindle. To stop this from happening:

- Use a plastic round lid off a spray can (a hairspray can or something similar). Punch a hole in the top of the lid the same size as the machine spindle.
- Punch a small hole at the bottom of the lid to push the thread through. Use sandpaper to smooth the punched holes.
- Place the lid on the machine spindle.
- Put the thread on the spindle inside the plastic lid.
- Feed the thread through the small hole and continue to thread the machine in the usual manner.

This stops the thread from becoming tangled around the spindle, it works much better than the gadgets I have purchased, and it's a lot cheaper!

Dorothy Annan, Durham, United Kingdom

punch holes

Mark it with an E

I use a permanent marker to mark a few of my bobbins with an E. This tells me that the bobbin has embroidery bobbin thread on it and is to be used only for embroidery. This is helpful because if I'm in a hurry, sometimes it's hard to tell if it's regular thread or embroidery bobbin thread.

Marilyn Kenzik, Elyria, Ohio

Kids' Hint
Embroiderer in training

My eight-year-old grandson loves to embroider on my sewing machine. Every time he comes over he wants to sew. I have memory cards with wild animals, sports themes, etc. I hoop the article and put the memory card in the machine for him, then he does the rest. He knows how to select colors, thread the machine, clip the threads, and start over again. We have a small basket in which he lines up his threads. When an article uses one thread number more than once in a design, we write the number on a piece of tape and stick it on top of an empty spool so he doesn't get mixed up.

Cynthia Kuglar, North Augusta, South Carolina

This seat is taken

When using a vertical thread holder on top of the sewing machine, I wasn't completely satisfied with the way the thread sat on the thread spool. So I used the large round disk that holds the thread on the thread spool. I turned it upside down so the rim was facing up. I find it's a perfect resting place for the larger spools of embroidery thread.

If your machine doesn't have a vertical spool holder, you may be able to adapt the machine to hold the thread in the vertical position. I remove the cover from my seam ripper, insert the seam ripper in one of the holes on the top of the machine, and use that as my spool holder.

Cathy McNabb, Cleveland, Tennessee

"Metal" of honor

In the past, whenever I used metallic thread for embroidery, the thread broke and left me frustrated. Now I use a spool of monofilament thread along with the metallic thread, threading both through the machine as if they were a single thread. This makes the thread much more resilient, eliminating the problem.

Sharron Murphy, Smiths Falls, Ontario, Canada

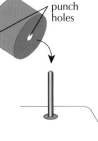

Note from **Nancy** *In addition to blending threads, make certain you're using a needle designed for metallic threads, such as a Metafil or Metallica needle.*

Roll tape!

All the little pieces of thread that get cut off between thread jumps always gave me problems. They were difficult to pick up and would get caught under the next color of stitching. My solution:

- Keep a roll of clear tape next to your machine.
- Use a pair of tweezers to hold the jump threads taut so you can cut them off close to the stitching.
- After snipping off the little thread jumps, tear off about a 2" strip of tape and sweep it over the embroidery.

The tape picks up all the loose threads and leaves a nice clean finish to begin stitching the next color. I even use this technique to remove tiny pieces of tear-away stabilizer. It is such a simple thing, but very effective and quite a time saver.

Bettie Frisby, Metairie, Louisiana

Put your tail between your stitches

When doing free-motion machine embroidery, it seems a nuisance to tie off and trim threads on the wrong side of the fabric. To eliminate that step, I pull up the bobbin thread, then grasp both the top and bobbin threads and pull them to the front of my project. I stitch over those threads, then clip off the thread tails. The tails are secured under the stitching. This works especially well when using satin or other filled-in stitches.

Gwen Tuthill, St. Petersburg, Florida

Stay inside the lines

When I do an embroidery design with my sewing machine embroidery unit I use black bobbin thread on both the top and in the bobbin for the final outline. The bobbin thread is thinner so the outline is not so heavy and bulky and doesn't overpower the design (especially on baby items). And because I am using the same color in the top and bottom, I don't have to worry about adjusting the thread tension. I keep two or three bobbins wound with black bobbin thread so I am always ready to finish the design in this way.

Deb Scherer, Lincoln, Nebraska

When all else fails, go to Plan B

In trying out some of the embroidery patterns on my sewing machine, I found I didn't have some of the correct colors of machine embroidery thread. I discovered that serger cone thread works well for a matte look, with just slight adjustments in the thread tension. I placed the thread cone on a cone thread adapter positioned next to my machine, threaded the machine, and sewed my design. The cones hold so much thread that I'm sure I'll save money with this idea.

Rose ChapdeLaine, Welch, Minnesota

Thread muffins

When I am doing a lot of embroidery that calls for many different colors of threads, I keep the threads in a small muffin pan and use them from there.

Carol Petronelli, Johnston, Rhode Island

I'm hooked!

One of my most useful tools for machine embroidery is a very small metal crochet hook! When I have to draw up the bobbin thread to the top of the design, the hook comes in handy in tight places. I also use this handy little hook to grab and hold up the jump threads for clipping on machine embroidery designs.

MaryLouise Karpenko, N. Richland Hills, Texas

What goes up must come down

When doing free-motion machine embroidery, generally we pull up the bobbin thread and then lower the presser bar. I reverse the sequence and lower the presser bar before I pull up the bobbin thread.

There are several advantages: The thread is easier to pull up, plus I don't forget to lower the presser bar. And because the upper thread has tension with the presser bar lowered, I don't use as much thread when I pull up the lower thread.

Nery Garcia, Miami Beach, Florida

Guest Spot

Eileen Roche, editor of Designs in Machine Embroidery *magazine, has appeared on two three-part series highlighting computerized embroidery, "Amazing Machine Embroidery" and "Amazing Machine Embroidery Encore." Here, Eileen recalls a "high-five" moment on the set.*

Eileen Roche

"I remember the first time I sat 'in the pit' (the bench area) on the set with Nancy. It was the first shot of my first taping on *Sewing With Nancy*. I thought to myself, 'I can't believe I am sitting here. I learned to sew from *Sewing With Nancy* and now I'm a guest!' I was trying really hard not to gush, and act as naturally as possible. Nancy and I had to sit really close to each other so the camera could catch us both. Nancy has done this so many times, yet she still ran through her lines before taping each segment. As I started to feel like I belonged there, I realized that Nancy's preparation put me at ease. I was glad that I could share my area of expertise with Nancy and her viewers, and in return, Nancy helped me understand what TV was like.

"Taping started rather smoothly; even the first computer screen segment televised on *Sewing With Nancy* came off without a hitch. At the end of that somewhat tense segment, I turned to Nancy and gave her a high-five. I wonder if any other guests have given Nancy a high-five on the set… she just made me feel right at home."

Test! Test! Test!

Relax – you will not be tested on the following material!
But you will learn some new ideas for testing designs, as well as
creative ways to turn test samples into gifts.

The case of the sewing machine cover

When monogramming a bridal set, my daughter and I used an old pillowcase for a test sample. You may ask, what did we do with the pillowcase? Simple: We cut it to fit the sewing machine, opening up the sides at the hemmed edge, creating an elegant cover for my sewing machine.

Pat Budzinski, Seven Hills, Ohio

Just in "case"

When I try different decorative stitches or designs on my embroidery machine, I put them on pillowcases. Each pillowcase is different and unique; I give them as gifts to children. I like this way of testing since I'm not discarding my test stitching.

Mary Herrmann, Evansville, Indiana

Guest of honor

I have the greatest display of guest towels! Instead of checking out a new design by trying it on a piece of muslin, I embroider a new guest towel with that design.

Sonya Breidbart, Scarsdale, New York

Say embroider!

As I sew embroidery designs or other special projects, I have a sheet with thread size, number, needle size, stabilizer, etc., listed and I just fill in the blanks and put it in a notebook with a picture taken using my digital camera. Then when I want to make that project again, I can just refer back to my notebook!

Kathy David, Franklinton, Louisiana

Note from
Nancy *Another good way to keep track of embroidery details is to use Embroidery Reference Cards. These 4" x 6", two-sided cards have plenty of space to document details such as stitching time, stabilizer type, and color order.*

Testing – it's not just for muslin!

I have two embroidery machines and do my own digitizing, so I do a "ton" of test stitching. I hit the remnant bins at the fabric store (often marked down 30 to 50%), and buy many different kinds of fabrics so I know how each design will stitch on a number of different types of fabrics.

Diane Milliron, Byron Center, Michigan

When I do a "test run" of a design, I use a piece of white or very light colored fabric approximately 8" x 10" from my scrap stash, note the thread color numbers on it, and insert it into sheet protectors in a three-ring binder. I can get several designs on one piece of fabric. I file them according to card numbers, and I can see at a glance if I like the thread colors, or want to make changes on the finished product.

Arlene Hagle, Akron, Ohio

See your designs in print

To keep track of embroidery designs, I started a three-ring binder with clear page protectors in it. I used a program such as Buzz Tools and printed out the designs I have on each disk. I put the printout and disk into one of the clear page protectors and I always know what is on each disk at a glance.

Teresa Pauline, Charleston, West Virginia

Be left holding the bag

When I do machine embroidery, I like to make a sample of the design first to check colors and size. To keep these for future use I insert them into a quart size zip-closure plastic bag along with the embroidery card or disk. Since I use these designs over and over, this saves me a lot of time.

Dorothy Piper, Bloomfield, Iowa

Be prepared or be square

I do "sew-outs" of all my new machine embroidery designs on 200-count muslin suitable for quilting. I use 6" or 8" squares and keep them for quilting projects. As the squares accumulate, I simply sort and store them in categories. When the need for a gift or special occasion quilt presents itself – voila – my sewing time is reduced considerably!

EuJane Taylor,
Houston, Texas

Rags to riches

To try out my machine embroidery designs, I purchase inexpensive cotton diaper (i.e. bird's eye) fabric. Since it comes in 34" wide, all I have to do is wash it, cut it in 20" lengths, and serge the raw edges. I have a stack of these on hand for my trials. I can then hem them and make nice dishtowels for gifts.

Jackie Rosier, Vancouver, Washington

Write the book on embroidery samples

Whenever I get a new creative card for my embroidery machine, I embroider each picture on a piece of muslin with the colors that are shown on the picture and the smallest size that is shown. When finished, I put them in a photo notebook that has plastic pages with pockets. When trying to decide what design to sew, I flip through the notebook until I find one that I like. The muslin examples are 4" x 6" and fit nicely in the plastic sleeves of the notebook that are 4¼" x 7". I label each example with the card number and the number of the template.

Judy Kane, Sumner, Washington
Shirley LeMasters, Anaheim, California

Take 19

We all start *someplace*

One of my favorite Chinese proverbs is, "A journey of a thousand miles begins with a single step." This simple phrase puts into perspective learning a new skill, starting a new job, beginning a new relationship… you just start by taking small steps!

My first experience with sewing was like that of many young girls of my era in rural communities. I grew up on a dairy farm in eastern Wisconsin and joined a 4-H club when I was 10 years old. My mom became the clothing leader for our club, diligently donating her time and talents. During the first year she taught us to sew a gathered skirt and a fringed scarf. (I never wore the scarf.) They were small projects… small steps forward. In the second year, we all made jumpers; you can see me hiding in the back row of this picture.

In college I majored in Clothing, Textiles, and Designs and minored in Journalism. The steps of my sewing journey led to a career and a lifelong hobby. Regardless of where you are in your sewing or quilting journey, don't stop. You never know what sites are ahead!

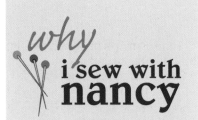

Cross Your I's & Dot Your Templates

Are you having problems putting your embroidery designs in their place? Use these trusty hints for making templates, and get your designs placed right on target.

In the clear

To create machine embroidery templates, I use a square of nine-gauge clear vinyl instead of sample cloth or muslin.

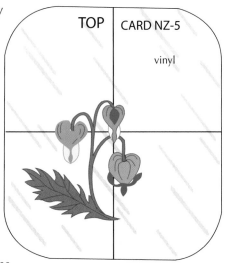

- Hoop a square of clear vinyl, placing tear-away stabilizer under the embroidery hoop.
- Using a permanent pen, mark the horizontal and vertical lines to indicate the center. Then draw a line around the inside of the hoop on the vinyl; this will be your cutting line when the embroidery is completed.
- Mark the top as a reminder of where the design will be stitched within the hoop. If you have many embroidery designs, you may want to also mark the template with the card or disk number as well as the design number for future reference.
- After completing embroidery on the vinyl, carefully remove the tear-away stabilizer and cut along the inside hoop line. You now have a clear template for embroidery placement – no more guessing!

Dorothy Waska, St. Paul, Minnesota

Placing designs is sheer delight!

To make a sample of all my embroidery patterns, I use a piece of white netting sandwiched between two pieces of water-soluble stabilizer. I use this to see how the design will look on my fabric and to help in determining the placement of the design on my garment.

Hazel Kidd, Jacksboro, Tennessee

Do your paper work

My tip is really a thread saver and eliminates many false tries and frustration as well as wasted time and fabric. When trying a new alphabet or embroidery design:

- Unthread your needle and use paper of any kind. (Junk mail or used adding machine paper works nicely.)
- "Sew" without thread on the paper. You now have your words or embroidery punched on the paper.
- Use the stitched paper to center or place the design where you want it.

This works great! It has saved me in so many ways.

Sharon J. Hughson, Piney Flats, Tennessee

Places, please!

To get easy, accurate placement of embroidery designs, I use inexpensive off-white (this color seems to be the easiest to see through) nylon organza to sew out the design. To save time, I use a medium-to-darker thread for contrast, and I don't change thread colors. I save even more time by just sewing out the segment that gives the basic outline. There is no need to stabilize this stiff organza.

- Before removing the fabric from the hoop, mark the hash marks from the hoop (the dots on the sides, top, and bottom of the hoop) right onto the organza, noting which one is the top of the hoop.
- Unhoop. Also, note directly on the organza to the inside of the hoop, whether the design was rotated, enlarged, reduced, mirror imaged, repositioned, or any other change you made at the sewing machine before sewing out.
- Cut roughly around the design, just slightly outside the hoop hash marks. Now you have an easy-to-see-through template to pin to your project.
- Hoop the fabric, matching to the hash marks, then unpin the template and you're ready to sew your design exactly where you want it.

As long as you didn't reposition the design before making the template, you can flip the template over and use it for the mirror image. When I am embroidering a collar, I pin the template to the collar before sticking the collar to the stabilizer. I take my trusty pen and outline the collar shape on the template. Then I can flip over the template and pin it to the other collar point and match the placement for both collar points exactly.

Becky Hopkins, Birmingham, Alabama

Window of opportunity

When I make shirt patterns with a hidden placket, I like to embroider on my fashion fabric in the front placket area before I cut out the right shirt front. This gives me plenty of fabric to hoop and eliminates the need to baste an extension onto the placket afterwards.

In placing my pattern on the fabric, however, I realized it was difficult to see exactly where the embroidery would end up. To help me position the

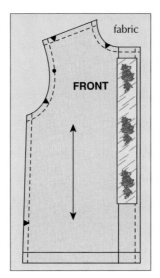

pattern on the fabric, I cut out a section from my paper pattern. In place of the cutout, I inserted a clear plastic "window" that allowed me to see the embroidered design and determine precisely where it would be located on the placket.

Mary Pongonis, Hallowell, Maine

clear plastic window

Copycat

Here is my method for making very accurate templates.

- Sew out a design, and while it is still in the hoop, make a copy. (I use my scanner, although a copier would work as well.)
- Cut out the copy just inside the hoop.

This makes a perfect template, and I can write about all the threads, tension settings, rotation, etc., on the back. Now I can get my design just where I want it on the fabric.

Helen Michalke, Weimar, Texas

Since some of my embroidery cards do not have templates, I tried a few ways to make my own. This is my most successful method:

- Stitch the placement lines and outlines of the patterns on white broadcloth with black thread.
- Press the fabric, tape it to a sheet of paper, make a photocopy, and make a transparency from the photocopy.
- Cut out the individual templates and place them on the fabric.

Doris Blundell, Kamloops, British Columbia, Canada

Connect the dots

When working with design cards, I often like to combine several embroidered elements in one project. Here is a helpful hint for placement on a project.

- Cut out several paper circles the same diameter as each portion of the design.
- Mark each circle, indicating which part of the embroidery design you will use.
- Place all the pattern pieces on the project to see how the finished design will look. The guesswork will be gone and all of your pieces will fit!
- Put a pinhole in the center of each circle, and use a marker to mark the exact spot for placement of each pattern piece.

Pat Hanrahan, Rochelle Park, New Jersey

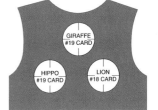

Embroidery Rx

Don't cry over broken needles – even the most experienced sewer makes mistakes every now and then. The following hints offer tips on everything from saving needles, to ripping out stitching, to removing marks.

Well-rounded personality

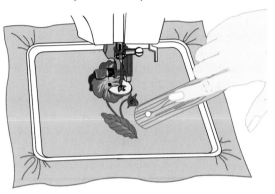

Even though I use an iron-on stabilizer as well as an additional one, sometimes while stitching a dense design the base fabric tends to buckle a bit. To prevent that from being a great problem, I use the rounded end of my Bamboo Pointer and Creaser to smooth out the fabric in front of the needle as the machine is stitching. It has made a world of difference and has made my life much simpler and less stressful.

Helena Bradford, Mt. Pleasant, South Carolina

Third time's a charm!

To iron out the wrinkles between embroidery stitching, I've found the Mini Iron® to be the solution. I've previously used this small iron to press seams on quilting projects and to attach fusible bias; now I have a third application.

Donna Schmidt,
Falls Church, Virginia

Keep an ear on your embroidery

As I am very busy around the house, I always have to run upstairs to check on how my machine embroidery is coming. My husband suggested that I use the baby monitor we use when our grandchildren visit. I put one part next to the sewing machine and slip the other part on my belt. It works great! I can hear immediately when the machine stops or beeps; it may be just time for a thread change, a bobbin change, or a broken thread. This saves me many steps to say the least. The monitor is now permanently in my sewing room as a new accessory.

Valerie Grimmer, Auburn, Michigan
Joyce Haggart, Rosebush, Michigan

Make a note of it

After ruining a blouse because the electricity blinked off while I was monogramming it, I now keep stick-on notes beside my machine.

Before sewing out a design, make a note of the location (vertical and horizontal position numbers), any rotations, tension adjustments, size changes, and all other special formatting. If you are interrupted or your electricity goes off, you can complete the embroidery later. Without this information it is difficult or impossible to align the design again.

Dianne Self, Dalton, Georgia

Give your needles a break!

When I'm doing machine embroidery and need to use something to help position threads or parts of a design, I prefer using a toothpick or wooden skewer rather than a stiletto. If the machine needle hits the toothpick, it just splits the tip. This not only saves on needles, it's also much safer.

Elise Scricco, Worcester, Massachusetts

In case of emergency, change your needle

When I embroidered a motif on Ultrasuede positioned on an adhesive-backed stabilizer with no other stabilizer underneath, my rayon embroidery thread kept shredding and breaking. I changed my needle from a machine embroidery needle to a size 75 leather needle. Like magic, there were no more breaks.

Virginia Amos,
Langley, British Columbia, Canada

One little, two little, three little needles

When doing machine embroidery, I change my needle every three hours of sewing time. This is especially important with densely filled patterns.

Sharon Pridmore, San Pablo, California

Roll with it!

To mark the spot for embroidery, I usually use a washable marker that has to be washed off when the embroidery is finished. It is very easy to remove the mark by washing out an empty roll-on deodorant bottle (unscrew the collar that holds the ball in to remove it), filling it with water, and then just "rolling" the marks away.

Carol Pearson, Diverton, Illinois

Throw in the Towel

Embroidering on towels can get hairy at times, but don't give up!
With the support of these hints, you'll be back in the ring in no time!

M is for monogram

Here are two tips I've found that make monogramming easier.

- When monogramming on a pile fabric, place a sheet of water-soluble stabilizer on the top as well as on the underside of the fabric. This tends to hold down those unruly lumps and makes the end result look so much more professional. This works especially well on terry towels, where it tends to be more difficult to make the monogram completely cover the base fabric.
- When monogramming letters that include curves or around the tops of hearts, I've found that reducing the pressure on the presser foot by one number makes turning so much smoother. It virtually eliminates the need to stop and reposition the needle.

Joanne Morgan, Kansas City, Missouri

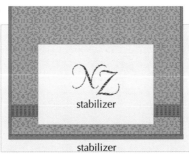

stabilizer

stabilizer

Staying on top of things

When embroidering on napped fabrics such as terry cloth, I put a tissue on top of the fabric. It holds the nap down so I get a better stitch. It's easy to remove the tissue when the stitching is complete. The heavier the terry, the better job the tissue does.

Evelyn Conner, Rockwood, Tennessee

When machine embroidering on terry cloth, I have found it helpful to apply to the surface a layer of bridal tulle or illusion (not English netting) in addition to the regular stabilizer. After completing the embroidery, I cut away the excess. The tulle will not show, and the stitching will not sink into the fabric.

Janet Leach, Janesville, Wisconsin

Loosen the towel strings

After machine basting thick towels to a sticky stabilizer for embroidering, following the sewing machine manufacturer's instructions, I knew that I would not be able to remove the stabilizer without removing some threads of the terry towels. I had also used water-soluble stabilizer on top of the towels. With spray bottle in hand, I decided to spray the backing too. As Nancy says, "Voila!" The backing adhesive loosened and was easy to remove.

Frances Rohling, Rohnert Park, California

What's cooking?

While trying to monogram some really thick bath towels, I was having a difficult time using transparent film stabilizer. After finishing one towel, then having to take the whole thing out, I tried using "fat free" cooking spray on top of the film stabilizer so the embroidery foot wouldn't stick to the film. I had perfect results. I just sprayed a tiny bit of cooking spray and spread it with my finger. I also made sure to wipe any spray from the embroidery foot when I finished.

Carrol Crump, Lynnwood, Washington

Guest Spot

It's always great to have friends in "high places!" For me, that phrase refers to receiving fashion forecast advice from Sewing With Nancy guest Gail Hamilton of The McCall Pattern Co., New York.

Gail first appeared on my show in 1985 for my first three-part series on serger/overlock sewing. She came prepared with cases of garments, all created with overlock seams, rolled edges, or an occasional accent of a flatlock stitch. As the process of serging was new for me, having a trunk filled with serged garments was a gift.

This series was my first experience with hiring professional models…Gail taught me the ropes. I learned the process of working through an agency, and choosing models who had TV experience (runway models "move" too much for TV). Plus, I realized that all the garments sewn for models were made 1" longer in the sleeves and 2" longer in the length to accommodate their long bodies!

Throughout the years, Gail has kindly nudged me in the current fashion direction, giving me the heads-up on what's hot and what's not. Her guidance from Manhattan to Beaver Dam, Wisconsin, has truly made a difference to viewers across the country.

At right: Two models (standing) join Gail and Nancy for a photo during a 1985 taping.

Gail Hamilton
The McCall Pattern Co.

Gail Y. Hamilton

Give Me a Hand

What do you do when you go south for the winter and forget your
embroidery floss, or need an easy way to mark snowflake positions on Polarfleece?
The following hints will solve these hand embroidery problems and more,
and keep you from flying off the "hand"le!

What's your number?

To keep track of my many different colors of embroidery thread, I keep a sample of each thread for future reference. For easy identification, I run a strand of thread through the paper band of each skein. This keeps the color of thread and its color number together for future use.

Virginia Ratermann, Breese, Illinois

Thrown for a loop

To keep thread tangle-free when working on a counted cross-stitch project, I save the white piece of cardboard that comes in the zipper packages:
- Punch a hole in the cardboard for each color of embroidery thread.
- Label each hole with the pattern, floss number, and color.
- Place the thread in each hole, and loop it so it holds.

When the project is finished, I leave the marked thread in the cardboard for future reference.

Beatrice Doig, West Seneca, New York

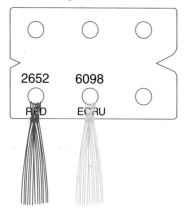

Let it snow!

Since I don't have an embroidery machine, I planned to hand embroider snowflakes on Polarfleece. To easily mark the position for each snowflake, I pressed a small bottle or bottle cap of the desired size onto the fleece where I wanted the stitching. A round imprint showed just long enough to stitch the snowflake, and I had no basting threads or marks to remove. I could only do one imprint at a time, but it worked like a charm!

Gloria Anderson, Marshall, Wisconsin

Buttons in bloom

To add a sweet touch to little girls' dresses, I like to embroider flower buttons.

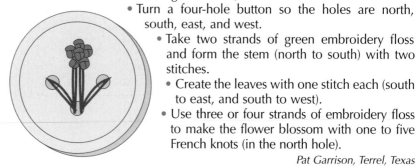

- Turn a four-hole button so the holes are north, south, east, and west.
- Take two strands of green embroidery floss and form the stem (north to south) with two stitches.
- Create the leaves with one stitch each (south to east, and south to west).
- Use three or four strands of embroidery floss to make the flower blossom with one to five French knots (in the north hole).

Pat Garrison, Terrel, Texas

Call for backup

When I went south for the winter, I left all my skeins of embroidery floss at home. While working on a quilting project, I needed a tiny bit of embroidery thread, so I improvised. I used regular sewing thread instead of the floss, threading it through a #8 embroidery needle. The color matched my project, and I didn't have to make a special trip to the store for another skein of embroidery thread.

Gertrude Zack, Tarpon Springs, Florida

It's all in your head

When making dolls like Raggedy Ann, I iron a piece of fusible knit to the headpieces. It makes the fabric much more sturdy when I am embroidering on the facial features and sewing in yarn for hair.

Fran Sines, Perkinston, Mississippi

Bring out the best in your garments

I've used threads drawn from the scraps of a garment as embroidery threads. The tone-on-tone embroidery is most elegant, both on garments and on things like place mats, totes, purses, or wall hangings. I use several strands of the drawn threads to stitch flowers, lazy daisy, French knots, and other embroidery stitches. Black-on-black is really dramatic, especially if I add a few shiny beads as centers of the flowers. Sometimes the lengthwise and crosswise threads are two different shades, and I've used that to good advantage, too. I've even clipped loops in the center of embroidered flowers to make fluffy fringe centers. (I also do this on a sewing machine by threading the machine with the same color thread as the fabric.)

Della Kirk, Issaquah, Washington

Decked Out Stitches

If you've been wishing for an embroidery machine, but your dream has not yet come true, be patient – someday your machine will come. While you wait, don't limit yourself to plain stitching, because just like a fairy godmother, these hints will have your stitching all dolled up and ready for the ball in no time!

Mind your own business

I have just started my own retail shop, selling items that I make. I am on a tight budget and cannot afford business cards or stationery yet. My alternative – I had rubber stamps made at our local business shop. The shop owner generously gave me a box of leftover card stock. Here's how I make my own business cards:

- Embroider down the side of each card using decorative machine stitches, chain stitching the cards much like in patchwork piecing.
- Cut the cards apart.
- Use rubber stamps to complete the business cards.

As I'm cutting the cards apart, I wind some bobbins. I feel I am accomplishing two things at once.

> Handmade by Judy
> 123 Main Street
> Skillman, NJ 08558
> Judy Kaufman
> Judy Kaufman

Judy Kaufman, Skillman, New Jersey

The name game

Here is a way I've found to make my own labels:

- Press backing onto a piece of lightweight muslin the size of computer paper.
- Insert the backed muslin into the printer.
- Make the labels you want to print on the word processor in the computer.
- Position the labels in rows, allowing room between the labels for decorative stitching.
- Cut the labels apart, trimming when necessary.

Add a small decorative design to enhance the labels. Presto, personalized labels!

> Made for you
> with love-
> Peggy Birdsong

Peggy Birdsong, Denver, North Carolina

Practice what you preach

When I started using the embroidery stitches on my machine, it was difficult to judge the pattern size using the illustration in the manual. I stitched every pattern on a piece of fabric. Under each pattern, I stitched the pattern number and the type of foot required. Now, instead of consulting the pattern plate on the machine, I look at my stitched patterns. It makes selecting a stitch much easier.

FOOT A 32	FOOT F 31	FOOT A 61
FOOT F 45	FOOT F 98	FOOT F 94

Gisela Weber, Hialeah, Florida
Esther Winfield, Planation, Florida

Bye for now

I hope that you've enjoyed the tour, and I hope to see you in my classroom very soon. Wear comfortable clothes, take the phone off the hook, and pour yourself a cup of tea or coffee. That's the best way to learn!

Don't be afraid to share with me the techniques or projects you've tried – I enjoy the feedback. Plus, keep those hints coming; I learn so much from you! You can reach me at:

Nancy's Notions
PO Box 683
Beaver Dam, WI 53916
sewhints@nancysnotions.com

Bye for now!

Nancy

PS: If you cannot find Sewing With Nancy on your local public TV station, check out the Sewing With Nancy web site for a listing of when the show airs and how to contact your local public television station:

sewingwithnancy.com

Nancy's *favorite* techniques

The Perfect Pattern to Showcase Designs!

As you may have guessed from reading this chapter, you can add embroidery to practically anything! To demonstrate the range of possibilities, I've chosen a striking pillow pattern, which is perfect for showcasing embroidery coordinates. The pillows featured here show how a simple change of fabric and embroidery designs can create two completely different looks. The delicate Bleeding Heart Pillow features beautiful flowers against a soft green, pink, and cream background. The Gone Fishin' Pillow offers a different view of nature, with its rustic green, blue, and tan fabrics, and fishing motif embroidery designs.

The best thing about this pillow pattern is that is allows your creativity to take over! Experiment with different combinations of fabric and embroidery designs to create the perfect accent to your decor, or create a one-of-a kind gift for someone dear to your heart.

Supplies needed:

- ¼ yd. Color A (light green)
- ⅛ yd. Color B (dark green)
- ¼ yd. Color C (pink)
- ⅛ yd. Color D (burgundy)
- ⅝ yd. Color E (cream)
- ¼ yd. fusible interfacing
- Amazing Designer Series "Nature's Reflections" Memory Card
- "Nature's Reflections" Templates

Optional: 2⅜ yd. cording, ¼" diameter

Choose the best interfacing and/or stabilizers for your project

- Before doing any embroidery, you must prepare the fabric by adding interfacing and/or stabilizers. One of the most common problems for beginning embroiderers is using insufficient stabilization. Always test the stitching on a sample before stitching on the actual garment or project to determine the best combination of stabilizers for the fabric and design.
- Add a layer of fusible interfacing. Interfacing prevents the temporary stabilizer from showing through after the stitching is completed. Select an interfacing weight compatible with the fabric: Use a lightweight interfacing such as Lightweight Pellon® for lightweight fabrics and a heavier interfacing like Pellon® ShirTailor® for heavier fabrics like denim.
- Add a temporary stabilizer to prevent stitch distortion. This stabilizer is generally removed after the stitching is completed. Choose a stabilizer appropriate for the fabric and stitch density.
  - Press-on stabilizer (for example, Pellon® Stitch-N-Tear®) is ideal for dense stitching where tearing won't distort embroidery stitches or the fabric.
  - Cut-away stabilizer (for example, Soft 'n Sheer™) is appropriate for delicate fabrics and designs that might be distorted by tearing away the stabilizer.
  - Water-soluble stabilizer (for example, Avalon® by Madeira) is for use on washable fabrics; it is easily removed by water, leaving no visible residue.
  - Sticky-backed stabilizer (for example, Filmoplast Stic) is used to stabilize fabric or garment sections too small to be hooped, or fabrics on which a hoop might leave an unsightly impression.

Preparing the pillow top:

Note: *The instructions that follow are for the Bleeding Heart Pillow. The Gone Fishin' Pillow is constructed the same way, using different fabrics and embroidery designs from the Amazing Designer Series Memories by the Shore Memory Card.*

1. Cut the pillow sections. If you are using Method 1 to construct the pillow, stitch your embroidery designs onto the fabric before you cut out the pillow sections. This is a great way to use all of those test samples of your designs.

a. **Color A**: Cut one 5" center square. *Optional:* Cut eight 1½" bias strips for piping.

b. **Color B**: Cut four 3" center corners.

c. **Color C**: Cut two 7½" squares. Cut and fuse the interfacing to the squares. Subcut the squares diagonally into four right triangles.

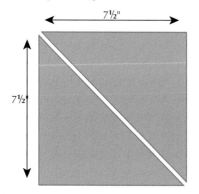

d. **Color D**: Cut four 3" corner squares.

e. **Color E**: Cut one 13½" strip. Subcut as follows:
- Two 18½" rectangles for pillow envelope back.
- Four 3" x 5" sashing strips.

Cut two 3" strips. Subcut into four 3" x 13¾" sashing strips.

selvage	13½" x 18½"	13½" x 18½"	3" x 5"	selvage
			3" x 5"	
			3" x 5"	
			3" x 5"	
	3" x 13¼"	3" x 13¼"		
	3" x 13¼"	3" x 13¼"		

2. Join the pillow sections, right sides together, using ¼" seams. Press the seams away from the center after each stitching.

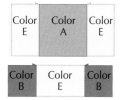

a. Stitch a Color E 3" x 5" sashing strip to each side of a Color A center square.

b. Stitch 3" Color B center corners to each end of the two remaining 5" Color E sashing strips.

c. Stitch these strips to the center block.

d. Stitch a Color C right triangle to each side of the pieced center block.

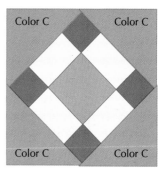

e. Stitch two of the 3" x 13¾" Color E sashing strips to the pieced block.

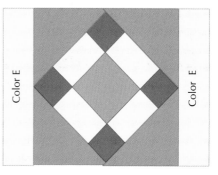

f. Stitch a 3" Color D corner square to each end of the two remaining Color E sashing strips.

g. Stitch these strips to the pieced pillow top.

h. If you are using method B to construct the pillow, add embroidery to the patchwork sections.

If you are using method A, proceed to Step 6 to complete the pillow.

3. Position the design on the fabric. Ensuring an embroidery design will be stitched precisely where you want it is one of the biggest concerns in machine embroidery. Here are three ways to help properly position the design.

a. Stitch out the design on test fabric. Trace around the inside of the hoop before removing the fabric from the hoop. Also mark horizontal and vertical center marks and the top of the design. Cut around the traced line and use that section as a placement guide, positioning it on the embroidery fabric.

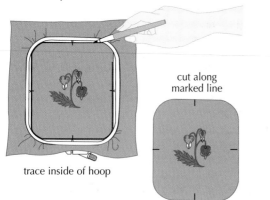

cut along
marked line

trace inside of hoop

b. Use a purchased template. These templates have a crosshatch with positioning holes as well as a center hole, making it easy to precisely position the design in the hoop. Tape the template in place with Sewer's Fix-it Tape

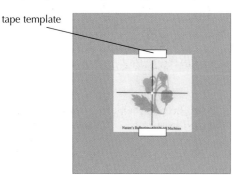

tape template

before hooping the fabric; remove the template after positioning the machine needle for the start of the design.

c. Use the trace or "walk-about" feature available on some machines. Insert a washable fabric marker in the hole of the embroidery foot. Press the appropriate button on the machine and the machine will trace around the perimeter of the design as well as indicate the center needle position.

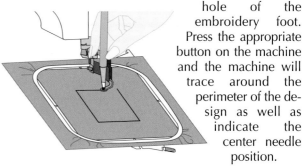

4. Insert the hoop in the machine.
a. Place the outer hoop on a flat surface.
b. Position the fabric over the hoop.

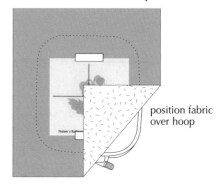

position fabric
over hoop

c. Place the inner hoop over the fabric and press down firmly with the heels of your hands, aligning the cross marks of the design or template with the markings on the hoop.

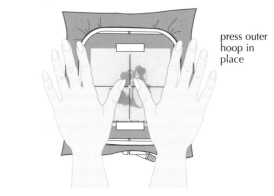

press outer
hoop in
place

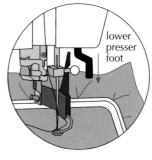

lower
presser
foot

d. Move the needle to the design's starting point.
e. Lower the presser foot to ensure the design is properly positioned. Remove any templates prior to stitching.

5. Stitch the design.

a. Organize your threads in sequential order before beginning stitching. Line them up in the order they will be stitched to make it easy to move from color to color.

b. Bring up the bobbin thread; sew a few stitches, and clip the thread.

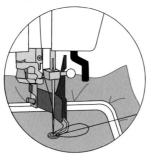

bring up bobbin thread

c. Stitch the first color.

d. To change threads, clip the needle thread at both the needle and the thread spool. Remove the thread by pulling it out through the needle. Doing so flosses the machine tension disks and prevents lint from being drawn into the machine mechanism.

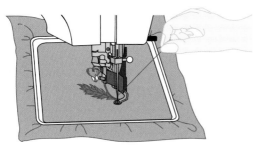

pull thread out through needle

Completing the pillow:

6. Assemble the pillow. *Optional:* Add piping to the outer edge of the pillow top.

a. Join the short edges of the piping strips to form a continuous strip. Joining the strips on the bias helps reduce bulk.

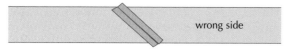

wrong side

b. Fold the strip in half, meeting the lengthwise edges.

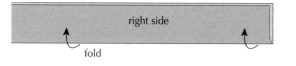

right side

fold

c. Position the piping on the right side of the pillow, beginning in the middle of one side, meeting cut edges. Overlap the ends of the piping, angling the piping to the outer edge. Machine baste in place.

d. Prepare the pillow back using your favorite technique. To continue the theme of the pillow, choose a closure that reflects the designs used on the front. For example, the Bleeding Heart Pillow uses color coordinated ties, while the Gone Fishin' Pillow features rustic looking wooden buttons.

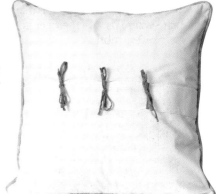

e. Join the front to the back with right sides together. Turn the pillow right side out.

$\mathcal{I}$ndex

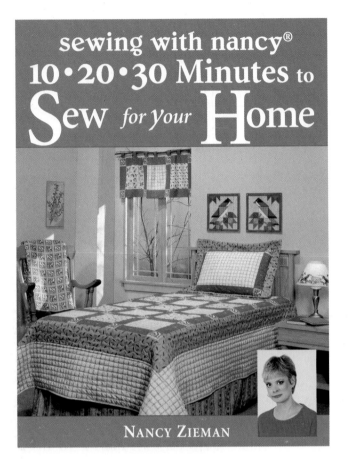